The Cambridge Introduction to
Chekhov

Chekhov is widely acknowledged as one of the most influential literary figures of modern times. Russia's preeminent playwright, he played a significant role in revolutionizing the modern theatre. His impact on prose fiction writing is incalculable: he helped define the modern short story. Beginning with an engaging account of Chekhov's life and cultural context in nineteenth-century Russia, this book introduces the reader to this fascinating and complex personality. Unlike much criticism of Chekhov, it includes detailed discussions of both his fiction and his plays. The *Introduction* traces his concise, impressionistic prose style from early comic sketches to mature works such as "Ward No. 6" and "In the Ravine." Examining Chekhov's development as a dramatist, the book considers his one-act vaudevilles and early works, while providing a detailed, act-by-act analysis of the masterpieces on which his reputation rests: *The Seagull, Uncle Vanya, Three Sisters*, and *The Cherry Orchard*.

JAMES N. LOEHLIN is Shakespeare at Winedale Regents Professor of English at the University of Texas at Austin. He is the author of *Chekhov: The Cherry Orchard* in the Cambridge Plays in Production series, and the editor of *Romeo and Juliet* in the Cambridge Shakespeare in Production series. He has also written books on Shakespeare's *Henry V* and *Henry IV, Parts I and II*. He has directed, acted in, or supervised productions of all Chekhov's major plays, as well as twenty-five of Shakespeare's plays.

The Cambridge Introduction to
Chekhov

JAMES N. LOEHLIN
The University of Texas

CAMBRIDGE
UNIVERSITY PRESS

CAMBRIDGE UNIVERSITY PRESS
Cambridge, New York, Melbourne, Madrid, Cape Town, Singapore,
São Paulo, Delhi, Dubai, Tokyo, Mexico City

Cambridge University Press
The Edinburgh Building, Cambridge CB2 8RU, UK

Published in the United States of America by Cambridge University Press, New York

www.cambridge.org
Information on this title: www.cambridge.org/9780521706889

First published 2010

Printed in the United Kingdom at the University Press, Cambridge

A catalogue record for this publication is available from the British Library

Library of Congress Cataloguing in Publication data
Loehlin, James N.
The Cambridge introduction to Chekhov / James N. Loehlin.
    p.   cm. – (Cambridge introductions to literature)
ISBN 978-0-521-88077-0 (hardback)
1. Chekhov, Anton Pavlovich, 1860–1904 – Criticism and interpretation.   I. Title.
II. Series.
PG3458.Z8L64   2010
891.72′3–dc22

                                                                        2010022722

ISBN 978-0-521-88077-0 Hardback
ISBN 978-0-521-70688-9 Paperback

Contents

Preface

Shortly before Anton Chekhov died of tuberculosis at the age of forty-four, he went for an evening carriage ride with a young writer, Ivan Bunin, who visited him frequently during his illness. They drove from the Crimean town of Yalta, where Chekhov was convalescing, to the nearby coastal village of Oreanda. A cliff-top prospect in this village is the setting of one of the most famous episodes in Chekhov's fiction: Gurov's seaside epiphany in "The Lady with the Little Dog." In Chekhov's story, the timeless, indifferent beauty of the sea leads Gurov to the realization that "everything was beautiful in this world, everything except for what we ourselves think and do when we forget the higher goals of being and our human dignity."[1]

Chekhov and Bunin drove the same route that Gurov and Anna, the lady with the dog, take in Chekhov's story. Bunin's description of the carriage ride has some of the lyricism and pathos of Chekhov's evocations of nature: "We were quiet, looking at the shining, matted-gold valley of the sea. We first passed by a forest that had a springlike air, tender, pensive, and beautiful." Bunin's account leads, like Gurov's view of the sea, to a reflection on time, change, and the impermanence of human achievement:

> We stopped the carriage and walked quietly under these cypresses, past the ruins of a palace shining bluish-white in the moonlight. Chekhov suddenly turned to me and said, "Do you know how long people will continue to read my works? Seven years, that is all."

Startled by this sudden assertion by a dying author whose works he greatly admired, Bunin asked, "Why seven?"

"Well, then," Chekhov responded wryly, "seven and a half."[2]

The sly, self-mocking irony in that added "and a half," the ability to find a joke in the midst of a reflection on his own death, is characteristic of Chekhov. His work is suffused with a consciousness of human suffering and stupidity, the sorry messes we make of our lives and the lofty indifference of the nature that surrounds us. Yet he avoids sentimentality or despair through the kind of acerbic wit he shows here, in recognizing and deflating his own vanity.

Chekhov was able to look at human folly, even his own, with cool detachment, and turn his observations into art.

Chekhov's sense of his impermanence was premature. At the time of this introduction's publication, Chekhov's work will have outlasted his own estimate by exactly one hundred years. He is recognized as Russia's preeminent playwright and is exceeded only by Shakespeare as a staple of the international dramatic repertoire. His impact on the writing of prose fiction is incalculable: he helped define the modern short story. With paradigm-shifting contributions to two fields, fiction and drama, Chekhov has remained one of the greatest influences on the literature of the past century.

His legacy is the product of a short but amazingly productive life. He wrote hundreds of stories, thousands of letters, and more than two dozen works in dramatic form, several of which helped revolutionize the modern theatre. Yet he did not, at least initially, see writing as his primary occupation, but as a way to earn extra money or refresh his mind from the strains of his medical practice. He worked as a doctor through most of his adult life and often asserted that "Medicine is my lawful wife, and literature is my mistress." He credited his medical training with sharpening his powers of observation and giving his literary work a sense of direction. His dual professions of doctor and author, together with his romantic life, early death, and humanitarian efforts, have made him an immensely attractive figure to subsequent generations. The persona of Chekhov has achieved a legendary status rivaling that of his literary productions. While his personality was complex, elusive, and perhaps ultimately unknowable, he is a figure who continues to fascinate, both as a writer and a human being.

This study aims to provide the beginning reader with a broad survey of Chekhov's literary achievement, both in fiction and drama. I have thought it more important to give a sense of the range and scope of Chekhov's work, and his astonishing prolificacy, than to go into a few representative works in great depth. Accordingly, I consider some fifty of Chekhov's stories and fifteen plays in this volume, although more time is spent on the four final plays than on anything else. I have not tried to advance a particular "reading" of Chekhov, but rather to introduce the reader to how the texts work, by calling attention to the particular details encountered in reading or staging them. In the major plays, in particular, I try to show how the texts unfold moment by moment in performance, while drawing out some of the common themes, dramatic devices, and poetic images Chekhov builds these works around.

I have tried to give some sense of Chekhov's life and cultural context, and the reception of his works, but these are necessarily very brief overviews. I am grateful for the scholarship of my predecessors and colleagues in the field of

Russian literature, in whose territory I still feel myself very much an amateur. I write for the English-language reader who is beginning to discover Chekhov, and my goal is to communicate what makes these texts special, how they achieve their effects, and why they continue to live in the study and on the stage. This is, unavoidably, a rather personal perspective, and any errors or misinterpretations are my own.

I am grateful to Vicki Cooper, Rebecca Taylor, and everyone at Cambridge University Press for their patience and help with this volume. Jacqueline French has been an exemplary copy-editor, eagle-eyed and judicious. I thank my family for their inspirational examples, and my wife Laurel for her unceasing love and support. Thanks also to my University of Texas colleagues who have helped guide me in this unfamiliar Russian landscape, notably Tom Garza and Elizabeth Richmond-Garza. I am deeply indebted to the students with whom I have learned about Chekhov over the years; and especially to Graham Schmidt, who has been a most thoughtful and constructive collaborator.

Chronology

1860   Anton Pavlovich Chekhov born on January 17 at Taganrog in southern Russia, third son of Pavel Chekhov, a small shopkeeper, and his wife Yevgenia

1861   Emancipation of the serfs by Alexander II

1867   Chekhov enrolled in Greek school in Taganrog

1868   Chekhov moves to Taganrog Gymnasium

1873   Chekhov sees his first play, Offenbach's *La Belle Hélène*, along with *Hamlet* and *The Government Inspector*

1875   Chekhov's older brothers go to Moscow to study; Chekhov sends them a home-made humorous magazine, *The Stammerer*, with sketches of Taganrog life

1876   Pavel Chekhov goes bankrupt; flees to Moscow with his family, leaving Anton behind to complete his education

1877   Publication of Tolstoy's *Anna Karenina* completed. Chekhov visits Moscow for the first time, where his family is living in poverty

1878   Chekhov writes the full-length play *Fatherlessness*, which is either destroyed or revised into the play now known as *Platonov*

1879   Chekhov matriculates from Gymnasium and wins scholarship to study medicine in Moscow; writes humorous pieces for magazine *The Alarm Clock*

1880   Publication of Dostoevsky's *The Brothers Karamazov* completed. Chekhov's first short story, "A Letter from the Don Landowner Stepan Vladimorich N., to His Learned Neighbor Dr. Friedrick," published in *The Dragonfly*; he publishes further stories under pseudonym Antosha Chekhonte

1881   Alexander II assassinated; severe repression follows under Alexander III. Chekhov begins contributing to magazine *Fragments*; offers the play known as *Platonov* to Maria Ermolova, but it is rejected

1882   Chekhov is able to support his family with his contributions to humorous weekly magazines

1884   Chekhov graduates and becomes practicing physician at Chikhino rural hospital; first signs of his tuberculosis. Publishes the collection *Tales of Melpomene* and *The Shooting Party*, his only novel

1885   Chekhov begins friendship with Suvorin, publisher of *New Times*, and has relationships with Natalia Golden and Dunia Efros; writes over a hundred stories in the next two years

1886   Brief engagement to Dunia Efros. Chekhov receives encouragement from writer Dmitri Grigorovich and begins publishing regularly under his own name, producing dozens of pieces and publishing the collection *Motley Stories*

1887   Chekhov makes trip to Taganrog and the Don steppes; collection *In the Twilight* published; Chekhov writes *Ivanov* in two weeks for Korsh Theatre in Moscow

1888   "The Steppe" published in *The Northern Herald*; Chekhov wins Pushkin Prize; farces *The Bear* and *The Proposal* successful; Chekhov revises *Ivanov* for Petersburg

1889   "A Boring Story" published; Chekhov meets Lydia Avilova; death of Chekhov's brother Nikolai; *The Wood Demon* a failure in Moscow

1890   Chekhov travels across Siberia to survey medical conditions on prison island of Sakhalin; return trip by sea (via Hong Kong, Singapore, and Ceylon) inspires story "Gusev"; collection *Gloomy People* published

1891   Severe famine; Chekhov organizes relief efforts. Relationship with Lika Mizinova. Chekhov publishes "The Duel" and writes "The Grasshopper"; travels to Western Europe

1892   Chekhov buys small estate at Melikhovo, near Moscow, where he lives with his parents and sister; Chekhov completes "Ward No. 6" and "Story of an Unknown Man"

1893   Serial publication of *The Island of Sakhalin*

1894   Death of Alexander III and accession of Nicholas II; Chekhov travels to Western Europe with Suvorin; publishes "The Student" and "The Black Monk," among other stories

1895   Chekhov visits Tolstoy at his estate, Yasnaya Polyana; publishes "Three Years"; works on *The Seagull* and the stories "The House with the Mezzanine," "Ariadne," and "Anna on the Neck"

1896   Chekhov builds schools near Melikhovo and donates books to Taganrog library; writes "My Life." Disastrous premiere of *The Seagull* at Aleksandrinsky Theatre, Petersburg

1897   Chekhov has severe lung hemorrhage; diagnosed with tuberculosis. Dreyfus affair causes rift with Suvorin over anti-Semitic stance of *New Times*. Publishes *Uncle Vanya* and "Peasants"

1898   Chekhov meets Olga Knipper. Moscow Art Theatre, founded by
        Stanislavsky and Nemirovich-Danchenko, produces *The Seagull* to
        great acclaim. "The Little Trilogy" published. Death of Chekhov's
        father

1899   Moscow Art Theatre produces *Uncle Vanya*. "The Lady with the Little
        Dog" and "The Darling" published, among others. Chekhov sells estate
        at Melikhovo, arranges for publication of his collected works by
        Adolph Marx

1900   Chekhov settles in Yalta, works on *Three Sisters*; "In the Ravine"
        published in Gorky's left-wing journal *Life*; Chekhov elected to Russian
        Academy

1901   Chekhov marries Olga Knipper; *Three Sisters* premieres at Moscow Art
        Theatre

1902   Chekhov resigns from Russian Academy over Gorky's exclusion;
        completes "The Bishop"; Olga suffers miscarriage

1903   Chekhov completes his last story, "The Fiancée," and his last play, *The
        Cherry Orchard*

1904   Premiere of *The Cherry Orchard* at Moscow Art Theatre; Chekhov's
        health worsens; he dies of tuberculosis at Badenweiler in Germany and
        is buried at Novodevichy Cemetery in Moscow

1905   Disastrous Russo-Japanese War; Russian Revolution of 1905 leads to
        establishment of Duma (Russian parliament) and limited
        constitutional monarchy

A note on translations and transliteration

Unless otherwise specified, all quotations from Chekhov's dramatic works are from Laurence Senelick, *Anton Chekhov: The Complete Plays*. For the stories, I have used the translations of Richard Pevear and Larissa Volokhonsky when available, otherwise, the Constance Garnett translations in the thirteen-volume Ecco edition. Citations from individual works are given in a note on first mention to clarify which translation is being used. For longer works, page references for all subsequent citations are given in the text. For shorter works and where acts are discussed individually, I have opted instead to give a page range in a note at first mention rather than cluttering the text with page references. For Chekhov's letters, I have used Rosamund Bartlett's *Anton Chekhov: A Life in Letters* where possible, giving the date in the body of the text.

In transliterating Cyrillic, I have tried to be consistent without being pedantic. Anglicized name forms are used for tsars (thus 'Alexander II', 'Nicholas I') and common Russian place names (e.g. St. Petersburg, Yalta), and I have used the established Western spellings of well-known figures (e.g. Fyodor Dostoevsky, Maxim Gorky, Leo Tolstoy), even though this may lead to inconsistencies. For the most part, I have reproduced character names as they are transliterated in the translations I am using, although I have tried to avoid too many confusing variants. I have standardized the transliteration "Chekhov" in quotations. The soft sign is not denoted with Russian words in the text (e.g. glasnost).

Chapter 1

Life

For many readers, Anton Chekhov's life has exerted nearly as much fascination as his works. Not only was he a major literary figure with an unquantifiable impact on the drama and fiction of the modern period, but he was an indisputably good man, who worked heroically, throughout his short life, for the benefit of other people. Listing him on a roll call of "modern saints," Chekhov scholar Charles Meister has asserted that "Even if he had not been a great writer, Chekhov would have deserved worldwide recognition for his role as a humanitarian."[1] His achievements are incontrovertible: he raised his family from poverty through his own effort and talent, built schools and hospitals, gave free medical treatment to thousands, helped change Russia's penal conditions through his report on the Sakhalin prisons, stood up against injustices of all kinds, and wrote some of the greatest stories and plays in the history of literature, all while, for much of his life, fighting a losing battle against the tuberculosis that killed him at forty-four. Recent biographical revelations that Chekhov could be irritable, vain, or selfish, and that he kept others, especially the women in his life, at an emotional distance while accepting their devotion, have done little to tarnish his overall reputation. The letters, memoirs, and reminiscences of his contemporaries leave little doubt that Chekhov was deeply and deservingly loved; and that love has been reaffirmed by generations of readers.

Because of the richness of his short life, the complexity and ambiguity of his work, and the volatility of his own times and those that followed, Chekhov has been subject to myriad interpretations that have allowed him to be many things

1

to many people. He has been hailed by Soviet ideologues as the harbinger of the Revolution, and by dispossessed aristocrats as the voice of twilight Russia. He has been seen as a timid recluse, kindly, shy, and sad, and as a brilliant *bon vivant*, the lover of fashionable writers and beautiful actresses. He has been a coolly objective doctor, ruthlessly anatomizing the ills of his society, and a passionate romantic, a nature-loving poet and environmentalist. He has been the toast of metropolitan society, and the offspring of serfs from Russia's impoverished margins.

Chekhov has himself provided various, often contradictory, ways for interpreting him. Though he professed himself a victim of "autobiographobia," he wrote about himself, his history, and his opinions in thousands of letters, as well as reflecting them, in mutated forms, in his stories and plays. One of the most compelling narratives of Chekhov's life is one that he offered to Suvorin, his friend and publisher, as a potential subject for a short story:

> Try writing a story about a young man, the son of a serf, a former shop boy and chorister, schoolboy and student, brought up to be respectful of his betters and to kiss the priest's hand, to submit to the ideas of others, to be grateful for every crust of bread, who is constantly thrashed, who goes out without galoshes to tutor other people's children, who gets into fights, torments animals, savours the taste of good dinners with rich relations, unnecessarily plays the hypocrite before God and his fellows purely from a realization of his own insignificance – and then go on to tell the story of how this young man drop by drop wrings the slave out of himself until, one fine morning, he awakes to feel that flowing in his veins is no longer the blood of a slave, but that of a complete human being …
>
> (January 7, 1889)[2]

One of the stories of Chekhov's life is this – his squeezing the slave out of himself. His social elevation from beaten shop boy to literary superstar (and his experience of both of these milieux) plainly informs his writing. But this life, fascinating as it is, does not in itself explain the work, nor is it always reflected in the work; Chekhov was, after all, a very private man. More illuminating are the artistic opinions and occasional manifestos he expressed in his letters. The best known, perhaps, is his declaration that "My holy of holies is the human body, good health, intelligence, talent, inspiration, love, and complete freedom, freedom from violence and lies, no matter what form these last two may take" (October 4, 1888). Chekhov's revulsion from "violence and lies" is discernable everywhere in his work.

The story of Chekhov's life is intensely compelling and accounts, in no small way, for his popularity and celebrity. From the moment of his death, his family members, friends, lovers, colleagues, and even his literary rivals began to try to account for him, to preserve and embellish their memories of him, and to create the shifting, multifaceted image that we must accept as all we can really know of Anton Chekhov.

Childhood and youth

The simple biographical facts can be readily established. Anton Pavlovich Chekhov was born in the town of Taganrog, a port on the Sea of Azov in southern Russia, in 1860. His father Pavel was a shopkeeper, the son of a serf who had bought his freedom. His mother Yevgenia gave birth to five sons and two daughters; Anton was the third child. His elder brothers, Aleksandr and Nikolai, preceded Anton into literary and artistic circles in Moscow, though not with their brother's success. His sister Masha devoted much of her life to Anton, managing his household and eventually guarding his legacy. Anton played a semi-paternal role with regard to his younger brothers, Vanya and Misha. His youngest sister Yevgenia died in infancy.

Pavel Chekhov was an incompetent merchant and a bullying father; memories of childhood beatings and domestic tyranny permeate Chekhov's works. "Despotism and lies" destroyed his childhood, he felt, "so much so that we become sick and fearful when we remember it," as he wrote to his brother Aleksandr (January 2, 1889). Anton and his brothers worked long hours tending the family shop, which sold tea, coffee, sugar, olive oil, preserved foods, soap, candles, and other household supplies, as well as Greek wine and vodka by the glass. Pavel, a sternly pious man, was enthusiastically devoted to the sung liturgy of the Russian church. He became a choirmaster and conscripted his sons as singers. While Chekhov hated performing in the early-morning services in freezing chapels – "we felt like little convicts," he recalled later – he did gain a love for the Church Slavonic liturgy that enriched his writing. Chekhov was probably, later in life, a nonbeliever himself, though his attitude to religion was complex: he wrote that "An enormously wide field lies between 'God exists' and 'there is no God,' one that the true wise man traverses with great difficulty."[3] Whatever his own beliefs, he depicted profound religious feeling in many stories, including "Easter Night," "The Student," and "The Bishop."

Taganrog was in many ways a provincial backwater of muddy streets and squat, graceless houses. Chekhov later derided it as coarse and benighted: "the 60,000 inhabitants of this town do absolutely nothing except eat, drink and procreate; they have no other interests whatsoever" (April 7, 1887). Yet Taganrog also had a cosmopolitan side. European merchants traded there,

Italian opera companies played at the theatre, and many of the leading citizens were Greeks. Anton and his brothers briefly attended the Greek school, which Pavel saw as the path to a mercantile career, but as they didn't speak the language, they were soon withdrawn and enrolled in the Taganrog Grammar School. Here Chekhov gained a good education, though he had to repeat two years because of his struggles with classical Greek. His schoolmasters, though they may have inspired some of the eccentric or pathetic figures of Chekhov's stories (notably Kulygin in *Three Sisters* and Belikov in "The Man in a Case"), seem on the whole to have been humane and diligent teachers. And while Chekhov's father may have tyrannized over his children, he did manage to secure for all of them the education he never had, and a chance to continue the family's move from serfdom to the middle classes. As a schoolboy, Chekhov began writing the humorous sketches that marked his early literary career; a handwritten magazine, *The Stammerer*, contained comic accounts of Taganrog life for the amusement of Chekhov's older brothers, who by then were studying in Moscow.

Although oppressed at home, bored at school, and worn out in the shop, Chekhov found solace in outdoor pursuits. He developed a lifelong passion for fishing, a sportsman's knowledge of animals and birds, and a keen sensitivity to nature and its changing moods. When he was eleven, he and his brother Aleksandr rode in an open cart to visit his grandparents, some fifty miles away across the steppe. This journey, with its vast skies and thunderstorms, its Scythian grave-mounds and humming insects, its natural grandeur and human squalor, left a permanent mark on Chekhov and years later inspired his breakthrough novella "The Steppe." Despite Chekhov's love for a vigorous outdoor life, he was often ill, even in his youth. On another summer excursion to a neighboring estate, he swam in a cold river and became very sick. He was diagnosed with peritonitis, but he may already have been infected with tuberculosis; the long, cold hours spent in shop and church cannot have aided his health. Back in Taganrog, Chekhov was treated by the school physician, Dr. Schrempf, whose kindness and diligence inspired him to study medicine.

One of the biggest influences on the young Chekhov was the Taganrog Theatre. Here he saw his first play, Offenbach's *La Belle Hélène*, as well as productions of Russian classics like Griboedov's *Woe From Wit*, Ostrovsky's *The Storm*, and Gogol's *The Government Inspector* (Chekhov also played the Mayor in an amateur version of the last of these plays). He saw Shakespeare's *Hamlet*, which cast a long shadow over *The Seagull* and several of his prose works. He read widely, recommending *Don Quixote* to his younger brother Misha, but rejecting *Uncle Tom's Cabin* as sentimental and cloying: "I experienced the disagreeable sensation, familiar to mortals, of having overindulged in raisins and currants" (April 5, 1879). Even in his earliest letters, his sharp opinions and dry wit are evident.

In 1876, his father went bankrupt. Having overextended his business just at the moment when Taganrog's economy was slowing down (neighboring Rostov-on-Don was usurping its status as the leading regional port), Pavel found himself unable to pay off the new house he had built for his family. With his main creditor threatening legal action, and in danger of imprisonment for debt, Pavel fled to Moscow. Sneaking out of town in a cart by cover of darkness, Pavel avoided the Taganrog railway station for fear of being arrested, joining the Moscow train further up the line. A lodger of the Chekhovs', Gavril Selivanov, paid off the 500-ruble debt but ended up taking possession of the house for himself. The furniture was impounded in lieu of unpaid interest, Yevgenia took the two youngest children to Moscow, and Vanya was sent to an aunt. At sixteen, Anton found himself alone, a lodger in his own house, tutoring Selivanov's nephew in return for room and board. The episode of his family's dispossession would provide material for Chekhov's final play, *The Cherry Orchard*.

Chekhov continued with his studies in Taganrog, supporting himself by tutoring and by selling what remained of the family's property. He was able to send some money to Moscow, where the rest of the Chekhovs were living in poverty in rented rooms. Visiting his family at Easter 1877, Chekhov was depressed by the squalor they lived in but impressed by the metropolis. He enjoyed the sights and the theatres, and began to think of moving there to study. Eventually Pavel got a live-in warehouse job, which had the double benefit of bringing in thirty rubles a month and keeping him out of his family's hair.

Medicine and literature

In 1879 Chekhov passed his exams, earning a scholarship from the city of Taganrog, and moved to Moscow to study medicine at the university. He also found himself effectively the head of a large household, earning the nickname "Father Antosha" from his brothers. While studying anatomy, chemistry, and other disciplines, he began writing short stories for popular periodicals in order to help support his family. His first story was printed in 1880 in the journal *Dragonfly*. "A Letter from the Don Landowner Stepan Vladimorich N., to His Learned Neighbor Dr. Friedrick" was a parody of popular scientific knowledge, the speculative musings of a provincial ignoramus. Chekhov received five kopecks per line, and the story appeared anonymously. Chekhov had no wish to compromise his position in the medical profession, though his pseudonyms eventually became rather transparent: "Antosha Chekhonte," a soubriquet from his schooldays, became the most prevalent. By 1883 he was publishing regularly in *Fragments*, the most popular journal of this type, and earning enough for his family to move to better quarters.

Chekhov's responsibilities as de facto head of the family led him to become frustrated with the dissolute lives led by his older brothers. He wrote them affectionate but sometimes strongly critical letters. He derided Aleksandr for the squalor in which he lived, arguing that he was setting a bad example for his infant daughter: "this kind of thing can ruin a little girl from her earliest years" (October 1883). He recognized that his brother Nikolai was wasting himself in drink and loose living. As Nikolai deteriorated, Chekhov remonstrated with him severely, once even sending him a list of requisites for the behavior of civilized people. This begins positively – "1) They respect human beings as individuals and are therefore always tolerant, gentle, courteous and amenable" – but soon moves into very specific attacks on Nikolai's lifestyle and companions:

> 8) They work at developing their aesthetic sensibility. They do not allow themselves to sleep in their clothes, stare at the bedbugs in the cracks in the walls, breathe foul air, walk on a floor covered in spit, cook their food on a paraffin stove. As far as possible they try to control and elevate their sex drive … Civilized people don't simply obey their baser instincts. They demand more from a woman than bed, horse sweat, and the sound of pissing … (March 1886)

He likewise reprimanded Aleksandr for his treatment of his common-law wife, a former girlfriend of Chekhov's named Natalia Golden:

> On my first visit to you, what wrenched us apart was your *appalling* treatment of Natalia Alexandrovna and your cook. Forgive me, but to treat women in such a manner, whoever they may be, is unworthy of a decent, caring human being. What heavenly or earthly power granted you the right to make them your slaves? Constant bad language of the most filthy kind, raising your voice to them, criticizing them, capricious demands at lunch and dinner, endless complaints about how your life is nothing but penal servitude and accursed drudgery – is not all that the mark of a coarse bully and despot? (January 2, 1889)

Chekhov's moralizing letters may have an element of priggishness, but they also give a strong sense of his own manners and values, as well as the pressures he felt in having been thrust into such a responsible position so early in life. His letters to both his elder brothers make evident Chekhov's concern for them and his fervent desire that they not waste their human possibility.

Chekhov himself was far from a prig; despite the demands of medicine and literature, he found time for enjoying Moscow nightlife and developing flirtations with many young women of his acquaintance. He seems briefly to have become engaged to a young Jewish woman, his sister's friend Dunia Efros, but nothing came of this, though they remained on friendly terms. Chekhov would spend the next twenty years attracting and repelling women, charming them into intimacy but then keeping them at arm's length: he repeatedly avowed that the married state was not for him. "Let me have a wife who, like the moon, will not appear in my sky every day," he wrote some years later, adding, "Having a wife won't make me write any better" (March 23, 1895).

After completing his medical certification in 1884, Chekhov became a practicing physician at Chikhino rural hospital near Moscow. His medical work gave him local color and incidents for his stories. He wrote to Nikolai Leikin, the editor at *Fragments*, about a grotesque open-air autopsy he performed on a factory worker, killed in a drunken brawl, whose injuries had been exacerbated by attempts to resuscitate him: "apparently the Manekhino peasants, when they found the body, rocked and pummeled it so enthusiastically for two hours that any future defense lawyer the murderer may have will have every right to call expert witnesses to state whether the ribs might not have been broken as a result of these attentions" (June 27, 1884). The absurd details and mordant tone might have come from one of Chekhov's stories, and indeed the episode is recalled in "On Official Business" some fifteen years later. For all his irony, Chekhov was a conscientious and sympathetic doctor, working exhausting hours and treating peasants free of charge. His medical training also, in his own view, had an impact on his writing. "It significantly enlarged the scope of my observations and enriched me with knowledge whose true worth to a writer can only be evaluated by somebody who is himself a doctor," he wrote, adding that his medical background provided "a sense of direction" and helped him "to avoid many mistakes."[4] Though Chekhov practiced medicine successfully for many years, he did apparently misdiagnose or deceive one of his patients: himself. By 1884 he was coughing blood from his lungs, but for years he refused to acknowledge that he was suffering from the tuberculosis that would eventually kill him.

Chekhov initially found the constrained format of *Fragments* a useful discipline, but he soon wanted an outlet for stories of greater scope and variety of tone. He wrote some more serious stories for the *Petersburg Gazette*, and then, in January 1886, he began to contribute to Russia's largest daily newspaper, the *New Times* (*Novoye Vremya*). Its publisher, Aleksey Suvorin, became Chekhov's most important patron and confidant. Though twenty-five years older than Chekhov, and of conservative political views that often led to conflict between the two men (especially over the Dreyfus case), Suvorin became a central figure in Chekhov's career as well as a close friend. *New Times* allowed Chekhov to expand and develop in both form and content, and exposed him to consideration as a serious author.

In March 1886, Chekhov received a letter from one of the most distinguished Russian writers of the time, Dmitri Grigorovich. In it the older writer praised Chekhov's talent and urged him to take it more seriously and cultivate it: "you must have respect for a talent which is so rarely granted. Stop doing hack work."[5] This letter struck Chekhov "like a bolt of lighting"; he wrote back with unfeigned gratitude, acknowledging that "until now I have approached my writing in a most frivolous, irresponsible and meaningless way," and he resolved to give more time and attention to his work (March 28, 1886). Soon thereafter, on Grigorovich's urging, he began regularly presenting his writings under his own name. He also began publishing works in collections, *Motley Stories* (1886) and *In the Twilight* (1887).

In this period Chekhov also began to become known as a dramatist. In his teenage years he had written a play, called *Bezottsovshchina* (*Fatherlessness* or *Without Patrimony*), which he had shown to his brother Aleksandr, who critiqued it harshly. This piece was either destroyed or transformed into the sprawling, untitled work, not performed or published in Chekhov's lifetime, generally known as *Platonov*. In 1887, the Moscow impresario Korsh encouraged him to write a play for his theatre; he produced *Ivanov* in less than two weeks. It was a mixed success, but with Suvorin's encouragement Chekhov revised it for Petersburg, where it fared better. However, it was Chekhov's one-act farce *The Bear* that established him in the theatre and became an ongoing source of income (he jokingly referred to it as "The Milk-Cow").

A return visit to Taganrog in 1887 inspired his longest and most original story to date, "The Steppe," which appeared in a Petersburg journal, *The Northern Herald*. Following a young boy's cart-trip to the faraway town where he will attend school, it displayed Chekhov's brilliance as a nature-writer as well as his experimentation with narrative form. Chekhov was now recognized as a leading talent of the day; he was awarded the Pushkin Prize for Literature in 1888 for *In the Twilight*. He wrote fewer, longer, and more ambitious stories. Another early masterpiece, "A Boring Story," explored the emotional barrenness of a dying medical professor. It manifested a growing psychological and philosophical sophistication in Chekhov's work, and perhaps intimated the author's desire for a radical break with his current way of living.

Sakhalin

The watershed year was 1890, when Chekhov suspended his writing and medical practice to make a five-thousand-mile trek across Siberia to the prison island of Sakhalin. Several factors may have contributed to his decision to embark on this extraordinary journey. He was sensitive to criticism that his writing lacked social convictions and may have felt impelled to put his personal values to the test through some ambitious humanitarian endeavor. He was disenchanted with the theatre; his play *The Wood Demon* had been rejected by the imperial theatres in Petersburg and performed unsuccessfully in Moscow. Chekhov's personal life was also becoming, perhaps, too involving. He had grown friendly with his sister's friend Lika Mizinova, from whom he sometimes felt a need to distance himself; he had also met the writer Lydia Avilova, who would later claim, probably in self-delusion, to have been the great love of his life. Finally, in 1889, his brother Nikolai had died horribly from tuberculosis – an event that must have confronted Chekhov with his own mortality and plagued him with a survivor's guilt.

Chekhov's proposed project was ambitious but ominous: to survey conditions on Sakhalin island, the penal colony for the most wretched prisoners of tsarist Russia. Sakhalin was an island in the Pacific, at the far end of the Russian landmass, as far from Moscow to the east as New York was to the west. After undertaking an in-depth study of Sakhalin's history and geography, Chekhov set off on a river steamer down the Volga, beginning his passage east. He went by boat as far as Perm, in the Urals – the provincial backwater that would later inspire *Three Sisters*. He went another 400 miles by train to the end of the railway line – the Trans-Siberian Railway would not be constructed for several years. By sledge or cart, through snow and mud, Chekhov made his way across Siberia. He carried a revolver, though he never drew it; he risked freezing and starvation, and survived a troika crash. He crossed Lake Baikal on a ferry, and took a steamboat down the Amur River, on the Chinese border. Finally, in July 1890, after two and a half months of travel, he arrived at Aleksandrovsk, the central settlement of Sakhalin.

Life in Sakhalin was even worse than Chekhov had expected. The convicts lived in extreme hardship, doing heavy manual labor and often wearing leg-irons. Physical conditions were appalling, with freezing temperatures for half the year. Exiles lived in poor cabins, beset by disease and alcoholism. Chekhov was struck by the number of children on Sakhalin, many of them offspring of prostitution or promiscuous cohabitation; Chekhov estimated that there were 25 women for every 100 men in the colony. For three months,

Chekhov conducted a painstaking census of the population, recording information through personal interviews with thousands of exiles. One of these conversations, with a ten-year-old boy, he recorded verbatim:

I   What is your father's patronymic?
He   Don't know.
I   What do you mean, you don't know? You're living with your father and you don't know his name? For shame!
He   He's not my real father.
I   What do you mean – not your real father?
He   He lives with my ma.
I   Is your mother married or a widow?
He   Widow. She came because of her husband.
I   What do you mean, because of her husband?
He   She killed him.[6]

After his return to Russia, Chekhov helped set up orphanages for the child beggars and prostitutes of Sakhalin, and sent thousands of books for the children of the convicts.

Chekhov went back to Russia by sea, via Vladivostok, Hong Kong, Singapore, and Ceylon. He witnessed two burials at sea, inspiring his story "Gusev." He made love to "a black-eyed Hindu girl … in a coconut grove, by the light of the moon," as he claimed he would one day boast to his children (December 9, 1890). Finally, he sailed through the Red Sea and Suez Canal, eventually landing in Odessa, and then making his way by train back to Moscow, with a pet mongoose as a souvenir of his trip.

He did not remain long in Russia, however. Having explored, as he put it, the hell of Sakhalin and the paradise of Ceylon, Chekhov now headed west, on a tour of Europe with Suvorin. He approved of the cleanliness of Vienna, where the churches looked "more like cakes than buildings"; he also noted that "It is a strange feeling to be able to read and say whatever one likes" (March 20, 1891). He was enchanted by Venice: "You drift along in a gondola seeing the palaces of the Doges, Desdemona's house, the homes of famous painters, churches … And inside these churches sculpture and paintings such as one sees only in dreams" (March 24, 1891). He wore himself out in the museums of Florence and the Vatican, and hiked up to the mouth of Vesuvius: "It is terrifying, and yet one is gripped by a desire to leap straight down into the monster's mouth. I now believe in Hell" (April 7, 1891). After traveling on to Nice, Monte Carlo, and Paris, Chekhov had finally had enough and returned to Russia more exhausted by the cosmopolitan life of the European capitals than by his trek across Siberia.

Country life

Chekhov resolved on a more relaxed life in the country. Now somewhat more financially secure, he was able to buy a small country estate at Melikhovo, near Moscow. While the cottage there was initially leaky and dilapidated, over the years he was able to make it into a comfortable retreat for himself, his family, and two pet dachshunds, Quinine and Bromide. Here, between 1892 and 1899, he completed his report on Sakhalin and wrote his greatest short stories, as well as *The Seagull* and *Uncle Vanya*. He also became very interested in horticulture – cultivating, among other things, a cherry orchard. Tending his gardens, he exercised the environmental sensibilities espoused by Dr. Astrov in *Uncle Vanya*. He provided free medical treatment to the local population and directed the medical response when a cholera epidemic hit the country in 1892. He later oversaw the census for the region, supervising fifteen enumerators and tabulating the data. He helped fund and build three schools for the peasants, and commissioned a bell tower for the local church.

Busy as his country life proved to be, Chekhov also continued to travel. He made regular trips to Moscow and Petersburg; he visited Tolstoy at his estate; he went to Yalta, in the Crimea, and he made another brief trip to France and Italy. But most of the time he spent at Melikhovo. His parents lived with him after his father's retirement; his sister Masha also spent weekends and holidays there, bringing along her Moscow friends, including Lika Mizinova. Chekhov continued to hold her at a distance, however, and she eventually took up with a married friend of his, Ignati Potopenko. They went off to Paris together, where she had a child out of wedlock; Potopenko returned to his wife, and the child later died.

Lika's story was mirrored in the play Chekhov was writing at the time, *The Seagull*. The play also reflected Chekhov's life on the estate – where he hosted actors and writers from Moscow's cultural world – and his own self-questionings as a writer. He described the play as "a comedy with three parts for women, six for men, four acts, a landscape (view of a lake); many conversations about literature, hardly any action and 185 pounds of love" (October, 21 1895). Apart from the story of Lika, two other episodes came from his life. His friend the painter Isaak Levitan, staying with him, shot a woodcock but was unable to kill the wounded bird. Chekhov had to do so: "There was one beautiful and loving creature less in the world, and two fools went home and sat down to dinner" (April, 8 1892). The other episode was inspired by the besotted Lydia Avilova, who purportedly sent Chekhov a medallion that made reference to a line from his story "Neighbors": "If ever you should need my life, come and take it."

Chekhov offered the play to the Aleksandrinsky Theatre in St. Petersburg. Its premiere, in October 1896, is one of the most famous flops in the history of world drama. As Donald Rayfield has commented, *The Seagull* was put on "in the wrong city, in the wrong month, at the wrong theatre, with the wrong cast, and above all before the wrong audience."[7] The play was performed as a benefit for an aging comedienne, who was performing in a farce on the same bill; her rowdy fans jeered openly at Chekhov's subtle and symbolic play. Many of the actors did not know their lines, and Chekhov felt that neither they nor the director Karpov understood the play. Even Vera Komissarzhevskaya, the brilliant young Nina who, in rehearsals, had moved onlookers to tears, was intimidated by the hostile audience and gave a tentative performance. The audience hissed and catcalled; Chekhov left the auditorium after Act II, waiting out the play in one of the dressing rooms. Afterwards, he wandered the streets of Petersburg, had a late dinner alone in the restaurant, and went back to Suvorin's, where he got in bed and pulled a blanket over his head. The next morning, without saying goodbye to anyone, he took the train to Moscow and on to Melikhovo. He sent a brief note to his brother Misha:

> The play flopped and was a complete disaster. The atmosphere in the theatre was strained, a mixture of incomprehension and ignominy. The cast's performance was dreadful and stupid.
> The moral is: don't write plays.
> Never mind. I'm alive and well and in good heart.
> Your big daddy
> A. Chekhov (October 18, 1896)

In its four subsequent performances, however, *The Seagull* achieved a considerable success. Karpov and Suvorin made some minor cuts and changes; Komissarzhevskaya gave an inspired performance, and the other actors improved. Houses were full, and the intelligentsia generally enthusiastic. Chekhov was philosophical. He defended his flight from Petersburg – "I acted with the cold reasonableness of a man whose proposal has been rejected, and for whom the only thing remaining is to go away" – but he consented to the play's publication and said he expected it to be produced in Moscow eventually (October 22, 1896).

On March 22, 1897, Chekhov was sitting down to dinner with Suvorin at the Hermitage restaurant in Moscow when blood began to gush from his lungs. He soon had to face the unavoidable fact: "The doctors have diagnosed active pulmonary tuberculosis at the apex of my lungs and ordered me to change my way of life" (April 1, 1897). After a summer in Melikhovo, he left for Nice; he would not be able to endure another Moscow winter.

While in France, Chekhov took an active interest in the case of Alfred Dreyfus, a Jewish officer in the French army who had been convicted of treason and sentenced to penal servitude for life. Along with Zola and other French intellectuals, Chekhov was convinced that Dreyfus had been falsely accused on anti-Semitic grounds. Suvorin's paper was harshly anti-Semitic in its coverage of the case, and hostile in its attacks on Zola. Chekhov wrote a measured, closely argued letter to Suvorin about it, but eventually gave up in frustration. "The attitude of *New Times* with regard to the Zola affair has been simply vile," he wrote to his brother Aleksandr (February 23, 1898). Nonetheless, he soon reestablished relations with Suvorin, who remained a friend to the end of Chekhov's life.

The Moscow Art Theatre

While Chekhov was in France, Vladimir Nemirovich-Danchenko wrote to him to request the rights to perform *The Seagull* at the Moscow Art Theatre (MAT), which he had recently founded with the actor and director Konstantin Stanislavksy. Despite its notorious failure, Nemirovich felt *The Seagull* was perfect for the new theatre: "I will stake anything you like that these hidden dramas and tragedies in every character of the play, given a skillful, extremely conscientious production without banalities, can enthrall the auditorium …"[8] Chekhov demurred, but Nemirovich insisted: "*The Seagull* is the only contemporary play that enthralls me as a director, and you are the only modern writer of great interest to a theatre with a model repertoire."[9] Chekhov gave in. In September 1898, he traveled to Moscow to watch a rehearsal of two acts of *The Seagull*. He was impressed with the care and diligence of the MAT company and became optimistic about the production. He also saw a full run of the MAT's production of Aleksey Tolstoy's *Tsar Fyodor Ioannovich*, in which the actress Olga Knipper played the Tsaritsa Irina. "Irina, I think, is splendid," he wrote to Suvorin. "The voice, the nobility, the depth of feeling is so good that I have a lump in my throat … If I had stayed in Moscow I should have fallen in love with this Irina."[10] Within two years Olga Knipper would become Chekhov's wife, while the Moscow Art Theatre would help launch Chekhov into the ranks of the world's leading playwrights.

With winter coming, Chekhov had to flee south to Yalta. On September 20, he wrote an affectionate letter to his father, who had mellowed in his old age after Chekhov had taken over as head of the household. Chekhov inquired about preparations for the fruit trees in the coming winter – like his son, Pavel Chekhov was an avid gardener – and concluded, "Keep well and happy and do not forget your homesick wanderer." Three weeks later, Chekhov's friend Isaak Sinani showed him a telgram he had received from Masha: "How has Anton Pavl. Chekhov taken the news of his father's death." No letter had yet arrived informing him. Stunned, Chekhov wired back: "Heavenly kingdom eternal rest to father sad deeply sorry write details health good do not worry take care of mother Anton" (October 13, 1898). After his father's death, Chekhov decided to sell Melikhovo and move his family to Yalta permanently, and began looking for a suitable place to build a house. To pay for this, and with a consciousness that he probably was nearing the end of his life, he began to make arrangements to sell the rights to his collected works to the Moscow publisher Adolph Marx. The contract turned out to be unfavorable to Chekhov – he could have made much more money by holding on to his rights himself – but it did provide him with capital and allowed him to revise and edit his works to his satisfaction.

Good news came from Moscow: the opening of *The Seagull* at the Moscow Art Theatre was a triumph, guaranteeing the theatre's future and altering the direction of Chekhov's personal and professional life. Olga Knipper played the actress Arkadina, though she was too young for the part; Stanislavsky, whose acting Chekhov never appreciated, played the successful writer Trigorin. Arkadina's son, the symbolist playwright Treplyov who calls for "new forms" in the theatre, was played by Vsevolod Meyerhold, who went on to play a similar role in real life. The following year the MAT staged *Uncle Vanya*, again with Knipper and Stanislavsky in leading roles. The play had already been successful in the provinces – Maxim Gorky saw it and "wept like a woman … as though someone were sawing at me with a blunt-edged saw" – but the Moscow premiere, though not quite as ecstatically received as *The Seagull*, confirmed Chekhov's status as Russia's leading playwright.[11] The Moscow Art Theatre came to Yalta in early 1900 on a Crimean tour, in part to perform for the man who had effectively become their house dramatist. The event exhausted Chekhov, and he was glad when they left, but it allowed him to become closer to Olga Knipper.

Olga was of German descent and had been the protégée, and perhaps the lover, of Nemirovich-Danchenko before emerging as the leading lady of the MAT. She became close friends with Chekhov's sister Masha – a friendship that became strained after Olga and Chekhov became lovers, and more so when they wed. Because of Olga's career and Chekhov's health, they were separated much of the time, a situation that seems to have mostly suited Chekhov. Their evolving relationship is documented in a correspondence of more than a thousand pages, often teasingly affectionate, sometimes exasperated and overwrought. Some of these letters are taken up with the development of Chekhov's play *Three Sisters*, which Olga, on behalf of the MAT company, urged Chekhov to hurry up and finish. The provincial Prozorov sisters' longing for Moscow in the play may have reflected Chekhov's own frustration with being stuck in Yalta, which he found vulgar and backward. When the play was complete, he brought it to Moscow himself in October 1900. The play initially baffled the company, and Chekhov withdrew to Nice to revise it. From there he sent repeated suggestions about the staging, evidently mistrustful of Stanislavsky. The play opened in January 1901 to a lukewarm reception but went on to become a mainstay of the MAT repertory, to the extent that Muscovites spoke of "paying a call on the Prozorovs" when they went to the theatre.[12]

For months Olga lobbied Chekhov to regularize their relationship by marriage, to which he finally consented in May 1901. Hating ceremony, he invited their friends and family to a dinner which they did not attend, then slipped off with Olga to be married quietly, with only Olga's brother and uncle and two students for witnesses. Their honeymoon was to a sanatorium in southern Russia where Chekhov took a cure of fermented mare's milk to try to regain some of his strength. He and Olga had only three years of married life, half of which they spent apart. Though they hoped for a child, her only pregnancy ended in miscarriage.

Last years

Chekhov spent the winter of 1901–02 in Yalta, working on his penultimate story, "The Bishop," a work in which he seemed to anticipate his own death. He also began developing ideas for *The Cherry Orchard*, his final play. These got further suggestions from a pleasant six weeks that he and Olga spent together that summer at Lyubimovka, Stanislavsky's country estate. Returning to Yalta for the winter, he completed his last story, "The Fiancée," which features a young woman who rejects a bourgeois marriage in favor of an activist life in Petersburg. This story, together with *The Cherry Orchard*, which heralds the fall of the Russian gentry, were taken by Soviet critics as evidence that the dying Chekhov had come to develop revolutionary ideals. There is little evidence for these in his letters and other writings of the time, though he did, on occasion, use his status as a prominent literary figure to fight against what he perceived as injustices. When the socialist writer Maxim Gorky was expelled from the Russian Academy in the summer of 1902 on the personal instructions of Tsar Nicholas II, Chekhov resigned from the Academy in protest.

Chekhov sent *The Cherry Orchard* to Moscow and was astonished by the response of Stanislavsky and company. He had intended the play as "a comedy, in places even a farce," and was amazed to hear that people had been weeping during the reading. The play's premiere in January 1904 was a painful occasion for Chekhov. Stanislavsky, who did not trust the play, had decided to try to ensure the success of the evening by also making it a jubilee celebration of Chekhov's twenty-five years as a writer. In the interval after Act III, an unsuspecting Chekhov was dragged to the stage, and forced to listen to endless speeches, one of which, by an unintended irony, began remarkably like Gayev's sentimental tribute to a bookcase in Act I of the play. Chekhov accepted these honors with good grace, but the evening exhausted and depressed him; he cannot have been blind to the funereal character of the occasion. And as he followed the progress of *The Cherry Orchard* after his return to Yalta, he concluded that "Stanislavsky has ruined my play."[13]

Chekhov's health continued to deteriorate. In the summer, on a doctor's advice, he went with Olga to the German spa at Badenweiler, in the Black Forest. Initially he seemed to improve, but he suffered a heart attack on June 29. Early in the morning of July 2, he asked Olga to send for a doctor, apparently the first time he ever asked for one. Finding the situation hopeless, the doctor sent for champagne, in accordance with medical tradition. Chekhov confirmed that he was dying – "ich sterbe" – and then had a glass of champagne. Smiling at Olga, he observed that it had been a long time since he had drunk champagne. Then he lay down on his left side and died.

As Janet Malcolm has pointed out in *Reading Chekhov*, the episode of Chekhov's death, related by Olga in her memoirs and amplified by many authors since (including Raymond Carver in his story "Errand"), has a literary quality.[14] Yet the account of Chekhov's equanimity in his final moments seems wholly in keeping with his character. And the aftermath of his death, as has often been noted, has an element of absurdity that might have come from one of Chekhov's own stories. His body was returned to Russia in a refrigerated train carriage marked "Fresh Oysters." The train was greeted by a large crowd and a military band, but it turned out they were there to commemorate a fallen general, not Chekhov. For Chekhov's protégé and admirer, the socialist writer Maxim Gorky, this episode exemplified the vulgarity of Russian life that his friend had always fought against: "The dirty green railway truck seems to me precisely the great, triumphant laugh of banality over its tired enemy."[15] Whether Chekhov would have shared this sense of defeat, or enjoyed the moment's macabre humor, we obviously cannot know.

Chapter 2

Chekhov in context

Two crucial historical events frame Chekhov's life, and between them they reveal much about the Russia in which he lived, practiced medicine, formed his opinions, and wrote his works. These were the Emancipation of the Serfs in 1861, a year after Chekhov's birth, and the Russian Revolution of 1905, a year after his death. Together they defined a Russia still heavily invested in a medieval past while on the precipice of revolutionary change; a Russia rooted in peasant agriculture but undergoing rapid urbanization and industrialization; a Russia ruled by an autocratic tsar but already devising the structures of Soviet communism. Just as Chekhov traced his own ancestry to servitude and shopkeeping, while coming to rub shoulders with industrialists and revolutionaries, so his Russia grew from a vast but remote feudal empire to a political powder keg that would rock the history of the twentieth century.

The Emancipation of the Serfs was the most important of the reforms undertaken by Tsar Alexander II. Millions of peasants, who had formerly been bound to the lands on which they were born and which they cultivated for the benefit of wealthy landowners, were granted the rights of citizens and allowed to buy the land they worked. While this action had many complex long-term effects and did not, at one stroke of the pen, transform the lives of Russia's peasantry, it set in motion fundamental changes to Russia's feudal economy and gave the possibility of geographical and class mobility to a huge segment of the population. It created the opportunity for people like Chekhov himself, and his character Lopakhin, to remake their social identity within a single generation. "I bought the estate where my grandfather and father were slaves, where they weren't even allowed in the kitchen," Lopakhin cries at the climax of *The Cherry Orchard*; yet elsewhere he feels that he is still, at heart, a peasant, a pig in a pastry-shop.[1] The Emancipation marked a decisive change, but it could not transform entrenched social and economic conditions.

The revolution of 1905 represented the first widespread and violent struggle against the tsarist regime. While it lacked a coherent organization and was ultimately unsuccessful, it revealed the powerful popular opposition that would bring an end to the Romanov dynasty twelve years later. The slow pace of the reforms heralded by the Emancipation, the crushing repressions inflicted by the autocratic Tsar Alexander III, and the crippling economic effects of the disastrous Russo-Japanese War of 1905 – together with the spread, after the mid-1880s, of Marxist doctrine among the militant intelligentsia – led to eruptions of violent conflict across the Russian empire, most notably the "bloody Sunday" massacre at the Winter Palace in St. Petersburg and the mutiny of Russian sailors aboard the battleship Potemkin.

Bracketed by these pivotal events, Chekhov's brief life encompassed some of the most significant developments in Russian history, as the empire of the tsars approached and entered the twentieth century. Yet the Russia that Chekhov depicted in his stories and plays was often that of a sleepy and settled provincial world, where ordinary people go about lives bound by tradition, and revolutionary change seems hundreds of years in the future. To understand the social and cultural world of these works, as well as the forces that would soon overturn it, it is necessary to consider the history and geography of the Russia into which Chekhov was born.

Land and people

In the mid nineteenth century, imperial Russia stretched from the borders of Western Europe to the Sea of Japan, from the Arctic tundra to the deserts of Persia. It comprised over 8 million square miles, more than a sixth of the world's landmass. Most of this territory was in Asia, east of the Ural Mountains, including the great Siberian plain that Chekhov crossed on his journey to Sakhalin. These lands were inhabited by a range of peoples – Tatars, Kazakhs, Bashkirs – who lived under the administration of the Russian empire. Western Russia was populated mainly by Slavs, but there were also large numbers of Jews, Germans, and Poles. Chekhov's Russia was a multicultural society, though it could not be called an especially tolerant or liberal one.

Chekhov's Russia was a patriarchal society – quite literally, in that religious life was under the jurisdiction of the Patriarch of Moscow, the leading figure of the Russian Orthodox Church, and all civil authority derived from the autocratic ruler, the tsar. Russian family life also centered on the father. One consequence of this fact is a distinctive feature of Russian culture that may be confusing for readers of Chekhov: the convention of Russian names. Along with their given name and surname, Russians used a patronymic, based on the father's first name: thus Chekhov, the son of Pavel Chekhov, was Anton Pavlovich Chekhov. Women also used a patronymic, but it was marked by gender, with the feminine ending -*a*. Chekhov's sister was thus Maria Pavlovna Chekhova. The most formal form of address was to call a person by his or her name and patronymic. Most names also had various diminutives with slightly different shades of meaning; Chekhov might have called his sister Masha, Mashenka, or Mashka, depending on his attitude at a particular moment. English translations sometimes try to reproduce these subtleties, sometimes do not. One feature of Russian social interaction that English really cannot reproduce is its use of formal (*vy*) and familiar (*ty*) pronouns, with their attendant verb conjugations. Speaking broadly, Russians of Chekhov's day observed quite a range of social distinctions in their daily interactions, and many of these have an impact on the behavior in Chekhov's works.

Chekhov's Russia was European Russia, the Western third of the empire; he sometimes decried what he saw as the Asiatic barbarity of the East. Western Russia was mainly a huge plain, of forests in the north and steppe to the south. Much of the middle of the country was fertile agricultural land, supporting an economy centered on wheat and other crops. Russia was connected by great rivers – the Dnieper, the Don, and the Volga – that allowed internal navigation, except in winter. Russian winters were long and rugged, with average temperatures in Moscow below freezing for five months out of the year. Yet the frozen roads actually made travel easier, as troikas could be pulled easily over the packed snow. Railroads were rare at the time of Chekhov's birth, though the vital line between the two capital cities, Moscow and St. Petersburg, had been established in 1851. The coming of the railway is a much-discussed cultural transformation in Chekhov's stories and plays; by the time of his death a broad network had been established, and the Trans-Siberian Railway was nearing completion.

Geography and climate obviously had a huge impact on Russian life, and correspondingly on Chekhov's works: in *Three Sisters* Masha remarks on the psychological effects of living in a climate where it might snow at any moment. One feature of Russia's geography is that in the population centers around Moscow and Petersburg, the amount of light undergoes tremendous seasonal variation, resulting in "white nights" in summer and long hours of darkness in the winter. This phenomenon results in surprising situations like the opening of *The Cherry Orchard*, where Lopakhin remarks that it is two o'clock in the morning, but the dawn breaks soon after.

In Chekhov's time, most Russians lived in the countryside, with peasants comprising 80 percent of the population. After Emancipation, peasant life was centered on the village commune, or *mir*, which took over tax-collecting and judicial functions formerly carried out by the landowners. At a higher level of administration was the *zemstvo*, a local council introduced as part of the reforms of Alexander II. Zemstvos oversaw education and social services, including medical treatment; Chekhov himself worked as a *zemstvo* doctor and contributed to the building of *zemstvo* schools in his district around Melikhovo. Another significant part of the social life of the countryside was the Orthodox Church; Chekhov's story "Easter Night" depicts a rural monastery's communal celebrations at Easter, a key event in the Russian calendar.

Over the course of the nineteenth century, an increasing percentage of the population moved to the cities. Most of these cities were small and had little social infrastructure; one-story wooden houses and unpaved roads were the norm. The exceptions were the two great cities of Moscow and St. Petersburg, each with its own distinctive personality. Moscow had been the capital from the fifteenth to the eighteenth century, and it retained some of its medieval character. Wealthy merchants, wearing huge beards and long Russian coats, held to traditional manners and values; on the other hand, the city had Russia's first university, and after the Napoleonic Wars it became a center for new ideas. St. Petersburg, established as the capital by Peter the Great in 1712, was an aristocratic European city, with elegant neoclassical architecture, grand imperial theatres, and the country's first and greatest art museum, the Hermitage, founded in 1764. The contrast between the two cities is an emblem of the evolving and complex relationship between Russia and the West. Chekhov sets most of his works in the countryside or in Moscow; only one, the uncharacteristic "Story of an Unknown Man," is set in Petersburg.

Russia and the West

Peter the Great wanted to modernize Russia by turning it more toward Europe; one of his chief means for doing so was building this new capital on the Gulf of Finland, where his navy would have access to the West. His successors, a series of empresses, kept their courts in Petersburg and maintained this Western outlook. Catherine the Great, herself a German Princess, imported many ideas of the European Enlightenment and corresponded with Diderot and Voltaire. French became the language of the upper classes. Throughout this period, Moscow maintained a more distinctly Russian identity. Napoleon's invasion of Moscow in 1812 had a decisive impact in many different ways. Muscovites withdrew from the city and set it alight, leaving Napoleon's forces stranded in a Russian winter without resources. Though two-thirds of the city was burned, Moscow had assured Napoleon's eventual defeat. This heroic achievement galvanized the city, filling it with patriotic self-confidence; it also caused it to be modernized through new construction.

Despite the resurgence of Russian nationalism after 1812, one effect of the Napoleonic Wars was to bring even more political influence from the West. Russian officers who had served in Europe were impressed by the freedom of Western institutions and began to push for the replacement of tsarist autocracy with a constitutional government. The new tsar, Nicholas I, suppressed the rebellion of the Decembrists in 1825, but the new ideas continued to ferment. Despite heavy-handed censorship and an official ideology of "Orthodoxy, Autocracy, and Nationality" (*Pravoslavie, Samoderzhavie, i Narodnost*), Moscow became the cradle of a new social phenomenon, the intelligentsia. These educated, reformist thinkers were not in agreement as to the best direction for the country, however. Some continued to look to the West for liberal, rationalist solutions to Russia's social problems, while others sought answers in uniquely Russian institutions such as the Orthodox Church and the village commune. These divisions between "Slavophiles" and "Westernizers" persisted into Chekhov's day, though both sides agreed that Russia was in need of reform.

Reform and reaction

This reform came in the 1860s under Tsar Alexander II. The autocratic Nicholas I had ruthlessly suppressed dissent in Russia and helped put down rebellions abroad, earning himself the nickname "the Gendarme of Europe." Yet he weakened his position considerably through his attempts to expand the empire, which resulted in Russia's ignominious defeat at the hands of British and French forces in the Crimean War. In 1855, near the end of the conflict, English ships bombarded Chekhov's hometown of Taganrog; the Chekhovs fled to the countryside, where Chekhov's eldest brother was born. When Nicholas I died the same year, Russia was clearly losing the war. His son and successor, Alexander II, turned his attention to Russia's problems at home, undertaking sweeping liberal reforms. Besides freeing the serfs, he developed the *zemstvo* form of local government, reformed the judicial system on European models, introduced a new penal code, and even drew up plans for an elected parliament, or Duma. But his changes did not go far enough for some, including the new type of radical thinkers that Turgenev termed Nihilists. The atmosphere of paranoia and persecution they instigated is suggested in Chekhov's bleak novella about a failed secret agent, "The Story of an Unknown Man." One such extremist group, the People's Will, determined to assassinate the tsar, and after several attempts, Alexander was killed in 1881 by a terrorist's bomb.

Reaction was swift and severe. The slain tsar's son, Alexander III, moved implacably to crush revolutionary organizations. He also curtailed civil liberties and undid many of his father's reforms. Censorship was strictly enforced, access to education was reduced, and Jews were subjected to brutal pogroms. This was the repressive atmosphere in which Chekhov came of age as a writer. While he was never, himself, a political radical, he was conscious that the freedoms of Russian writers and thinkers were being systematically taken away; later in his life, when he had achieved a position of respect and authority, he defended the rights of younger writers against such persecutions.

The structure of society

Despite the reforms of Alexander II, the Russia of Chekhov's lifetime remained a highly structured hierarchical society, with the rural peasantry by far the largest segment of the population. Chekhov wrote about people from every level of Russian life. A sampling of the titles of some of his stories illustrates the breadth of his view: "The Huntsman," "The Cook's Wedding," "The Privy Councilor," "The Chemist's Wife," "The Chorus Girl," "The Schoolmaster," "The Cossack," "The Doctor," "The Princess," "The Horse Stealers," "The Head Gardener's Story," "Peasants," "The Lady with the Little Dog." His stories provide a fairly comprehensive picture of the life of late nineteenth-century Russia, while his major plays encompass the range of individuals – young and old, rich and poor, educated and illiterate – who might make up a typical household of the Russian gentry.

At the top of the social scale was the aristocracy, the class with which Chekhov concerned himself the least. Titled nobility turn up rarely in his stories, and there is evidence that Chekhov took a rather critical view of their inherited privilege; in "The Princess," a cynical doctor ridicules the philanthropic pretensions of the weak, self-deluding heroine. The broader estate of the gentry was an important one in Russia, producing most of its artists and intellectuals as well as the bureaucrats who ran the empire. Membership of this class could be inherited or achieved through military or civilian service. Russia's social hierarchy was based largely around a "Table of Ranks" that had been introduced by Peter the Great and remained an important index of one's identity even two centuries later. This table comprised fourteen levels of the civil service, equivalent to military ranks, from commander in chief down to second lieutenant. Achieving the rank of titular councilor, equivalent to staff captain, earned one personal membership in the gentry; the rank of actual state councilor made this status hereditary (as did the military rank of major general). Civil servants, like members of the military, wore uniforms and decorations and were entitled to official privileges: in *Three Sisters* the schoolmaster Kulygin proudly sports the Order of Stanislav, and Andrey Prozorov snaps at Ferapont for not addressing him as "Your Excellency." Obsession with rank was almost a cliché in Russian culture, being fully explored, for instance, in the *Petersburg Tales* of Nikolai Gogol. Many of Chekhov's early stories mock this rank reverence, a phenomenon so common as to have its own name, *chinopochitanie*. In "The Death of a Clerk," the lowly hero sneezes on a high-ranking official who is sitting in front of him at the opera; his mortification at this is so extreme that he eventually dies from it. In "Fat and Thin," two former school-friends meet on a railway platform; when one of them (the thin one) learns that the other is a privy councilor, he becomes awkward and constrained, his garrulous good nature freezing into obsequious awe.

As in other European countries, Russia's gentry were the land-owning class. Even after the Emancipation, and consequent sale of land to the newly freed peasants, many Russian gentry owned large estates, where they either lived full-time or spent the summers, wintering in Moscow, Petersburg, or the Crimea. With the increase in social mobility in the later nineteenth century, however, members of the merchant classes and urban bourgeoisie began acquiring summer houses, or dachas, in the country. These are the *dachniki* for whom Lopakhin wants to cut down and subdivide the cherry orchard in Chekhov's final play; their encroachment on the countryside was literal evidence of Russia's changing social landscape.

The Russian country house is the setting for most of Chekhov's plays and many of his stories. The lives of the landed gentry, especially in summer, were often spent in leisure pursuits, many of which Chekhov enjoyed himself: hunting, fishing, gathering mushrooms, playing cards, music, reading, and writing letters. Both during and after serfdom, any estate had many servants, managers, and workmen. Even poor families often had at least one household servant, as Chekhov's did in his childhood. The wet nurse or nanny was a mainstay of Russian domestic life – most members of the gentry were closer to their nannies than to their mothers. As elsewhere in Russia, life on the country estates was strongly affected by the seasons, with the severe fluctuations of the climate dictating the rhythms of the working year.

The officer class of Russia's military were also members of the gentry, and were seen by Chekhov as a civilizing force in Russia's regions. They were often well educated and cosmopolitan, and they brought various technical and cultural improvements with them when they were billeted in remote areas. It was, after all, the officers who had served in the campaigns of 1812 who were the strongest advocates for liberal reforms, and it was through military service that many Russian gentlemen developed sympathetic relationships with their peasant soldiers. In writing *Three Sisters*, Chekhov was moved by his admiration for the cultural value of the army, and he even brought an officer in to Moscow Art Theatre rehearsals to make sure the actors would accurately represent military behavior.

Besides the gentry, the other privileged estate – so called because of exemption from taxation, flogging, and military conscription – was the clergy. The Russian Orthodox Church was itself a complex hierarchy, governed by the Holy Synod in Moscow, with regional bishops and local parish churches, as well as a range of monasteries, seminaries, and other religious houses. There were also dissenting "Old Believers" who held to a more conservative faith. Chekhov, though not religious himself, found much to admire in the Russian church. Many of the clergy in his stories are shown as creative artists – the dead poet-monk in "Easter Night" and the sensitive seminarian in "The Student" combine spiritual yearning and artistic achievement.

The class into which Chekhov was born was that of the merchants. His father had worked his way up into the Second Guild, but as his business failed he was unable to pay his dues and fell back to the level of *meshchane*, or petit-bourgeoisie. He never attained to the First Guild, which was for quite wealthy merchants, often those engaged in international trade. These urban classes became increasingly important as more and more of Russia's population moved into cities – from around 4 percent at the beginning of the nineteenth century to 13 percent by the end.[2] Some merchants, in Moscow especially, became very wealthy as Russia developed a more modern commercial economy; Stanislavsky was a member of this class, as his father, a textile manufacturer, was the head of Moscow's merchant guild. Russia was well behind Western Europe when it came to industrialization, but by the end of the century there were large factories and the beginnings of an industrial proletariat. Several of Chekhov's stories, notably "A Woman's Kingdom" and "A Medical Case," detail the dehumanizing effects of factory work, and Chekhov himself had to contend with the medical consequences of mechanization.

The peasants

Peasants unable to make a living on the land found work in factories, or traveled to the towns to take low-paying service jobs as waiters or hotel clerks – Chekhov's story "Peasants" follows the fate of one such family. Most of the peasants, however, still lived in the countryside in small villages. By far the largest social group in Russia, making up some 80 percent of the population, the peasantry was largely illiterate, and many lived at a subsistence level. Emancipation had allowed a few to become wealthy *kulaks*, but many had been unable to keep up with the payments on the land they were buying from their former masters, and all were subject to the exigencies of rural life. Bad harvests in 1891–92 caused a widespread famine across the Russian country-side; Chekhov was one of many who helped organize relief efforts, but thousands of peasants starved to death.

The condition of the Russian peasant was a subject for intense debate among the intelligentsia to which Chekhov belonged. Peasants were sometimes romanticized or sentimentalized; to Slavophiles they were the true Russians, and their industry, simplicity, and integrity were a reproach to the decadent elites. Others considered them benighted and oppressed, and pushed for greater political representation and social services for the peasantry. Romantic students in the 1860s had declared themselves *narodniki* or Populists and gone to live in rural communes, trying to bring revolutionary social consciousness to the bemused and suspicious peasants in a movement called "going to the people." Writers like Dostoevsky promoted a "native soil" movement in the arts to rediscover the Russian soul among the peasantry. Chekhov himself built schools and hospitals and lent his services to the *zemstvo*, but his stories suggest a more pessimistic perspective. His experiences on his estate at Melikhovo led to several works that shocked the reading public with their picture of the brutality and squalor of peasant life. "The New Villa," "Peasant Women," "In the Ravine," and especially "Peasants" all present class conflict, physical degradation, domestic violence, ignorance, poverty, and alcoholism as basic facts of peasant existence.

"Peasants" created a national outcry when Chekhov published it in *Russian Thought* in 1897. It deals with a Moscow waiter named Nikolai who, because of ill health, has to return to his village with his wife and daughter. His extended peasant family lives in a simple hut and endures a harsh winter, deprivations by the *zemstvo* taxman, and a fire in the village. But these peasants are not the stoical victims or salt-of-the-earth heroes of the Russian peasant myth. Nikolai's mother is a vicious old harridan who beats his bewildered daughter, his brother is an abusive drunkard, and his sister-in-law is a foul-mouthed tramp. In the end, Nikolai dies and his wife and daughter have to return to Moscow as beggars; Chekhov intended to show them descending into prostitution but could not get this ending past the censor. Yet Chekhov's story, harsh as it is, does not blame the peasants for their condition but recognizes the inherent injustices in a society that keeps them ruthlessly at the bottom. As Nikolai's wife leaves the village, she reflects on the lot of the peasantry in terms that Chekhov presumably endorsed:

> In the course of the summer and the winter there had been hours and days when it seemed as though these people lived worse than the beasts, and to live with them was terrible; they were coarse, dishonest, filthy, and drunken; they did not live in harmony, but quarrelled continually, because they distrusted and feared and did not respect one another. Who keeps the tavern and makes the people drunken? A peasant. Who wastes and spends on drink the funds of the commune, of the schools, of the church? A peasant. Who stole from his neighbours, set fire to their property, gave false witness at the court for a bottle of vodka? At the meetings of the Zemstvo and other local bodies, who was the first to fall foul of the peasants? A peasant. Yes, to live with them was terrible; but yet, they were human beings, they suffered and wept like human beings, and there was nothing in their lives for which one could not find excuse. Hard labour that made the whole body ache at night, the cruel winters, the scanty harvests, the overcrowding; and they had no help and none to whom they could look for help.[3]

Some critics on both the right and left applauded Chekhov for revealing the degraded condition of the peasantry, but Tolstoy called the story "a sin before the people," and many joined in his condemnation.[4]

Literary heritage

Chekhov was writing in a period of great richness and achievement in Russian culture and the arts. During the nineteenth century, the attempt to incorporate Western artistic influences while seeking an authentically Russian art in native traditions had resulted in a flourishing cultural scene, centered on Moscow. In music, Slavophile composers like "The Five" (Balakirev, Borodin, Cui, Mussorgsky, and Rimsky-Korsakov) drew on folk tunes, peasant dances, and church bells to create a "native" alternative to European-style conservatory music. In art, the Wanderers (including Ilya Repin and Chekhov's friend Isaak Levitan) rejected academic traditions and painted historical works and landscapes celebrating the Russian land and people. Much of the artistic productivity was sponsored by the new wealth of Moscow's rising merchant classes, who were interested in fostering what they perceived as an authentically Russian culture. Pavel Tretyakov, a textile baron from an Old Believer merchant family, patronized Russian painters and established the Tretyakov Gallery in Moscow. Savva Morozov, a Moscow factory owner, was the principal backer of the Moscow Art Theatre, and Stanislavsky came from a wealthy merchant family, the Alekseyevs. Many emerging writers came from the merchant class, including Chekhov himself and his fellow dramatist Alexander Ostrovsky, who detailed the lives of the bourgeoisie in plays like *A Family Affair* and *The Storm*.

Russia's greatest cultural achievement in the nineteenth century, however, was probably in the field of literary prose, and this was where Chekhov would himself first make his mark. The father of Russian literature was the Romantic poet Alexander Pushkin, who wrote stories and plays but is best known for verse narratives like *Eugene Onegin*. But the literary giants who followed him, and who most influenced Chekhov, were the great Russian fiction writers, Gogol, Turgenev, Dostoevsky, and especially Tolstoy. Each of these figures had an impact on Chekhov's career, and his work must be seen in relation to the literary landscape they defined.

Nikolai Gogol (1809–1852) established his reputation as a writer with fantastic tales set in his native Ukraine. His most famous work, however, draws on the world of officialdom that he encountered when he moved to St. Petersburg under the patronage of Pushkin. His satirical stories of rank-obsessed bureaucrats detail the shallowness of life in the capital, often with an undercurrent of gothic horror. In "The Nose," a Collegiate Assessor wakes to discover that his nose has left his face and is leading a life of its own in St. Petersburg; when he finally locates it, it initially refuses to reattach itself because it has attained a higher rank. In "The Overcoat," the hapless clerk Akaky Akakievich is robbed of his fine new coat, and when he attempts to enlist the help of an "Important Personage," he is so crushed by his condescension that he dies – only to return as a ghost to steal the Personage's coat from him. Tales like these had a clear impact on early Chekhov stories like "The Death of a Clerk." Gogol also wrote a play, *The Government Inspector*, which was a standard of the Russian repertoire. Chekhov acted in an amateur production when he was a boy, and Gogol's satire on small-minded obsequiousness probably had an impact on some of his vaudevilles such as *The Jubilee* and *The Wedding*. Chekhov's regard for Gogol is evident in a remark he addressed to Nemirovich-Danchenko, regarding the latter's interest in a populist theatre: "All that is foolishness, sugar-candy for the people. You must not lower Gogol to the people, but raise the people to the level of Gogol" (November 2, 1903).[5]

Ivan Turgenev (1818–1883) came from a wealthy family of landed gentry but developed a close sympathy with the peasants he encountered while hunting on his estates. His observations of nature and peasant life formed the basis for *Sportsman's Sketches*, his first major work. This collection of stories reveals a sensitivity to landscape and climate that anticipates some of Chekhov's nature writing, especially "The Steppe." The sketches also picture the harsh lives of the peasants in terms so severe that they may have helped contribute to the abolition of serfdom; they certainly got Turgenev in trouble with the censor, which resulted in his house arrest. One of the stories, "Hamlet of the Shchigrovsky District," parodies upper-class idleness and introduces the disaffected but ineffectual Hamlet figure who turns up regularly in the literature of this period, a variation on the Russian archetype known as the "superfluous man." Turgenev was fascinated by the character of Hamlet and wrote an influential essay, "Hamlet and Don Quixote," which Chekhov admired and recommended to his brothers. Bazorov, the nihilist hero of Turgenev's major novel *Fathers and Sons*, is an ambiguous Hamlet figure. Turgenev anticipated Chekhov through his depiction of life among the gentry on a country estate in his novel *A Nest of Gentlefolk* and especially his play *A Month in the Country*, which is structurally similar to Chekhov's major plays.

While Chekhov admired Gogol and Turgenev, he was not partial to Dostoevsky: he found him "very long and self-indulgent. Very pretentious," as he wrote to Suvorin (March 5, 1889). Fyodor Dostoevsky (1821–1881) was a vigorous Slavophile who was once sentenced to death for revolutionary activities and only pardoned on the scaffold. His novels *Crime and Punishment*, *The Idiot*, and *The Brothers Karamazov* all deal with tormented souls confronting the spiritual vacuity of Russian life. The psychological intensity of Dostoevsky's work may have rubbed off on certain episodes in Chekhov's stories, but the older writer's investment in Russian Orthodox Christianity had little appeal for him.

Tolstoy, on the other hand, was a powerful influence on Chekhov. Count Leo Tolstoy (1828–1910) was the most important figure in nineteenth-century Russian literature and remains one of the greatest of all novelists, chiefly on the strength of his masterpieces *War and Peace* (completed in 1869) and *Anna Karenina* (1877). The social breadth and psychological depth of these works established them as cornerstones of Russian culture, but Tolstoy's importance went well beyond them. He was a prolific writer who produced plays, stories, and essays on a wide range of philosophical, political, and religious topics. His views on art and society changed significantly over the course of his long life. In his youth a dashing officer, a gambler, and a libertine, he eventually renounced his aristocratic heritage (along with the royalties from his works) and became a kind of moral sage and champion of the people. He sought the Russian soul among his former serfs; he grew a long beard and wore peasant clothes; sometimes he even scythed hay in the fields, as his character Levin had done in *War and Peace*. He believed in personal spiritual and moral reform, which included vegetarianism and celibacy. He developed a doctrine of non-resistance to evil that influenced Gandhi.

Chekhov revered Tolstoy both as a writer and a man. He considered him the dominant figure in Russian culture, and wrote of his story "The Kreuzer Sonata" that "it would be hard to find anything to compare with the importance of its theme or the beauty of its execution," though he found some of Tolstoy's polemical views on sex both arrogant and ignorant.[6] Chekhov was for a time influenced by Tolstoy's philosophy; stories like "The Duel" and "My Life" show him wrestling with questions about quietism versus activism, or the intelligentsia's finding common cause with the peasantry. After confronting the brutalities of Sakhalin, he began to reject Tolstoy's views, finding "The Kreuzer Sonata" senseless and ridiculing Tolstoy's austere habits in a letter to Suvorin:

> Reason and justice tell me there is more love for mankind in electricity and steam than there is in chastity and abstaining from meat. It is true that war is evil and courts of law are evil, but that does not mean I have to go about in bast shoes and sleep on top of the stove with the labourer and his wife, and so forth. (March 27, 1894)

A year or so later, however, Chekhov met Tolstoy in person, visiting his estate at Yasnaya Polyana. The two developed a close friendship; Chekhov was particularly struck by the devotion Tolstoy inspired in his daughters. After Chekhov was hospitalized for tuberculosis, Tolstoy visited him, and the two writers argued about the immortality of the soul. Tolstoy felt that after death the soul continued to exist in some primal form, but Chekhov rejected the loss of individual consciousness this would entail: "I don't feel any need for immortality in this form" (April 16, 1897). Chekhov was himself concerned for Tolstoy's health, though the older man would outlive him by six years. "If he were to die, a large empty space would appear in my life," Chekhov wrote in 1900, adding, "there is no other person whom I love as I love him." Regarding Tolstoy's place in Russian letters, Chekhov wrote that "Were it not for him the world of literature would be a sheep without a shepherd, a morass in which it would be hard for us to find our way" (January 28, 1900). For his part, Tolstoy worried about what he saw as the increasing immorality of Chekhov's later works, and he was never a fan of the plays. After seeing *Uncle Vanya*, Tolstoy is reputed to have remarked to Chekhov, "You know I can't stand Shakespeare, but your plays are even worse than his."[7]

Tolstoy was something of a mentor and father-figure to Chekhov, and Chekhov played the same role with regard to another Moscow Art Theatre playwright, Maxim Gorky (1868–1936). Though Chekhov was only eight years older than Gorky, he made him a sort of protégé, advising him on his writing and nurturing his career. Gorky's revolutionary politics and social coarseness sometimes frustrated Chekhov – "he bristles like a porcupine" – but he recognized the younger writer as a real talent: "There is not a shadow of a doubt that he is made of the dough of which artists are made. He is the real thing" (January 24, 1900). His advice to Gorky on one of his stories reveals much about both writers:

> When you read proof, cross out as many modifiers of nouns and verbs as you can. You have so many modifiers that the reader has a hard time figuring out what deserves his attention, and it tires him out. If I write, "A man sat down on the grass," it is understandable because it is clear and doesn't require a second reading. But it would be hard to follow and brain-taxing if I were to write, "A tall, narrow-chested and red-bearded man of medium height sat down noiselessly, looking around timidly and in fright, on a patch of green grass that had been trampled by pedestrians." The brain can't grasp all of this at once, and the art of fiction ought to be immediately, instantaneously graspable. (September 3, 1899)

For all of his concerns about Gorky's prose style, Chekhov recognized him as a writer of talent and recommended him to the directors of the MAT. Moreover, Chekhov may have been influenced by Gorky's politics. It was on Gorky's invitation that Chekhov submitted the story "In the Ravine," about the impact of capitalist greed on the peasantry, to the radical journal *Life*. Gorky's plays explored issues of class and politics more explicitly than those of Chekhov. *The Lower Depths*, with its picture of exploitation and violence among the urban underclass, was a politically daring work when the MAT staged it in 1903, but it became one of the company's most famous productions. Gorky subsequently broke with the MAT over a quarrel with Nemirovich, so no more of his plays were produced there, but during the Soviet period the theatre was renamed in his honor.

The birth of a modern theatre

Along with Gorky, Chekhov participated in, and helped to bring about, a revolution in the modern theatre. Through their work with the Moscow Art

Theatre, they defined a new naturalistic style that had a widespread impact across Europe and defined the new realism of the twentieth century. But Chekhov's influence went beyond this, though he did not live to see it. The poetic and symbolic aspects of his work, his innovative approach to dramaturgy, and his atmosphere of existential longing: all these may be seen as precursors of a modern theatre that moves well beyond realism.

The Russian theatre in the nineteenth century was still primarily a relic of the imperial regime of Catherine the Great. In the 1870s, many nobles established private theatres on their estates for coterie performances by educated serfs. In Moscow and Petersburg, official state theatres, regulated by the tsarist bureaucracy, staged neoclassical tragedies and sentimental comedies on European models. Major Russian writers did engage with the drama – Pushkin, Gogol, Turgenev, and Tolstoy all wrote important plays that have remained in the repertoire – but much of what was on offer was weak and derivative. In 1882, the tsar ended the state monopoly on theatre in the capitals, but the imperial theatres – the Maly in Moscow and the Aleksandrinsky in Petersburg – still dominated the theatrical scene. Well-made plays, with melodramatic plotlines and showy opportunities for glamorous actresses, held the stage. Of the two new "people's" theatres that emerged in Moscow after 1882, Lentovsky's was oriented more toward sensation and spectacle, Korsh's toward serious drama. Korsh staged Tolstoy's *Power of Darkness* and Ibsen's *A Doll's House*, as well as Chekhov's *Ivanov*.[8] But there was still a perceived need for a new theatre that would challenge the stultifying traditions of the nineteenth-century stage, with its conventional stage business, standardized roles, and self-indulgent stars.

At a legendary lunch meeting at the Slavyansky Bazaar Hotel in Moscow in 1897, Vladimir Nemirovich-Danchenko and Constantin Stanislavsky drew up plans for a theatre that would break with the conventions of the Russian stage. Stanislavsky, a successful actor and director who would later revolutionize actor training through his psychological "method," had been greatly struck by the meticulous naturalism of the Meininger troupe, a German company that had toured Russia. Nemirovich-Danchenko, a playwright and teacher, was also a shrewd and forward-thinking critic of contemporary drama, with a taste for poetic and mystical plays. Between them they established the principles of a new theatre. It would be a collective effort, fully synthesizing all of the aspects of theatre toward a common artistic goal. There would be no stars showing off to applauding spectators, but a disciplined ensemble of highly trained theatre artists. There would be no artificial acting or reliance on convention; lengthy rehearsal periods, as well as lectures and discussions, would allow the actors to grasp every role in the most concrete detail. Sets and costumes would be carefully researched and crafted to support the overall goals of the production. Lighting would be appropriate and atmospheric, with no footlights or follow-spots. The theatre would be a "temple of art," where the audience would sit in concentrated silence and darkness; no conversations, curtain calls, nor late-comers would disturb the focus of the play. The repertoire would combine the best new writing from Russia and the West with fresh-eyed versions of classics. Opening in 1898 with Aleksey Tolstoy's historical drama *Tsar Fyodor Ioannovich*, the MAT went on to stage Shakespeare and the Greeks along with Ibsen, Hauptmann, Maeterlinck, and other innovative playwrights. But almost from the beginning, the staple of its repertory was Chekhov.

At the time Nemirovich-Danchenko approached Chekhov to ask him to let the MAT produce *The Seagull*, Chekhov had already been involved with the Russian theatre, off and on, for many years. In his medical school days, he had published numerous short pieces related to the theatre, ranging from criticism to gossip. His first collection of stories, *Tales of Melpomene*, dealt with backstage life. He had had some success as a playwright with *Ivanov* and the vaudevilles, though he had endured celebrated failures with *The Wood Demon* and *The Seagull*. But the MAT offered him another kind of opportunity, and he was moved by the passion and idealism Nemirovich displayed. Though he was not one to write manifestos or make sweeping pronouncements, Chekhov recognized that the theatre was ripe for reform and might provide possibilities for a new kind of writing. He wrote to Nemirovich that "The Art Theatre is creating the most glorious pages of the book that will in time come to be written of contemporary Russian theatre,"[9] and he himself contributed the most important of them.

Chekhov's originality as a playwright will be discussed more fully in the chapters to come, but it is worth saying a little about where his work fits in the century of intensive innovation it helped to usher in. Chekhov's work is generally associated with the rise of naturalistic drama at the end of the nineteenth century. The manifestos of Émile Zola, the productions of André Antoine, and the plays of Henrik Ibsen and August Strindberg were part of a pan-European movement to depict reality convincingly in the theatre. Chekhov was sympathetic to the aims of this movement, and expressed a desire to represent life on the stage in a new way:

> After all, in real life, people don't spend every moment in shooting at one another, hanging themselves, or making declarations of love. They do not spend all of their time saying clever things. They are more occupied with eating, drinking, flirting, and saying stupidities, and these are the things which ought to be shown on the stage … People eat their dinner, just eat their dinner, and all the time their happiness is taking form, or their lives are being destroyed.[10]

But Chekhov went beyond simply the subject matter of what was depicted onstage: he depicted it in a new way. As Martin Esslin has pointed out, Ibsen and other naturalistic playwrights still wrote variations on the well-made play, with tightly constructed plots and articulate characters whose desires drove the action in a clear direction. Chekhov's plays, by contrast, work by indirection, dramatizing the apparently inconsequential interactions of everyday life. Chekhov's plays, in David Magarshack's term, are "plays of indirect action," depicting not the most dramatic moments of a story, but the hidden impulses behind them. Chekhov's characters often seem not to know what they want, and though they sometimes talk incessantly, they are unable to give voice to their deepest feelings. Chekhov's drama emerges, not just in passionate speeches, but in the "subtext" below seemingly trivial remarks and enigmatic actions. Chekhov's approach anticipated not only the more or less realistic dramas of playwrights like Arthur Miller and Tennessee Williams, but the more elliptical works of Harold Pinter and even the absurdist dramas of Samuel Beckett. As Esslin writes, "*Waiting for Godot* carries Chekhov's technique of characters in apparently idle and trivial chatter to its extreme, creating a dramatic structure without action and completely open-ended."[11] In any event, there seems to be little doubt that the theatre of the twentieth century would not have been the same without Chekhov. His innovations in the writing of both drama and fiction continue to exert their influence on the writers of the new millennium.

Chapter 3

Early stories

Chekhov's literary style evolved over the course of his life, as he went from writing short, mostly comic, pieces for newspapers like *The Dragonfly* and *The Alarm Clock* to more sustained and serious pieces for the so-called "thick journals" like Suvorin's *New Times* or *Russian Thought*. His fiction does maintain certain characteristic features throughout his career. His stories deal almost exclusively with the lives of ordinary Russians in the contemporary world that Chekhov knew. An economical opening, with little exposition; a concern with the interior life of the characters, revealed through tellingly chosen details; a carefully crafted ending, whether surprising or deflationary: all of these are constants in Chekhov's fiction. This chapter will cover the range of Chekhov's earlier stories, up to his first sustained masterpiece, *The Steppe*, from 1888. The works discussed will give a sense of the range of Chekhov's subject matter as well as the characteristic literary devices that emerge over the first decade of his career.

The most obvious feature of Chekhov's early stories is their economy, forced on him by the rigid line-counts of the papers for which he wrote. The need to jump right into the action of a story led to his characteristically brief openings, which he retained even when he had more column inches to work with. A piece of advice he often gave to beginning writers was to tear out the opening pages of a story: "One should write in such a way that the reader understands what is going on not through any explanation on the part of the author, but rather through the movement of the story and through the conversations and actions of the characters. Try tearing out the first half of your story; you will only have to change the beginning of the second half a bit, and the story will be completely understandable."[1] By quickly jumping to the crucial action, Chekhov was able to sketch out the essence of a character in a story of only a hundred lines or so.

Rank reverence and social satire

Chekhov's early stories address a range of topics and situations, some of which will continue to be explored in his later stories and plays. One recurrent theme is rank reverence or *chinopochitanie*, the extreme self-consciousness of civil-service officials, particularly those relatively low in the bureaucratic hierarchy. Perhaps his best-known early story, "The Death of a Clerk" (1883), concerns a Gogolian bureaucrat who inadvertently sneezes on a high official while attending the opera. He is so mortified that he makes repeated attempts to apologize, making the situation worse and worse until finally, after the official snaps at him in impatience, he goes home and dies. His sudden and unexpected death, revealed in the last word of the story, produces both a comic surprise and a startling revaluation of the intensity of the clerk's obsession.

Another story from 1883, "Fat and Thin," portrays two former schoolmates meeting on a railway platform many years later. Initially they embrace enthusiastically and happily recall old times, but when the thin man realizes that the other has become a privy councilor, he immediately becomes constrained. Addressing his old friend as "Your Excellency," he reintroduces his wife and child in a stilted and formal way. "The fat man was about to make some protest, but the face of the thin man wore an expression of such reverence, sugariness, and mawkish respectfulness that the privy councilor was sickened."[2] In "Fat and Thin," Chekhov indicts the way rank-consciousness causes slavish and servile behavior toward those above one in station, but he is also concerned with the way it leads to mistreatment of those below. Chekhov's works are full of instances of petty tyranny, of those low on the social scale venting their resentments on those unfortunates who are even lower. "Small Fry" (1885) depicts a lowly clerk who has to work on Easter eve, and in a few pages the story reveals all of the frustrations and aspirations of his meaningless job. As he sits at his desk, the clerk notes a cockroach running about and pities it as a fellow-sufferer. He works on a flattering letter to a hated superior; he complains to the porter about the festivities he is missing out on; he considers leaving his post, absconding with funds and fleeing to America, or rising through the ranks by spying and back-stabbing. Suddenly he notices the cockroach again; he swats it and tosses it into the lamp, which flares and sputters. "And Nevyrazimov felt better," the story grimly concludes.[3]

The contrasting behavior of the rank-conscious official toward those above and below him in station is turned to comic effect in "A Chameleon" (1884), one of Chekhov's most frequently anthologized stories from this period. A puppy has been apprehended for biting a goldsmith on the finger. The police superintendent changes his opinion about the dog back and forth five times, depending on whether he believes it belongs to a general or is merely a stray. The story is told almost entirely in dialogue, with little comment from the narrator. The reader must fill in the private motivations of the policeman, as he alternately orders the dog strangled or pets it and threatens the goldsmith. These oscillations have a grotesque note of comedy about them, but the dog itself evokes pathos. While the reader must guess at the feelings of the policeman from his speech, the narrator's description leaves little doubt as to the feelings of the dog:

> The culprit who has caused the sensation, a white borzoy puppy with a sharp muzzle and a yellow patch on her back, is sitting on the ground with her fore-paws outstretched in the middle of the crowd, trembling all over. There is an expression of misery and terror in her tearful eyes.[4]

The theme of the chameleon runs through many of Chekhov's early stories of rank and status. Within a hierarchical, status-conscious society, characters adapt themselves to their surroundings, changing their behavior according to the rank of those with whom they interact. One prominent character from this period, however, stands out for his inability to change: the eponymous antihero of "Sergeant Prishibeyev" (1885). This retired soldier, accustomed to giving orders and enforcing discipline, is unable to adjust to life in a peasant village. His monomania leads him to break up unauthorized gatherings, spy on the village women, and eventually to beat up the village elder and policeman. While the story has humorous elements, it suggests a serious political comment on the dangers of a society built on authoritarianism. The story ends with the tables turned, with the bewildered Prishibeyev sent to jail for a month for disturbing the peace. Chekhov revised the story with a brief coda in which Prishibeyev, on his way to jail, is still unable to resist ordering a crowd of peasants to move along and stop making trouble. Prishibeyev became a byword in Russian society for the slave to authority who himself enforces it upon others; the story was reputedly a favorite of Stalin's.[5]

"Sergeant Prishibeyev" takes place in a courtroom. Chekhov had covered many trials as a journalist, and judicial settings figure in many of his early stories, especially those involving social satire. The hero of "The Malefactor" (1885) is a peasant who is on trial for unscrewing a nut from the railroad tracks to use as a sinker for his fishing line. Confronted with his crime against the railroad – a symbolic threat to Russia's modernization – he stolidly protests his innocence and refuses to be cowed by the judge. While at one level he is refusing to kowtow to authority, at another he is still very much invested in the Russian social hierarchy, as his final protest makes clear: "Judges indeed! Our master the general is dead – the Kingdom of Heaven be his – or he would have shown you judges … Flog if you like, but flog someone who deserves it, flog with conscience."[6] This same commitment to traditional authority structures will be heard in Chekhov's final work, *The Cherry Orchard*, where the old servant Firs regrets the Emancipation and looks back with nostalgia to a time when masters and servants both knew their places. Consciousness of social hierarchy remained a theme for Chekhov throughout his career.

Comic stories and jokes

While some of Chekhov's comic stories had a serious social or political undertone, many were written purely to entertain. Some of his most appealing stories from this period are basically extended jokes. Writing in 1929, the Russian Formalist critic Viktor Shklovksy observed that "The fundamental structural device used by Chekhov is the 'error.'"[7] Some simple mistake – of identity, social misrecognition, or even a misplaced object – leads to further misunderstandings. The basic situation is elaborated to lead to a comic payoff, which often comes in a surprising or unexpected manner, so that the reader's expectations are both frustrated and satisfied. In "Boots" (1885), the story involves the attempts of a rheumatic piano tuner named Murkin to recover his boots, which have been mislaid by a drunken hotel porter, who accidentally returned them to the wrong room after cleaning them. Going to the room, Murkin receives a pair of boots from the actress who lives there, but they turn out to be those of an actor with whom she is having an affair; he has gone off in Murkin's boots, which are in better condition. Putting on the actor's worn boots (both are for the left foot), Murkin limps to the theatre. He finds the actor in his dressing room, costumed as Bluebeard, trying to sell a revolver to another actor. This is one of the first instances of Chekhov's following his own advice about not introducing a gun into a literary work unless it is to be used subsequently: "If you hang a pistol on the wall in the first act, then it has to be shot in the last act."[8] As Murkin takes off the actor's boots and explains the situation, it becomes evident that the other actor is the husband of the woman Bluebeard has been visiting. A fracas breaks out, with Bluebeard protesting his innocence and threatening the hapless Murkin. In the last paragraph, Chekhov uses the narrative trick of zooming out to a more objective distance, leaving the reader to imagine the noisy climax of the story: "And all the persons who were promenading that evening in the town park by the Summer theatre describe to this day how just before the fourth act they saw a man with bare feet, a yellow face, and terror-stricken eyes dart out of the theatre and dash along the principal avenue. He was pursued by a man in the costume of Bluebeard, armed with a revolver. What happened later no one saw …"[9]

Part of the merit of these stories, in addition to their comic plots, lies in their development of type characters, often fussy and anxious creatures like Murkin, whose personal obsessions lead them into compromising situations that strip them of their hard-won dignity. In "Nerves" (1885), an architect who has attended a séance finds himself frightened to be alone in the dark. His wife is away at an all-night church service, so he repeatedly invents excuses to call on the German governess for company, who indignantly assumes he is trying to seduce her. Finally he sneaks into her room and falls asleep, to be found at dawn by his wife:

> On the bed lay stretched Rosalia Karlovna fast asleep, and a couple of yards from her was her husband curled up on the trunk sleeping the sleep of the just and snoring loudly.
> What she said to her husband, and how he looked when he woke, I leave to others to describe. It is beyond my powers.[10]

Again, Chekhov leads just up to the final punchline of the story, but then leaves it to the reader to imagine it.

The "surprise ending" is one of the defining features of Chekhov's early work. One of the best examples of a story in which Chekhov creates an expectation, then fulfills it in a surprising but satisfying way, is "Overdoing It" (1885), about another nervous man undertaking a journey by cart through a dark forest. Smirnov, a land surveyor, hires a peasant named Klim to take him to a remote estate, but on the way he begins to fear that his driver will rob him. In order to protect himself, he begins talking about his revolvers, his valor in combat, and the number of robbers he has vanquished. Growing more and more alarmed as night falls and the taciturn Klim drives them deeper into the woods, Smirnov elaborates his boasts ever further. Suddenly, Klim jumps off and bolts into the woods, crying, "Help! Take the horse and the cart, you devil, only don't take my life. Help!" The reader, seeing through Smirnov's empty boasting, perhaps expects that he *will* be robbed, but it turns out his words have been so effective that he finds himself alone and defenseless in the wilderness. Smirnov has received the expected comeuppance, but in an unexpected way (though he is eventually able to coax the driver out of the forest, after which "The road and Klim no longer seemed dangerous to him").[11]

Perhaps the most satisfying example of a Chekhovian surprise ending that is both unexpected and appropriate is that of "A Work of Art" (1886).[12] In this story, a doctor is given a present by the son of an antique dealer, whom he has saved from typhus. The gift is a bronze candleholder depicting two women in "the costume of Eve" and in quasi-pornographic attitudes. While the doctor finds it well-crafted and titillating, he protests that he cannot have it in his office. The young man presses it on him, insisting that it is a beautiful work of art, and he only wished that he had the other one of the pair of candlesticks to give him. The doctor decides to give it to his friend the lawyer, who then passes it along to his friend the actor, who, at a loss, takes it to the antique dealer from which it came originally. The next day the doctor's office door is flung open by the antique dealer's son. The reader expects him to be angry at the return of his gift; instead, he exclaims delightedly that he has found the partner to the original candlestick and thrusts the offending item on the doctor once more.

While Chekhov's early comic stories often have surprise endings, some of them also have surprise beginnings. As noted before, the strict limits on length at papers like *Fragments* meant that Chekhov had to jump right into the action of his stories, without giving much in the way of context or character background. This technique frequently produces an amusing effect, as the very limited exposition is combined with action. "In the Dark" (1886) begins with the memorable sentence, "A fly of medium size made its way into the nose of the assistant procurator, Garin."[13] The fly turns out not to be important to the story, except insofar as it causes Garin to sneeze, waking his wife, who soon becomes convinced a burglar is in the house. It turns out not to be a burglar but the lover of the cook; Garin's wife decides that this is an even worse violation of their home.

Women of strict virtue and propriety are frequent targets of Chekhov's comic stories. In "In an Hotel" (1885), the Colonel's wife complains about the boorish behavior of her neighbor until she learns he is a young unmarried man, at which point she begins trying to engineer a match between him and one of her daughters. In "The Marshal's Widow" (1885), the heroine has a memorial party on her husband's name-day every year but refuses to serve alcohol, since it had been his undoing. The guests, all pillars of the community, take turns making excuses to go out into the hall, where one of them has secreted several bottles in his fur coat. The humor of the story comes in part from the very absence of authorial comment. The story ends with a letter from the Marshal's widow to a friend, in which she describes events at the party that the reader understands more fully than she does:

> Father Yevmeny, that delightful little old man, sat down by me, and looking tearfully at me kept babbling something like a child. I did not

> understand what he said, but I know how to understand true feeling. The police captain, the handsome man of whom I wrote to you, went down on his knees to me, tried to read me some verses of his own composition (he is a poet), but … his feelings were too much for him, he lurched and fell over …[14]

The reader enjoys the widow's misperceptions of the drunken antics of her guests. Many of Chekhov's stories of this period employ this technique, where the narration is filtered through a consciousness that lacks a full understanding of the situation described, an understanding the reader is able to supply. Sometimes the effect is comic, sometimes poignant; and in some cases the misperception invites the reader to see things in a new and perhaps revealing way. This strategy is used with particular effectiveness in Chekhov's stories involving children and animals.

Stories of children

Chekhov had great imaginative sympathy for the perspectives of children, and they turn up repeatedly in his fiction, especially early on. Sometimes they are innocent, sometimes selfish and cruel, and sometimes they have been forced to grow up too quickly; but their worldview is nearly always, in some way, an indictment of the everyday life of adults. In "Grisha," the third-person narrator adopts the perceptions of a little boy, less than three years old, whose world has heretofore consisted largely of his nursery. Grisha's worldview sometimes implies a commentary on Russian domestic life: "Nurse and mamma are comprehensible: they dress Grisha, feed him, and put him to bed, but what papa exists for is unknown."[15] At other times, the story creates humor, and a sense of wonder, by painting the familiar in unfamiliar terms, as when, on his first walk in the town, Grisha sees "A crowd of soldiers, with red faces and bath brooms under their arms," and observes as "Two big cats with long faces run after each other across the boulevard, with their tongues out, and their tails in the air." Innocent of the harsher adult world of guns and dogs, Grisha interprets these things in terms of the known objects of his nursery. Eventually Grisha and the nurse visit the kitchen of another house, where they drink with the cook and a male companion. Grisha is stifled by the heat of the stove and chokes on the drink the adults mischievously give him. No great harm is done, but that evening, Grisha is feverish and is unable to relate his experiences to his mother beyond wailing, "Go away, stove!" The dry conclusion to the story enlists the reader's sympathies on behalf of the mistreated Grisha: "'He must have eaten too much …' mamma decides. And Grisha, shattered by the impressions of the new life he has just experienced, receives a spoonful of castor-oil from mamma."

The use of an innocent child protagonist often sets up some disturbing discovery about the adult world. In "The Cook's Wedding" (1885), another Grisha – or perhaps the same one at seven years old – eavesdrops on the marriage arrangements for the family cook, Pelageya, but can make no sense of the apparent injustice of this adult institution: "Pelageya was living in freedom, doing as she liked, and not having to account to anyone for her actions, and all at once, for no sort of reason, a stranger turns up, who has somehow acquired rights over her conduct and her property!"[16] In this story the reader is free to reject Grisha's perspective as limited and unformed, though we are forced at least momentarily to look at marriage in a new light. In "A Trifle from Life" (1886), the disillusionment is harsher, as a boy wrestles with the familial repercussions of adultery and divorce. Alyosha has his confidences betrayed by his mother's lover, who is concerned only with his own sense of grievance. Alyosha is shocked at the way adults seem to violate the values they try to impose on children: "It was the first time in his life that he had been brought into such coarse contact with lying; till then he had not known that there are in the world, besides sweet pears, pies, and expensive watches, a great many things for which the language of children has no expression."[17] This is one of what Vladimir Kataev has termed "stories of discovery," in which some every-day incident causes a character to reassess his or her previously complacent view of life, and to confront the world in all its complexity and malignity.[18]

Chekhov's children are not always quite so innocent. In "An Incident" (1886), Chekhov contrasts the world of adults with those of both children and animals, and these with each other. The story begins with the children of a well-to-do family declaring, with joyful absurdity, that "The cat has got puppies!"[19] The narrator editorializes that "Domestic animals play a scarcely noticed but undoubtedly beneficial part in the education and life of children," but the story implies that this education often comes at great cost to the animals in question. The enthusiasm the children have for the new kittens does not prevent their tormenting them: Vanya treats one as an experimental subject, trying to force its eyes open, and then "watching its movements, and thrusting first a pencil, then a match into its little mouth …" The children save the kittens from being drowned in the cesspool, only to learn that they have been eaten by Nero, the family dog. The consumption of the kittens is announced with a "snigger" by the footman, to the horror of the children:

> The children expect that all the people in the house will be aghast and fall upon the miscreant Nero. But they all sit calmly in their seats, and only

express surprise at the appetite of the huge dog. Papa and mamma laugh. Nero walks about by the table, wags his tail, and licks his lips complacently … the cat is the only one who is uneasy. With her tail in the air she walks about the rooms, looking suspiciously at people and mewing plaintively.

Both the indifference of the adults and the outrage of the children are contrasted with the baffled grief of the mother cat. The story is amusing in its matter-of-fact tone and startling denouement, but the mother cat's loss has genuine moral weight.

The sincere feelings of an animal are more fully explored in "Kashtanka" (1887), a story intended for children, which has a dog for its protagonist. Part of the pleasure of the story comes from the surprising ways the leading character interprets the world, just as in "Grisha." But the reader is also invited to question the events in ways beyond the scope of Kashtanka's own understanding of them; and like "An Incident," the story may leave a feeling of moral unease. Kashtanka ("Rusty") is a reddish mongrel belonging to a drunken carpenter and his son; she is devoted to them despite the fact that they evidently abuse her. One day she gets lost in the city; cold and hungry, she is adopted by a curious gentleman who treats her kindly and gives her a place to live. The reader gradually realizes the gentleman is a circus artiste of some kind; he also has a cat, a goose, and a pig in his establishment, and he trains all of them, including Kashtanka, to perform tricks. Kashtanka soon becomes adjusted to this new milieu, though she still, in dreams, recalls the smells of glue and varnish that she knew from the carpenter's shop. The growing attachment of Kashtanka (now called Auntie) to her new world is marked by her emotional response to an event she does not understand – the death of the goose, Ivan Ivanitch. In an effective if sentimental touch, the third-person narrator filters the trainer's grief through Auntie's uncomprehending but empathetic consciousness: "And shining drops, such as one sees on the window-pane when it rains, trickled down his cheeks. Not understanding what was the matter, Auntie and Fyodor Timofeyitch snuggled up to him and looked with horror at the gander."[20]

The climax of the story comes when Kashtanka is brought to the circus to take over Ivan Ivanitch's place in the act. The unreality of the scene is depicted in the images Kashtanka uses in her struggles to process it: the circus tent is like an inverted soup tureen, an elephant is a monster with a "fat, huge countenance with a tail instead of a nose, and two long gnawed bones sticking out of his mouth"; even her master becomes grotesquely transformed into what the reader, but not Kashtanka, recognizes as a clown: "The white-faced, sack-like figure smelt like her master, its voice, too, was the familiar master's voice, but there were moments when Auntie was tortured by doubts, and then she was ready to run away from the parti-coloured figure and to bark." Just as "Auntie" comes into the ring and begins her act, she hears two voices calling out her old name from the gallery:

> Auntie started, and looked where the shouting came from. Two faces, one hairy, drunken and grinning, the other chubby, rosy-cheeked and frightened-looking, dazed her eyes as the bright light had dazed them before … She remembered, fell off the chair, struggled on the sand, then jumped up, and with a delighted yap dashed towards those faces.

Kashtanka returns gladly to her old masters, and as she leaves the circus following "the people who smelled of glue and varnish," the whole episode seems to her "like a long, tangled, oppressive dream." The reader is invited to question whether she is really better off, since indeed both her masters exploit her in different ways. Vladimir Kataev has pointed out that the story has received a wide range of political interpretations from Soviet and Russian critics. There is certainly an element of social critique in the story, as evidenced by the narrator's parenthetical observation that "(All mankind Kashtanka divided into two uneven parts: masters and customers; between them there was an essential difference: the first had the right to beat her, and the second she had the right to nip by the calves of their legs.)" Yet as Kataev emphasizes, "Kashtanka" is not, at least primarily, a political allegory, but a story about a dog; and Kashtanka's return to her original masters, while it may raise moral questions about their right to her, provides a satisfying structural completion similar to many of Chekhov's other early stories.

Some of Chekhov's stories with child protagonists have a more aggressively sociopolitical tone. "Vanka" (1886), about a young village boy who has been apprenticed to a shoemaker in Moscow, has an element of Dickensian sentiment and bits of ironic humor, but it clearly reveals the plight of child workers and the newly urbanized peasantry. For most of the story, Vanka writes a letter to his grandfather, begging him to come take him away: "Have pity on an unhappy orphan like me; here everyone knocks me about, and I am fearfully hungry; I can't tell you what misery it is, I am always crying. And the other day the master hit me on the head with a last, so that I fell down."[21] His letter is interspersed with happy, somewhat idealized memories of life in the village, such as cutting down a Christmas tree for the masters' house. The reader recognizes that the reality of village life might not be much better than his present situation, and that Vanka's grandfather is probably a bit of a rogue. Nonetheless, Chekhov's final twist comes as a rather cruel joke. Vanka addresses his letter merely "*To grandfather in the village*" and drops it into a post box, from which it will simply be thrown away. As Vanka settles into happy dreams of home, the reader knows that it is too late for him, that his childhood is over and he will awake again into the bleak light of a menial working-class existence.

One of Vanka's chief complaints about his employers – "when their wretched brat cries I get no sleep at all, but have to rock the cradle" – became the main plot for one of Chekhov's most famous stories of children, written just over a year later. "Sleepy" (1888) tells of Varka, another abused orphan, whose principal job is rocking the cradle of her employers' infant. As in "Vanka," the story contrasts the child protagonist's visions of home and family with the exhausting misery of servant life. Yet while Vanka daydreams about pleasant village memories, Varka has actual dreams that obsessively rake over the tragedies that led to her present situation. Her father's death and her pilgrimage, with her mother Pelageya, to town in search of work recur in her visions as concrete sensory images, which mix and blend with her actual surroundings as she rocks the baby and fights to stay awake. The lullaby she is singing – "*Bayu-bayushki-bayu*"– becomes the chattering of her dying father's teeth ("*Bu-bu-bu-bu*") as she slips in and out of sleep. The other dream to which she repeatedly returns is a Dantean "broad highway of liquid mud"; down this highway "stretches a string of carts, people trudge along with bundles on their backs, and some sort of shadows flit back and forth."[22] The shadows are really there in the room with Varka; they come from diapers drying on a clothesline and are cast by a flickering icon-lamp, which also throws a green patch of light on the ceiling. (Green is generally an ominous color in Chekhov's work, often associated with death.) One of the technical achievements of the story is the way in which these two interwoven dreams absorb and interact with Varka's present reality: "The green spot and the shadows begin to move, getting into Varka's fixed, half-open eyes and forming dim reveries in her half-sleeping brain." During the episode of her father's death, Varka is vaguely aware of a baby crying, and of someone singing a lullaby "in her own voice": evidently she is still just awake enough to continue doing her job. The present-tense narration duplicates the sleepy confusion in Varka's own mind as she struggles to process her dreams and the sensory stimuli around her: "Varka goes into the woods and weeps there, but suddenly somebody hits her on the back of the head so hard that she bumps her forehead against a birch. She lifts her eyes and sees before her the shoemaker, her master." Until Varka has identified her master, she is still in the woods; and therefore it must be a birch tree on which she has hit her head, rather than the cradle.

The remainder of the story follows Varka through her grueling day of menial tasks – cleaning galoshes, lighting the samovar, fetching vodka for the master's guests – until night falls and she is again minding the cradle:

And the baby cries and gets exhausted from crying. Again Varka sees the muddy highway, the people with bundles, Pelageya, her father Yefim. She understands everything, recognizes everyone, but through her half sleep she simply cannot understand what power binds her hand and foot, oppresses her, and keeps her from living. She looks around, seeking this power in order to rid herself of it, but she cannot find it. Finally, worn out, she strains all her powers and her vision, looks up at the flickering green spot, and, hearing the crying, locates the enemy that keeps her from living.
    That enemy is the baby.

And so, "after strangling him," Varka lies down on the floor and immediately, "laughing with joy," falls asleep. The melodrama of the murder is vitiated by Chekhov's dispensing with it quickly in a participial phrase in the story's final sentence. And while the murder provides a shock ending that is perhaps necessary for Varka's predicament to have its full impact, the story itself is much more concerned with the poetic rendering of her exhausted delirium. Through the repeated use of a few striking images – the green light, the infernal highway, the drum-roll of the father's teeth – and the fugue-like oscillations between dream and reality, Chekhov creates an unforgettable impression of a mind *in extremis*, and evokes remarkable sympathy for his young protagonist. "Sleepy" depicts not one child murder, but two.

Sympathy with the downtrodden

Several of Chekhov's stories, like "Sleepy," are built on the sympathetic iden-tification with those on the margins of society. Like "Sleepy," these are brief snapshots of unhappy lives caught at moments, great or small, of decisive, unavoidable suffering. Such subjects, by their nature, incur the dangers of saccharine sentimentality, on the one hand, or strident social moralizing, on the other. Chekhov generally avoids these pitfalls through the use of unex-pected and sometimes grim humor, and through the resolute objectivity of his dispassionate narrative voice. Though some of his early stories have heavy moralistic comments from the narrator, he increasingly learned the value of leaving the reader to provide the ethical response to the action. In advice he gave to the writer Lydia Avilova, Chekhov wrote, "When you describe the miserable and unfortunate, and want to make the reader feel pity, try to be somewhat colder – that seems to give a kind of background to another's grief, against which it stands out more clearly. Whereas in your story the characters cry and you sigh. Yes, be more cold … The more objective you are, the stronger will be the impression you make."[23]

"Sorrow" (1885) and "Misery" (1886) both, by their very titles, might seem vulnerable to the above-mentioned problems of sentiment or preachiness. Both are stories of elderly working-class men, alone in the world and beset by loss. In "Sorrow" a village lathe-turner loses his wife; in "Misery" a Moscow cab driver mourns the death of his son. The former story uses the familiar Russian literary device of a sledge drive in a snowstorm (reused by Chekhov in "On Official Business" and made famous by Tolstoy in "Master and Man") to recount the forty-year marriage of Grigory and Matronya, whom he is taking to the hospital. As he jokes to his wife about the insults the doctor will hurl at him for not bringing her sooner, "prattl[ing] on mechanically to get a little relief from his depressing feelings," Grigory recognizes that he is facing a loss for which he is wholly unprepared. He has mistreated his wife almost from the moment of their marriage, and his self-justifying monologue gives some sense of the misery of her life while achieving a semi-comic tone: "if Pavel Ivanitch asks you whether I beat you, say, 'Never!' and I never will beat you again. I swear it. And did I ever beat you out of spite? I just beat you without thinking. I am sorry for you. Some men wouldn't trouble, but here I am taking you ... I am doing my best."[24] Grigory has been talking without any response since the beginning of the story, and the reader's suspicions are confirmed by a masterful detail: "It struck him as strange that the snow on his old woman's face was not melting." Confronting the reality of her death does not cure him of his self-ishness – it seems to him she has done it to spite him – but he recognizes that his marriage, and his life, have somehow been wasted: "He remembered that forty years ago Matryona had been young, handsome, merry ... All the essentials for a happy life had been there, but the trouble was that, just as he had got drunk after the wedding and lay sprawling on the stove, so he had gone on without waking up till now." The story seems heading for sentimentality and moralizing, but Chekhov brutally interrupts it with a casual reminder of the cold physiological facts of mortality: "A knocking was audible behind him, and though he did not look round, he knew it was the dead woman's head knocking against the sledge." By refusing to forgive Grigory or allow him to wallow in self-pity, Chekhov draws the reader's sympathy to him more sincerely. When Grigory wakes up in the hospital, half-dead from frostbite, the callous frankness of the doctor makes us feel that poor Grigory is entitled to a little more of the human warmth that he perhaps denied to his wife : "Say good-by to your arms and legs ... They've been frozen off. Come, come! ... What are you crying for? You've lived your life, and thank God for it! I suppose you have had sixty years of it – that's enough for you! ..." The mixture of ironic judgment and sympathetic understanding that the story extends toward Grigory will be revisited by Chekhov in one of his later masterpieces,

"Rothschild's Fiddle" (1894), another story about a dying widower reflecting on his life.

"Misery" is perhaps more sentimental, in that the protagonist is not depicted in the same ironic light as Grigory. We are told nothing of Iona the cabman's relationship with his dead son, so we cannot judge him in the way "Sorrow" invites us to judge Grigory. From the beginning of the story we are invited to sympathize with Iona as he sits huddled in the snow, with his horse, waiting for a fare. The mare, subtly introduced as a character from the beginning, is granted equal sentience with her master: "She is probably lost in thought. Anyone who has been torn away from the plough, from the familiar gray landscapes, and cast into this slough, full of monstrous lights, of unceasing uproar and hurrying people, is bound to think."[25] Iona encounters various people over the course of the evening and makes tentative attempts to talk to them about the recent death of his son. He is always rebuffed and finally returns to the cab-yard. As he feeds the mare, he begins, tentatively at first, to speak to her about his sorrow: "Now suppose you had a little colt …" The absurdity of the moment helps mitigate the sentimentality of it; the reader can share in the humor but may also be prepared to go along with the hopeful conclusion, with its hint of relief: "The little mare munches, listens, and breathes on her master's hands. Iona is carried away and tells her all about it."

Several of Chekhov's sympathetic stories call attention to the plight of young women who are essentially prostitutes, though they may cling to the fringes of more respectable society as seamstresses, dancers, or actresses. Chekhov had personal as well as professional experience with women of this class, and his attitude toward them was ambivalent; his later story "A Nervous Breakdown" (1889) mocks the crusade of a law student to save "fallen women" but expresses real, somewhat guilty outrage as to their plight. Chekhov's interest in prostitutes had a literary basis as well, as they are often featured characters in the works he most closely emulated, the stories of French writer Guy de Maupassant. In "Anyuta," "A Gentleman Friend," and "A Chorus Girl" (1886), Chekhov demonstrates the moral superiority of three such women to the men who exploit them. Anyuta is an impoverished young woman who lives with a medical student named Klochkov, helping support their meager household through embroidery work. She has lived with five such students previously, all of whom have now moved on to respectable lives in a class she can never join. In the course of the story Klochkov decides to tell her to leave, but then weakens and decides to let her stay another week. The satirical bite of the story comes from the way that Klochkov and his fellow students exploit Anyuta, not sexually, but by reducing her to an object for use in their studies. Preparing for an anatomy test, Klochkov makes Anyuta take her blouse off and draws charcoal lines on her chest tracing the position of her ribs; he becomes "so immersed in this occupation that he did not notice that Anyuta's lips, nose, and fingers had turned blue with cold."[26] His friend, the painter Fetisov, comes in and "borrows" Anyuta to pose for a painting of Psyche. Despite her demurral, Klochkov sends her off with high-minded words – "The man's asking for the sake of art, not for some trifle" – though there is every implication that he will send her to her next lover, perhaps Fetisov, in just the same way. The men of science and art pay lip service to their high-minded professions, while having their way with the body of Anyuta for pleasure or profit. Her sincere wish for Klochkov to succeed in his exams is contrasted with his vain daydreams of wealth and respectability. The story ends unresolved, with life going on as before – an instance of what the Soviet critic Viktor Shklovsky identified as the Chekhovian "zero ending" – and the seemingly random detail of someone in the boarding house hallway shouting about a samovar.[27]

Sympathy is mixed with satire in "A Gentleman Friend," in which the prostitute Vanda, penniless and just out of hospital, decides to ask for money from a Jewish dentist "who six months ago had given her a bracelet, and on whose head she had once emptied a glass of beer at the supper at the German Club."[28] She plans a playful and seductive appeal but then becomes self-conscious about her poor attire, cowed by the maidservant, and embarrassed by her position in life. The dentist does not recognize her, and meeting him on his territory rather than her own, Vanda cannot summon her usual teasing manner; she finds him cold and intimidating. In the end, rather than reveal herself, she lets him pull a healthy tooth and gives him her last ruble as a fee. The episode combines comic irony and pathos; it represents another of those moments of discovery where a character confronts the true awfulness of her situation: "She walked along the street, spitting blood, and brooding on her life, her ugly, wretched life, and the insults she had endured, and would have to endure tomorrow, and next week, and all her life, up to the very day of her death." But Chekhov does not end the story here, instead adding a reminder that these moments of awakening, though they may be true and profound, do not necessarily have a lasting impact: "Next day, however, she was back at the 'Renaissance,' and dancing there. She had on an enormous new red hat, a new fashionable jacket, and bronze shoes. And she was taken out to supper by a young merchant up from Kazan."

A companion piece to "A Gentleman Friend" is "The Chorus Girl," which replays a similar situation with a more sympathetic heroine. Pasha is entertaining her middle-class lover when his wife knocks on the door. While the husband hides in another room, the wife berates Pasha and demands that she return the gifts he has given her; he has evidently put the family at risk by embezzling from the office. Pasha protests that she has received nothing from him but ends up giving the wife all of her valuable possessions. After the wife leaves, her lover spurns her as a "low creature," aghast that his respectable wife "would have gone down on her knees … and to you!"[29] In the final paragraph Pasha, left alone, is unable to recover her self-possession as Vanda had; Chekhov leaves her reflecting bitterly on her condition, perhaps seeing its true cruelty for the first time:

> Pasha lay down and began wailing aloud. She was already regretting her things which she had given away so impulsively, and her feelings were hurt. She remembered how three years ago a merchant had beaten her for no sort of reason, and she wailed more loudly than ever.

The story gets its social edge from the high-handedness with which the husband and wife both treat Pasha; like Anyuta and Vanda, she is mistreated by those who consider themselves to be above her, in spite of her being more generous and moral than they. Chekhov recognized not only the vulnerability of those who were marginalized by gender and class, but the complacency and self-righteousness of the ostensibly "respectable" world.

Stories of women, marriage, and adultery

Chekhov's attitude to women was complicated and ambiguous throughout his life, and at times verged on misogyny. As a medical student, he contemplated writing a treatise on "sexual authority," influenced by Schopenhauer, contending that though evolution had reduced sexual difference in humans compared to other animals, there were still essential distinctions that prevented equality between the sexes. Oddly, this somewhat misogynistic view was tied up with one of Chekhov's fervent progressive beliefs, that women should have access to the same kind of education as men. In his personal life, while Chekhov was very appealing to women and enjoyed their company – he helped along the careers of a number of female writers – he was mistrustful of intimacy and was both attracted and repelled by female sexuality. Nevertheless, he portrayed female characters with remarkable complexity and insight, and many of his most important stories have women protagonists. He was keenly aware of the barriers to happiness posed by bourgeois marriage and its alternatives, while at the same time being attuned to the interior psychological traps women set for themselves in pursuing emotional satisfaction. In the period 1886–88, he wrote several studies of unhappy women caught at impasses – mundane or catastrophic – in their relationships with men.

Two of these stories, "The Huntsman" (1885) and "Agafya" (1886), helped launch Chekhov on his serious writing career. Both caught the attention of Grigorovich, a dean of Russian letters who became one of Chekhov's early allies and encouraged him to treat his writing more diligently. Both are influenced by Turgenev's *Sportsman's Sketches*, particularly the story "A Meeting." Like that story, both depict the unhappiness of peasant women who love callously indifferent men. "The Huntsman" portrays a brief meeting between Pelageya and her husband Yegor, and contrasts her fervent desire with his bored complacency. "Agafya" follows an essentially similar relationship, though in this case the heroine is married to a railway signalman and comes to the coolly contemptuous Savka on a fervid assignation. In both cases, the desired man has an affinity for nature, and a sense of freedom and self-worth, that leads him to reject or devalue the desperate sexual longing of the woman. Yegor takes pride in his ability as a hunter, the best shot in the district: "I'm free, spoiled, loose, and you're a barefoot farm worker, you live in dirt, you never straighten your back," he tells Pelageya.[30] Their meeting takes place on a road running between the forest where he hunts and the field where she is working; he has his gun, dog, and game bag, she carries a scythe. Though she begs him to return to their house in the village, he goes off on his free-spirited way. In the close of this brief story, Chekhov combines its simple elements with great artistic skill: Pelageya's sensual longing, Yegor's animal vigor, an insight into human relations combined with detailed observations of nature. Her eyes "caress" his departing figure, "his moving shoulder blades, his dashing head, his lazy, nonchalant stride." He stops and for a moment seems to want to speak to her, but he only gives her a ruble and walks off. In her final view of him, Chekhov incorporates a consciousness of the faculties of visual perception that suggests an impressionist painting: "But now the red color of his shirt merges with the dark color of his trousers, his steps can no longer be seen, the dog is indistinguishable from his boots." Suddenly he turns and disappears into the greenery; Pelageya "stands on tiptoe so as at least to see the white cap one more time."

While the story invites sympathy for Pelageya, it also honors the freedom to which Yegor aspires. Savka, the peasant lover of Agafya, is a more crassly selfish and destructive figure, though like Yegor he is a skilled hunter. Irresistible to women, he nonetheless has contempt for them; he prefers the challenge of catching a nightingale with his bare hands to accepting the caresses of the besotted Agafya. The story is set at a village allotment where Savka serves as a watchman and scarecrow. The narrator, an aristocratic huntsman in the manner of Turgenev, has come to fish with Savka and is an uncomfortable observer of his relations with Agafya. She stays with him at his hut through the night, in spite of the passing of the mail train that indicates that her husband will soon be home. Her conflicting impulses and intense passion are carefully delineated: "Agafya, intoxicated by the vodka, by Savka's scornful caresses, and by the stifling warmth of the night, was lying on the earth beside him, pressing her face convulsively to his knees."[31] After the train passes, she starts to leave: "For half a minute her whole figure, as far as I could distinguish it through the darkness, expressed conflict and hesitation. There was an instant when, seeming to come to herself, she drew herself up to get upon her feet, but then some invincible and implacable force seemed to push her whole body, and she sank down beside Savka again." Giving way to her desires, she utters "a wild, guttural laugh" conveying "reckless determination, impotence, and pain." The story ends the next morning as Savka and the narrator watch her walk through the fields to where her husband is waiting to beat her.

> In the village, near the furthest hut, Yakov was standing in the road, gazing fixedly at his returning wife. He stood without stirring, and was as motionless as a post. What was he thinking as he looked at her? What words was he preparing to greet her with? Agafya stood still a little while, looked round once more as though expecting help from us, and went on. I have never seen anyone, drunk or sober, move as she did. Agafya seemed to be shrivelled up by her husband's eyes. At one time she moved in zigzags, then she moved her feet up and down without going forward, bending her knees and stretching out her hands, then she staggered back. When she had gone another hundred paces she looked round once more and sat down.

Her strikingly described, back-and-forth movement communicates her internal anguish, though the story ends with her gathering the strength to confront her situation head-on: "Agafya suddenly jumped up, shook her head, and with a bold step went towards her husband. She had evidently plucked up her courage and made up her mind." Her courage in this moment makes a final contrast with the lazy selfishness of Savka.

While the desiring women of these stories are treated sympathetically, a related trio of stories from 1886 depicts female sexuality as more dangerous and destructive. In "The Witch," "A Misfortune," and "Mire," the women have more agency, and the men are threatened, manipulated, or humiliated by their sexual power. The title character of "The Witch" is the sensual young wife of an impotent sexton; he comes to believe that her unsatisfied desire is luring young men to their remote hut. There is no suggestion of the supernatural in the story, but Chekhov effectively exploits the romantic "pathetic fallacy" of having external nature match the emotional condition of the protagonist. The snow-storm that rages at the beginning of the story matches the furious passion of

Raissa; at the same time, it provides a convincing catalyst for her cabin fever and frustration, as well as a plausible motivation for the arrival of a strapping young postman out of the night. The threatened adultery never occurs, but the sexton is confirmed in his suspicions. To his alarm, however, the diabolical evil he associates with his wife's sexuality only makes her more attractive to him – but she repels his advances with an elbow to the nose. The story recognizes the unhappiness of both partners in this loveless marriage, though it casts the sexton's as comic, Raissa's as near-tragic.

The tragic and destructive dimensions of rampant female sexuality are invoked again in "A Misfortune," a story strongly influenced by Tolstoy's *Anna Karenina*, Russia's great novel of adultery. Sofya Petrovna, the young wife of a notary, is flattered by the attentions of the brooding lawyer Ilyin. Their first encounter takes place near a railway line, an ominous symbol given its importance in Tolstoy's novel (the adulterous Anna throws herself under a train). Sofya rejects Ilyin's advances, but he accuses her, correctly, of unconsciously leading him on. At their dacha, Sofya is suddenly disgusted by her husband's manner of eating, just as Anna Karenina is revolted by her husband's ears. The limited-omniscient narration skillfully shows that Sofya is half-aware of the effects of her behavior and the ultimate direction of her impulses; but she is acting a part even to herself: "'Poor Andrey!' she said to herself, trying as she thought of her husband to put into her face as tender an expression as she could."[32] When Ilyin arrives with guests in the evening, she indulges "the pettiness and egoism of youth," and flirts with him; "she felt sorry for him, but at the same time the presence of a man who loved her to distraction, filled her soul with triumph and a sense of her own power." Despite a few half-hearted attempts to remain faithful, by the end of the story she is walking through the night to meet Ilyin: "She was breathless, hot with shame, did not feel her legs under her, but what drove her on was stronger than shame, reason, or fear." Sofya is shallow, hypocritical, and driven not only by lust but by the power her sexuality gives her. That Chekhov is making her out to be an archetype of woman is suggested by associations with the biblical Eve; her desire is likened to a boa constrictor, and she is charmed by Ilyin's tiepin, a red snake with diamond eyes.

An even more aggressively allegorical version of the tempter Eve is provided by Chekhov's story "Mire." Its seductive Jewish protagonist, Susanna Rothstein, may have been influenced by Chekhov's sometime-fianceé Dunia Efros, with whom he seems to have had a stormy relationship. In "Mire" a young officer goes to Susanna, a successful vodka distiller, to recover some family debts that he needs in order to marry. Susanna teases and provokes him with her cynical wit, and he finds himself both revolted and tempted by her.

Her appearance is presented with a wealth of synesthetic detail: in her tight black dress, her figure "looked as though it had been turned in a lathe"; her head is "black and as curly as lamb's-wool"; her white face "for some reason suggested the cloying scent of jasmine"; and her nose and ears "were astoundingly white, as though they belonged to a corpse, or had been moulded out of transparent wax."[33] Chekhov makes her surroundings an expression of her sensual and financial rapacity, overcrowded with gilt and chintz; her lack of gentility is evident in "the gilt cornices, the gaudy wall-paper, the bright velvet table-cloths, the common oleographs in heavy frames." When she suddenly snatches back the IOUs he has brought, the officer seizes her in a physical confrontation redolent of animal sexuality: her face and bosom quiver "with a spiteful, catlike expression"; her fist with the IOUs "struggled convulsively for the pocket, like a fish in the net"; "she wriggled like an eel in his arms with her supple, flexible body, struck him in the chest with her elbows, and scratched him, so that he could not help touching her all over, and was forced to hurt her and disregard her modesty." Needless to say, he fails to recover the IOUs or the money; his cousin later finds himself seduced in the same way. The story ends with most of the men in the district in Susanna's house, enticed by the mire of sexuality and intoxicated by "the same sickly smell of jasmine." When the cousin returns for another visit, his response is one of sexual shame:

> He was on terms of friendly intimacy with all the men in the room, but scarcely nodded to them; they, too, scarcely responded, as though the places in which they met were not quite decent, and as though they were in tacit agreement with one another that it was more suitable for them not to recognise one another.

While Susanna's Jewishness is stressed throughout the story as a part of what makes her alien and enticing, there is also the suggestion that her unbridled sexual aggression is a quintessential part of her identity as a woman: "Well … she *is* a fe-e-male, I beg to inform you!" the cousin tells the officer after his encounter with her. On the other hand, as a woman and an outsider, Susanna Rothstein has few weapons to use against the chauvinistic Russian landowners who despise her; and so her use of her sexuality can be seen as an act of social defiance. Chekhov's friend Maria Kiseleva wrote to him protesting about the immorality of the story, leading Chekhov to respond with one of his most famous dicta, comparing the writer to a chemist: "To a chemist there is nothing impure on earth. The writer should be just as objective as the chemist; he should liberate himself from everyday subjectivity and acknowledge that manure piles play a highly respectable role in the landscape and that evil passions are every bit as much a part of life as good ones" (January 14, 1887).

Chekhov did not shrink from portraying controversial subjects, and his coolly dispassionate tone allowed him to explore sexuality with unusual frankness.

"The Steppe"

In 1888, Chekhov published what would be a major turning point in his literary career: the novella "The Steppe". It was his first work for one of the "thick journals" that dominated the more elevated literary scene. It represented an attempt to process his debts to forebears like Gogol – it echoes the natural descriptions of "Sorochintsy Fair" and the peripatetic structure of *Dead Souls* – while finding his own distinct voice. Chekhov wrote that "I know in the next world Gogol will be angry with me. He's the Tsar of the Steppes in our literature" (February 5, 1888).[34] It was the longest and most lyrical work Chekhov had produced, with an experimental, episodic structure that Chekhov himself had some doubts about, though he wrote to Grigorovich that he felt the story was his masterpiece. It was a deeply personal work, drawing on childhood memories of the steppe and, more directly, on a six-week journey he had made to Taganrog in 1887, which provided him with detailed notes about the nature and people of the South.

"The Steppe" is subtitled "The Story of a Journey," and as such it is part of a tradition that goes back to Homer's *Odyssey*. Its protagonist is a nine-year-old boy, Yegorushka, and its only real plot is his trip by cart from the provincial town where he grew up to the city, presumably Kiev, where he will attend school. Along the way, a series of loosely linked episodes impress themselves on the young hero. "The Steppe" is a coming-of-age story; Yegorushka leaves his childhood behind and struggles to process the vastness of the world and the complexity of human affairs. The story begins and ends with discussions of the boy's schooling, but it is the journey itself that provides his education.

Chekhov's observations of southern Russia produced some of his most precise and lyrical nature writing. "The Steppe" begins with the carriage in which Yegorushka is riding, accompanied by his uncle and a priest, Father Khristofor, leaving the town and entering the vastness of the steppe. The town is defined by institutions of confinement, labor, and death – the travelers ride past the prison, the smithies, the cemetery, and the brickworks – but the steppe is filled with mysterious life. It becomes a character in the story, changing its mood with the weather and time of day. As the sun rises it smiles and sparkles with dew, but soon "the deceived steppe assumed its usual July look," and Yegorushka finds it "stifling and dismal."[35] The heat, the humming of insects, the flights of birds, the desultory encounters with other people, all contribute to

Yegorushka's dreamy torpor. The size and strangeness of the steppe is conveyed through the image of a distant windmill, which, as they approach it, seems to move to the side to avoid them. The presence of Kurgans – Scythian burial mounds – serves as a *memento mori*; at other times, the steppe seems eerily alive. In one surreal instant, the grass seems to be singing, though its song eventually merges with that of a young peasant woman.

The most sustained human interaction the travelers have occurs when they stop at a wayside inn run by a Jewish couple. The episode recalls an incident from Chekhov's childhood in which he became ill on a journey and was looked after by a Jewish tavern-keeper and his wife. The couple in the story are similarly kindly, if sycophantic, but the central figure of the episode is the innkeeper's brother Solomon. He is a Dostoevskian malcontent who rejects his brother's concern for material wealth – he has burned his inheritance in the fire and now lingers at the inn to subject passersby to his sarcastic jibes. He baffles and discomfits those around him, but his relentless negativity casts a shadow over the story's human interactions that is never quite dispelled.

At the inn, Yegorushka also meets a young Polish countess whose beauty elicits from him a hint of emerging sexuality. She is there seeking the mysterious Varmalov, an elusive, Godot-like figure who seems to rule the steppe, and to whom Yegorushka's uncle and Father Khristofor are also bound. They make a side-trip in search of him, leaving Yegorushka to continue his journey in the company of a wagon train taking wool to market. The cartloads of wool provide a snug haven for Yegorushka, while the drivers of the train represent a range of ages and backgrounds, adding to the boy's understanding of Russian peasant life. Hearing their complaints and reminiscences, he assumes that all have had splendid lives in the past but have now fallen on hard times; the narrator observes that Yegorushka had not yet learned that the Russian loves recalling life but does not love living.

Sometimes, as in Chekhov's other stories of children, the boy's naiveté is exploited for an ironic point; in other cases Yegorushka seems precociously perceptive. In an episode recalling Tugenev's story "Bezhin Lea," the drivers sit around a campfire telling frightening tales of murders and apparitions. The elderly Pantalei tells repeated stories about merchants menaced by robbers with "long knives" and delivered by providential means. Yegorushka is intrigued, but eventually begins to suspect their veracity, and to reflect on motivations behind such narratives: "it seemed strange to him that a man who had traveled all over Russia in his lifetime, who had seen and known so much, whose wife and children had burned up, devalued his rich life so much that, whenever he sat by the campfire, he either kept silent or spoke of something that had never been" (75). Chekhov's own beliefs about the need for verisimilitude and objectivity in fiction emerge in the mind of his child protagonist.

The climax of the story is a thunderstorm that breaks over the steppe just as the simmering and conflicted emotional life of Yegorushka breaks to the surface. He has an enemy in the wagon train, a cruel, aggressive, and free-spirited young man named Dymov, who has the callous vigor and selfishness that Chekhov seems both to admire and resent in characters like Yegor in "The Huntsman." Dymov dominates and humiliates Yegorushka, along with other weaker members of the train, until the boy retreats to the wagon in tears. To Yegorushka's surprise, Dymov offers to let him hit him; at the same moment, there is a flash of lighting, sparking off one of the most famous thunderstorms in Russian literature. "As if someone had struck a match against the sky, a pale phosphorescent strip flashed and went out. There was a sound of someone walking on an iron roof somewhere very far away. He was probably walking barefoot, because the iron made a dull rumble" (89–90). The storm is another instance of Chekhov's pathetic fallacy, but the atmosphere of stifling heat and charged energy that proceeds the storm contributes to, as well as matching, the volatile frustrations of a boy who is very conscious of not yet being a man.

Yegorushka becomes ill after his night in the storm, and Chekhov employs his skill at depicting abnormal mental states in his descriptions of the boy's delirium. Chekhov mixes the senses of hearing, touch, taste, and smell to convey Yegorushka's feverish perceptions: "Something weighed on his head and chest, crushing him, and he did not know what it was: the old people's whispering or the heavy smell of the sheepskin? There was an unpleasant metallic taste in his mouth …" (97). Characters and incidents from the journey reappear in distorted form; characteristically, Chekhov represents them in flatly objective terms, with the same reality as anything else in the story: "Titus came up to the bed on skinny legs and began waving his arms, then grew up to the ceiling and turned into a windmill" (113). The illness marks a final phase in Yegorushka's transformational journey; when he awakes one morning fully recovered, he has arrived in the city where he is to study.

Like many of Chekhov's stories, "The Steppe" ends with a beginning. Left behind at the house where he will lodge, Yegorushka rushes after his departing uncle and Father Khristofor, only to see them disappearing out of sight around the street corner.

> Yegorushka felt that with these people, everything he had lived through up to then had vanished forever, like smoke; he sank wearily on to a bench and with bitter tears greeted the new, unknown life that was now beginning for him …
> What sort of life would it be? (113)

This sense that a new and different future awaits the characters in his stories, who have been changed by the apparently inconsequential events they have lived through, is very common in Chekhov. Nothing decisive has happened to Yegorushka on his journey, other than the journey itself: he has left home and gone to school. But the richness with which Chekhov has described the boy's perceptions along the way suggests some altering of his consciousness, a putting away of childish things. It is notable how much of a blank slate Yegorushka is, a wide-eyed drinker-in of the fullness of the world. In this way, perhaps, the story is emblematic of a key transition in Chekhov himself, an end of his literary apprenticeship. With "The Steppe," Chekhov ended his series of stories focused on child protagonists, and he never again wrote as fully about nature or the southern Russia of his youth. Like the English Romantic poet William Wordsworth, Chekhov in his later stories turned his attention away from childhood and nature to "the still, sad music of humanity."[36]

Chapter 4

Early plays

Dramatic sketches and monologues

While Chekhov's reputation as a playwright rests on the four major plays he wrote in the last decade of his life, his earlier dramatic work shows both his developing style and his iconoclastic attitude to the theatre of his time. Chekhov's early plays can be divided into two categories: full-length plays and one-acts. The longer plays lead more directly into the mature works for which Chekhov is best known, and they will be considered last in this chapter; the shorter works relate more closely to Chekhov's stories. Indeed, some of Chekhov's early plays are simply dramatizations of particular stories, such as "Along the Highway," one of his first dramatic efforts, written in 1884. Subtitled "A Dramatic Sketch in One Act," it stages the story "In the Autumn," about a ruined landowner seeking shelter in a wayside tavern. It was rejected by the censor as too squalid and gloomy for performance and never staged in Chekhov's lifetime. Nevertheless, Chekhov persisted with experiments in the short dramatic form, some of which bore fruit as highly successful commercial entertainment.

The one-acts fall into a variety of styles and types, many of which have not always been considered part of Chekhov's dramatic output. While working for comic newspapers like *The Alarm Clock* and *Fragments*, Chekhov wrote several short pieces in dramatic form, many of them parodying popular drama of the day. While these were not, presumably, intended for performance, at least one of them – *The Sudden Death of a Steed* (first published in 1888) – eventually made it to the stage. Chekhov's parodies reveal his eye for stagecraft and his derision of the conventions of the well-made plays and melodramas that dominated the Moscow and Petersburg theatres. The most extensive, *Unclean Tragedians and Leprous Playwrights* (1884), mocks the over-the-top plots and scenic spectacles of Romantic drama, specifically targeting Tarnovsky's *The Clean and the Leprous*, which had just played in Moscow. The opening stage direction gives some of the flavor of Chekhov's parody: "*The crater of a volcano. At a desk, covered in blood, sits TARNOVSKY; instead of a head, a skull sits on his shoulders; sulphur blazes in his mouth; out of his nostrils leap sneering green imps.*"[1] Although only a few pages long, Chekhov's playlet is so packed with action that it takes up six acts; it ends with "*Thunder, lightning, hoarfrost, the murder of Coverley, a great migration of peoples, shipwreck and the tying up of all the loose ends*" (277). Chekhov's mockery plainly indicates his impatience with the conventions of the popular theatre of spectacle; his views parallel those of the naturalist theatre movement underway in Northern and Western Europe. *Unclean Tragedians* was written in 1884, three years after Ibsen's *Ghosts*, and three years before Strindberg's *The Father* and the opening of André Antoine's Théâtre Libre in Paris. While Chekhov had mixed feelings about Ibsen and Strindberg and was not a self-consciously "naturalist" playwright, many of his earliest quasi-dramatic writings evince dissatisfaction with the nineteenth-century theatrical status quo.

One of the strangest of Chekhov's early plays is *Tatyana Repina* (1889), which is a kind of one-act sequel to the melodrama of the same name by Chekhov's friend and publisher Aleksey Suvorin. This play was never intended for public consumption – Chekhov had it privately printed in an edition of three copies as a gift for his friend – but it is arresting in its original structure and quasi-surrealist touches. Suvorin's play is about a jilted actress who poisons herself onstage; Chekhov's sequel takes up the story as the actress's former lover is being married to an heiress. Like many of Chekhov's later one-acts, it features a broken ritual, as the wedding is interrupted, first by rumors of a suicide epidemic among Russian women, then by a mysterious "Lady in Black," whom the bridegroom believes to be the dead Tatyana. The whole play is interspersed with the words of the marriage ceremony and the liturgical chantings of two church choirs, evidence of Chekhov's ongoing fascination with Orthodox ritual. The actual dialogue of the characters makes up less than a third of the play and is always in ironic counterpoint to the sacraments of marriage going on simultaneously. The tone of *Tatyana Repina* is a mixture of sardonic humor and uncanny horror. At the end of the play, the bridegroom hastens to the cemetery to order a requiem for Tatyana, while the mysterious lady in black dies in the church after the wedding guests have departed. As in many of

Chekhov's stories of mystery and suspense, nothing genuinely supernatural is known to have occurred; but the final effect is eerie and deeply unsettling.

Chekhov also wrote several of what are, for all intents and purposes, monologues, though they may contain one supporting character to be a feed to the protagonist. One of these, *Swan Song* (1887), continues to develop Chekhov's interest in the theatrical milieu; it is based on his short story "Calchas," one of his many tales about the stage. An elderly actor, costumed as the soothsayer Calchas from Offenbach's operetta *La Belle Hélène*, stumbles drunkenly onto the stage, having fallen asleep in his dressing room after the performance. While the old prompter Nikita tries to get him to go home, the actor, Svetlovidov, rambles about his life in the theatre. He recalls his early years as an artillery officer, before he "fell into the pit"; reminisces about a woman who loved him for his acting but wanted him to give up the stage; and relives his triumphs in the classical repertoire. The play contains extensive quotations from Shakespeare that chart the course of Svetlovidov's disappointed life: he rails against the heavens as Lear, verbally duels with Nikita as Hamlet, and finally renounces his former glories with Othello's "Farewell the tranquil mind; farewell content." *Swan Song* is a funny but poignant piece that honors the theatre while recognizing its frequent crassness and vulgarity. Svetlovidov is no tragic hero, but his final coming to terms with his life on the stage gives him a certain tattered grandeur.

The second quasi-monologue, *An Involuntary Tragedian* (1890), is also a chronicle of disillusionment. Despite the title, it has nothing to do with the theatre, although the protagonist does end up maniacally quoting Othello's demand for "Blood, blood, blood!" The hero, Tolkachov, is complaining about his life as a Petersburg bureaucrat, commuting from the dacha where his family is spending the summer. He is burdened with purchases he has been told to make in town, ranging from face powder and castor oil to crimson silk, carbolic acid, and a toy bicycle. He enumerates the woes of train travel, amateur theatricals, and mosquitoes, as well as the frustrations of office work in the sleepy Petersburg summer. He is talking to a Petersburg friend named Murashkin, from whom he is trying to borrow a revolver to shoot himself. As in *Swan Song*, the interlocutor is there mainly as a "feed," but he does serve an ironic plot function. After Tolkachov's diatribe, Murashkin asks him whether he can take a sewing machine and a caged canary out to a lady friend renting a dacha nearby; this is the final straw that sends the hero into his homicidal rage. The piece is basically comic from start to finish, but the proliferation of incongruous and unwieldy objects Tolkachov is to carry has a touch of the theatre of the absurd, and his despairing exasperation with his life hints at tragedy.

These darker tendencies are carried further in *The Evils of Tobacco*. This piece, a true monologue that Chekhov revised five times, reveals the further evolution of his interest in the alienated and neurotic individual, and points toward twentieth-century works by authors like Pirandello and Kafka. The initial version (1886), which Chekhov allegedly wrote in two and a half hours, is a comic monologue in which the speaker Nyukhin never quite gets to the subject of his lecture, wandering into digressions about his wife's boarding school. He stumbles over his pseudo-scientific jargon, complains about the bratty schoolgirls, and tries to interest the audience in marrying his nine daughters. This first version is a satirical but basically light-hearted piece, comparable to Robert Benchley's classic American monologue "The Treasurer's Report" (1928). In successive revisions, however, Chekhov made the piece more and more serious, as the henpecked hero's frustrations evolved into full-fledged existential despair. In the final version, written in 1902, Nyukhin shows the same kind of horror over his life and revulsion from his wife as Andrey in *Three Sisters*, written shortly before. In the last version of *The Evils of Tobacco*, the comic exasperation of the hero eventually turns into a shocking tirade of fear and hate, and a desperate desire for flight:

> It doesn't matter where … just to run away from this shabby, vulgar, despicable life, which has turned me into an old, pathetic idiot, an old, pathetic imbecile, to run away from that stupid, shallow, penny-pinching bitch, bitch, bitch, my wife, who has made my life a living hell for thirty-three years, to run away from the music, the kitchen, my wife's money, from all that inanity and banality … and come to a halt somewhere far, far away in a meadow and stand like a tree, a pillar, a scarecrow in a cornfield, under the broad sky … (970)

Nyukhin's anguished desire for freedom and peace elevates *The Evils of Tobacco* into a cry of protest against the vulgarity or *poshlost* that Chekhov condemned in so many of his works.

Vaudevilles

The vaudevilles proper were written as curtain raisers or benefit pieces, designed to be part of a longer theatrical evening. They were among the most popular of Chekhov's works in his lifetime and remained so in the early Soviet period. Avant-garde directors like Vsevolod Meyerhold and Yevgeny Vakhtangov found the fast pace and exaggerated absurdity of the vaudevilles more to their taste than the careful naturalism of the full-length plays. One of Meyerhold's most celebrated productions was a program of

Chekhov vaudevilles entitled *33 Swoons* because of the number of times characters in the plays faint out of hysteria or exasperation.

Of Chekhov's four major vaudevilles, two of them, *The Bear* and *The Proposal*, are tight three-handers that were successfully performed around Russia from the late 1880s onward. The other two, *The Wedding* (1890) and *The Jubilee* (1891), were not staged until a special Chekhov evening at the Moscow Hunt Club in 1900. They are more experimental in form and have more of the qualities associated with Chekhov's later plays.

The Bear – unambiguous in Russian (*Medved*) but sometimes translated as *The Boor* or *The Brute* – was the most commercially successful of Chekhov's plays during his lifetime and has remained the most popular of his shorter works. Its strong characterizations, satisfyingly simple plot, and farcical denouement have long appealed to both actors and audiences. Laurence Senelick sees in it an echo of Petronius' ancient Roman story of the Widow of Ephesus, whose grief for a dead husband is quickly overcome by an ardent soldier (J. M. Synge's 1903 Irish play *In the Shadow of the Glen* seems to draw on the same story).[2] The heroine of *The Bear* is a strong-willed young widow "with dimples in her cheeks" (417), Yelena Popova. Another landowner, her neighbor Smirnov, comes to ask for repayment of a debt owed by her husband, but she is too consumed by her mourning to attend to him. It becomes evident that her devotion to the dead husband is misplaced – he was an unfaithful swindler – but Popova persists, to the increasing exasperation of the obstreperous Smirnov, who is desperate for his money. In the end, the conflict between the two escalates into an imminent duel, despite the pacifying efforts of the servant Luka, the only other speaking character. Popova's violent spirit wins the admiration of Smirnov, who proposes to her; and, in the comic denouement, the pair are engaged in *"a prolonged kiss"* when Luka and the other servants burst in with pitchforks to try to drive the Bear out of the house.

The idea of a romance between strong-willed characters who are initially at odds is a staple of romantic comedy, dating back to Shakespearean couples like Beatrice and Benedick or Kate and Petruchio. Popova's maudlin reclusiveness also recalls Shakespeare's Olivia in *Twelfth Night*, who refuses to admit suitors while in mourning but eventually succumbs to love. Popova's mourning has an element of self-righteousness, and even passive-aggressive hostility toward her worthless husband. "He was nothing but unjust to me, cruel and … even unfaithful," she declares, "but I shall be faithful to the day I die and show him that I know how to love" (418). Her stubbornness is perfectly pitched to set off the belligerent Smirnov, who represents himself as an old campaigner in the battle of the sexes: "I loved passionately, madly, you-name-it-ly, damn it, squawked like a parrot about women's rights, spent half my fortune on hearts and flowers, but now – thanks but no thanks!" His misogynistic pose – "all women, great and small, are phonies, show-offs, gossips, trouble-makers, liars to the marrow of their bones" (425) – comes across as protesting too much. Soon after meeting Popova, Smirnov has already noticed her attractively dimpled cheeks and become self-conscious about his own clothes and appearance. Chekhov makes much of the incongruity between Smirnov's bear-like qualities and the drawing-room setting. Twice he *"Grabs the back of a chair, the chair creaks and breaks"* (425); when wooing Popova he *"Grasps her by the arm, she shrieks in pain"* (431). His bull-in-a-china shop boorishness as a would-be romantic hero is recalled years later in the figure of Lopakhin in *The Cherry Orchard*.

The comic climax of the play, the intended duel, also neatly serves as its turning point, when the characters become conscious of their mutual attraction. Popova's request that Smirnov show her how to shoot allows his masculine vanity an opportunity for gallantry and showing off, as he admires her husband's pistols and enumerates their finer points. On the stage, the shooting lesson also allows for a physical proximity between the characters that raises the sexual tension. When Smirnov makes his surprising declaration of love – surprising to him and to Popova, though not to the audience – the characters fall into a parodic inversion of gender roles. Smirnov grovels on his knees, declaring "I've gone all touchy-feely, I've turned to sugar, I'm limp as a dishrag" (431), while Popova brandishes her phallic pistol like Ibsen's Hedda Gabler, demanding that he get up and fight. Their conflict ends in a kiss just as Luka bursts in: a farcical situation later recreated in Vanya's inopportune entrance in Act III of *Uncle Vanya*.

Despite the occasional long-windedness of the protagonists' tirades, the play is very economically constructed. The thermometer that Chekhov uses to chart the progress of Popova's thawing-out is the treatment of the offstage carriage-horse, Toby, who is associated throughout with the dead husband (in his production, Meyerhold reinforced this association by having the stage dominated by a portrait of the husband with Toby). Early in the play, Luka suggests hitching up Toby to pay a call on the neighbors, leading Popova to recall her husband's fondness for the horse in lachrymose terms. She orders Luka to give Toby an extra portion of oats. When Smirnov mentions oats in connection with the husband's debt, Popova again calls for extra oats for Toby. But after the concluding kiss, Popova declares, *"with downcast eyes,"* that "Toby gets no oats today." By making Toby metonymic of the dead husband, Chekhov neatly marks the shift in his heroine's affections and provides a crisp laugh-line for the final curtain.

The Proposal was a transparent attempt to cash in on the success of *The Bear* by repeating the same basic formula. Chekhov disparaged it as "a vulgarish and boringish vaudeville, but suitable for the provinces" (434); in fact, it had its first performance at the imperial residence at Tsarskoe Selo before Tsar Alexander III, who enjoyed it immensely. While it was not quite the cash cow that *The Bear* was, it enjoyed similar success on provincial stages around Russia. It serves as a companion piece to *The Bear*, in that its story goes in the opposite direction; while the former play has adversaries falling into one another's arms, the latter turns an intended marriage proposal into a violent quarrel.

The Proposal matches *The Bear* in its economy and sharply drawn characters. Lomov, a hypochondriacal young landowner, has come to propose to Nataliya Stepanovna, daughter of his neighbor Chubukov. Before he can get around to it, however, he inadvertently begins a dispute about the ownership of some fields between their estates. After Lomov has been driven off in a burst of recriminations, Chubukov reveals to his daughter the purpose of his visit. She recalls Lomov and attempts to make small talk, hoping he will come around to the proposal, but the conversation strays into a new argument on the relative merits of the dogs Splasher, Dasher, and Smasher (in Russian, *Otkatay*, *Ugaday*, and *Razmakhay*). Lomov gets so worked up that he appears to die of a heart attack, while Nataliya goes into hysterics. Both recover just enough that Chubakov can unite their hands and declare them engaged; he calls for champagne as they recommence their quarrel about the dogs.

Much of the comedy in *The Proposal* is of the type characterized by the French philosopher Henri Bergson, in his 1901 essay "Laughter," as "the mechanical encrusted on the living."[3] For Bergson, human beings become funny when they behave in a mechanical way, like puppets or automata, reacting with jerky predictability to external stimuli. Repetition and physical slapstick are hallmarks of this kind of humor, and *The Proposal* has both. Lomov's hypochondria is manifested in various physical tics in response to his imagined symptoms. All three characters constantly work themselves into emotional and physical frenzies, which they attempt to counter by mechanically drinking water and collapsing into armchairs. The characters are visually incongruous as well, with Lomov in tails and white gloves while Nataliya is in an apron and housedress from shelling peas. Their attempts at social interaction are constantly overwhelmed by the violence of their emotional responses: the swift alteration of tears and embraces, small talk and fainting fits, highlights the absurdity of the plot.

One thing that is notable about all of the vaudevilles is their emphasis on crude materialism. The characters have little of the philosophical and aesthetic mindset of the protagonists of the major plays – rather than concerning themselves with new forms in art or speculating about life in two hundred years, they are strictly interested in getting money, social position, food, sex. The characters in *The Proposal* fight over property and hunting dogs, symbols of their aristocratic pretensions. Chekhov's *The Wedding*, meanwhile, is similar in many ways to Bertolt Brecht's one-act on the same general subject, *The Petit-Bourgeois Wedding*, though I know of no evidence that Brecht was familiar with Chekhov's work. The vaudevilles do sometimes seem to be overt satires on bourgeois values: this may be one reason the plays retained their popularity in the Soviet era.

Like *The Proposal*, both *The Wedding* and *The Jubilee* center on violated rituals – the ceremonial act evoked by the title is either thwarted or turned into a fiasco. Chekhov's vaudevilles make a mockery of the rituals of social life. In *The Wedding*, a lower-middle class couple is marrying off their daughter to a minor bureaucrat in return for a dowry of household articles and lottery tickets. The comic energies of the play are driven by the characters' social aspirations: everyone is out for status or cash. In order to make the wedding a more high-toned affair, the mother has given a family friend money to invite someone of the rank of general; he, in turn, has pocketed the money and brought a retired second-class naval captain. In the end, the fraud is exposed, and the captain's incomprehensible nautical jargon causes an uproar among the guests, leading to his premature departure from the party. There is no other plot.

The Wedding may reflect the class aspirations of Chekhov's own merchant family. One of his earliest comic pieces, which got him into trouble with his relatives, was a parody of his family's behavior at a wedding party, illustrated by his brother Nikolai. The characters in *The Wedding* are the kind of coarse provincials Chekhov would have interacted with in his youth: a telegraph operator, an insurance agent, a midwife, a sailor in the volunteer fleet. One of them, the Greek caterer Dymba, is a reminder of Chekhov's Taganrog upbringing.

Dymba's garbled attempts at speechmaking add to the linguistic chaos of the play. Language itself becomes a part of the comic design, anticipating the mature Chekhov's concern with the banalities of everyday interactions, as well as the rich texture of apparently random words and sounds that contributes to the effect of his great plays. In *The Wedding*, the guests continually interrupt each other and talk at cross-purposes – the deaf captain is always misunderstanding what is said to him – while the music of the band frequently intrudes on the action. The pretentious bridegroom peppers his speech with bad French, Dymba stumbles over his Russian, the telegraphist raps Morse code on the table, the captain's naval orders are like a foreign language in themselves – "Haul taut the foretop and main braces on the starboard" – the midwife is always bursting into song, and the poor Best Man never gets to finish his speech (578). This innovative mixture of incomprehensible speech and noise resembles the careful use of music and sound effects in *Three Sisters* and the almost surreal sound of the "breaking string" in *The Cherry Orchard*.

While the satire in *The Wedding* is mostly relatively good-natured – the characters are fools rather than monsters – it occasionally takes on a harsher edge. The chaos that concludes the play has an element of the grotesque, reminiscent of Gogol's *The Government Inspector*, another skewering of bourgeois aspiration that became popular with the theatrical avant-garde of the early twentieth century. Yevgeny Vakhtangov's 1920 Moscow production of *The Wedding* found in it a savage caricature of the pre-revolutionary bourgeoisie, where individualistic desires reduced people to the level of grunting animals. When the captain tries to extricate himself at the end of the play, he cries out, "*Chelovek, Vyvedi menya! Chelovek!*" The primary meaning of "*Chelovek*" here is presumably "Waiter" – the captain is calling for a waiter to show him the way out. But in Vakhtangov's production, "*Chelovek*" also reverted to its core meaning of "human being"; in his desperate cry, the captain was calling on humanity to help him escape from the brutal, animalistic appetites *The Wedding* had portrayed.

The Jubilee, sometimes translated as *The Celebration* (Senelick) or *The Anniversary*, depicts a similarly crass bourgeois milieu. In this case, the setting is a bank, and the ritual involved is the celebration of its fifteenth birthday with testimonials and a speech to the shareholders. The Bank Manager is continually interrupted in the preparation of his speech by his wife, his bookkeeper, and an old woman who keeps asking him for money. The misunderstandings and accusations build to the point of threats, hysteria, and fainting fits, and at the moment of greatest chaos, the deputation of shareholders arrives. In its use of parallel intersecting speeches and its near-tragic yet farcical climax, *The Jubilee* in some ways parallels Chekhov's full-length plays, but its unrelieved caustic tone is unique in Chekhov's drama.

The vaudevilles afforded Chekhov an opportunity to comment on the theatre and society of his time, to extend the themes and situations of his stories, and to develop the techniques that would define his full-length plays. As Vera Gottlieb notes in her study of the vaudevilles, these shorter works enabled Chekhov to find the element of balance that characterized his drama: "a balance between objectivity and commitment, comic detachment and sympathetic involvement, the creation of theatrical illusion, and the exposure of social reality."[4]

Platonov

Chekhov's earliest extant play was also his last to be published. Based on a manuscript preserved in a safety-deposit box, this play first appeared in print in 1923. It has no certain title, but it is generally known as *Platonov* after its protagonist; it may be identical with the play called *Bezottsovshchina* (*Fatherlessness* or *Without Patrimony*) that Chekhov first drafted in 1878 while in high school in Taganrog. Chekhov offered the manuscript to a leading actress of Moscow's Maly Theatre in 1881; after she rejected it, he seems to have laid it aside. It is a sprawling four-act melodrama, about three times the size of Chekhov's other full-length plays. It has twenty characters and would take five or six hours to perform uncut. Nonetheless, it is distinctively Chekhovian in both form and content. It contains many hints of Chekhov's nascent playwriting style, along with character types and plot elements that were to appear in his mature drama. It has also, in various adapted forms, had a surprisingly successful history on stage and screen.

Like most of Chekhov's later plays, *Platonov* is set on a country estate, over which hangs the burden of debt and the malaise of idleness. The play begins with arrivals, small talk, and the rekindling of old relationships; the leisurely first act, which includes a chess match and a long-delayed luncheon, is a fairly effective piece of unforced exposition. As the chattering characters come and go from the drawing room – Chekhov is already experimenting with simultaneous, overlapping conversation – the romantic and economic relationships begin to emerge. The mistress of the estate is Anna Petrovna, a general's widow, who adroitly plays the vivacious hostess in order to keep her various creditors and suitors at bay. Her erotic interest is centered on Platonov, a schoolmaster and superfluous-man type who is an object of desire for all of the women in the play. Though he has a wife and young son, Platonov becomes entangled with a young chemistry student, Mariya Grekova; with Sofya, the wife of Anna Petrovna's stepson; and with Anna Petrovna herself. Platonov is intelligent, witty, and charismatic, but with a brooding sense of failure and a dangerous streak of cynicism: he is clearly a disruptive force within the gathering. It transpires that Sofya knew him in his dashing student days, and the two rekindle an affair during an evening party in Act II, setting in motion a chain of melodramatic events. Platonov's wife Sasha attempts suicide by throwing herself under a train, and is saved at the last moment by the horse-thief Osip, who subsequently tries to kill Platonov out of jealousy over Anna Petrovna. In Act IV, Platonov, drunk and depressed, considers suicide himself, but cannot bring himself to do it; instead he takes up with Grekova, only to be shot by the jealous Sofya.

Despite some of the contrivances of its plot, *Platonov* manages some effective theatrical moments through its mixture of farce and melodrama. The spectacle of Platonov, drunk and delirious, being doggedly pursued by women who want alternately to possess him or kill him, has an anarchic energy that almost justifies the extravagances of the plot. With Platonov himself, Chekhov begins his exploration of a certain type of attractive, well-meaning but potentially destructive protagonist that will dominate all of his early plays, reworked again in the Hamlet-like Ivanov and the wood-demon doctor, Khrushchov. "I've destroyed, snuffed out weak women, who weren't to blame for anything," Platonov chides himself while contemplating suicide. "It wouldn't have been so pathetic, if I'd killed them some other way, driven by monstrous passions, sort of Spanish style, but I killed them just like that … any stupid old way, Russian style" (189). Platonov's lines suggest that he sees himself as a Russian Don Juan. While this kind of engaging antihero has a certain theatrical appeal, Chekhov's drama takes a step forward when he moves this character out of the limelight and into a more complex and balanced web of relationships. There are shades of Platonov in Trigorin, Astrov, and Vershinin, but in the later plays Chekhov has moved beyond a dramatic structure centered on a single charismatic male protagonist.

After being forgotten for decades, *Platonov* enjoyed a surprising afterlife in various transmuted forms. First staged in a cut and rewritten version in Germany in 1928, it was subsequently produced in Czechoslovakia, Italy, France, and the United States, where it appeared at the Provincetown Playhouse in 1940 in an Americanized version entitled *Fireworks on the James*. It was not staged in Russia until 1957 and was dismissed by Soviet critics. In London, however, it scored a commercial success in the unlikely venue of the Royal Court Theatre, home of Britain's angry-young-man revolution in kitchen-sink drama. The 1960 production was entitled *Don Juan in the Russian Manner* (after the lines quoted above) and featured the urbane Shavian actor Rex Harrison in the lead part. Another British adaptation, Michael Frayn's *Wild Honey*, became one of the National Theatre's most successful Chekhov productions in the 1980s, transferring to the West End and Broadway. Frayn, a distinguished comic playwright and noted translator of Chekhov, streamlined and focused the unwieldy text, suffusing it with a sultry summer atmosphere that gradually darkened into tragic farce. Rather than being shot by Sofya, Ian McKellen's incorrigible Platonov wandered onto the railroad tracks to be hit by an oncoming train in a memorable *coup de théâtre*. The National staged another *Platonov* adaptation in 1990, this time by the Marxian playwright Trevor Griffiths, who had done a notoriously politicized version of *The Cherry Orchard* in the 1970s. Entitled *Piano*, it was based not on Chekhov's play but on a Soviet film version from 1976, *Unfinished Piece for Mechanical Piano*. This loose adaptation by the great Russian director Nikita Mikhalkov is one of the most successful cinematic realizations of Chekhov. The range and variety of these adapted versions suggest the intense desire of directors and audiences to discover a "new" Chekhov play, as well as the theatrical vitality latent in Chekhov's earliest dramatic work.

Ivanov

Chekhov's next full-length play, *Ivanov*, was commissioned for Korsh's Theatre in Moscow in 1887, and allegedly written in under two weeks. Its protagonist is also a charismatic malcontent, a "superfluous man" entrapped by the stultifying atmosphere of the 1880s, a period of political repression and spiritual malaise. The name Ivanov, one of the most common Russian surnames, literally equivalent to "Jones," suggests that the hero is something of an Everyman, representative of the paralysis gripping Russia's intelligentsia. Ivanov is an educated landowner whose ideals and aspirations have gone sour. His estate is in debt, he has abandoned his schemes for improving life for the peasants, and he has grown weary of his consumptive Jewish wife Sarra, whom he married in a fit of idealism and thus cut off from her family and fortune. Over the course of the play he becomes, rather reluctantly, involved with Sasha, the young daughter of a neighboring landowner. In the final act, after his wife's death, he is getting ready to marry Sasha when he is confronted by Lvov, a young doctor who had attended Sarra. Lvov gives voice to the accusations whispered by gossip-mongers throughout the play: that Ivanov is a cad, that he drove his wife to her death, that he married for money and intends to do so again. While Ivanov does not exactly dispute these accusations, he makes clear that they are far from adequate to explain his behavior; nonetheless, they bring about his death. In the original version, he dies from a heart attack just before his wedding; in the revision, Chekhov has him rush offstage and shoot himself.

In writing about the play, Chekhov insisted on its originality in eschewing the morally defined character types of conventional Russian drama: "I did not portray a single villain or angel (though I could not refrain when it came to buffoons)" (October 24, 1887). Chekhov does not try to excuse Ivanov for his behavior: the scenes with his wife Sarra are among the most painful in his drama. The Act II curtain, with Sarra bursting in just as Ivanov is embracing Sasha, tends toward melodrama; this stock situation works better as farce in *The Bear* and *Uncle Vanya*. But the confrontation between husband and wife at the end of Act III is truer and more heart-rending. Sarra loses some of her own dignity in her angry denunciations of Ivanov. She confronts him with the fact that she left her family and her faith for him, and accuses him of gold-digging: "You married me and thought my father and mother would forgive me, give me money … When you realized there was no money, you came up with a new game" (512). Ivanov tries to convince her of his good faith toward both her and Sasha: that however destructive and selfish his actions, his motives were not mercenary. But as she continues to accuse him, he finally lashes out savagely: "Sarra, shut up, get out, or else I'll say something I'll regret! It's all I can do to keep from calling you something horrible, humiliating …" And then he shouts, "*Zamolchi, zhidovka!*" Senelick's translation, "Shut up, you kike bitch!" (513) is perhaps over-aggressive but has appropriate shock value. The word Ivanov uses is a feminine version of "*zhid*," a derogatory term for a Jew, related to English "yid," but without the same level of offensiveness in nineteenth-century Russia. (Chekhov used the word himself occasionally in his letters, though he actively opposed anti-Semitism and was for a time engaged to a Jewish woman – a situation that may be reflected in *Ivanov*.) But Ivanov's explosion of anti-Semitic vituperation does not mark the limit of his cruelty in this scene. As Sarra still will not back down, he coldly announces: "Then know that you … will die soon … The doctor told me that you'll die soon …" At this, she falters, and Ivanov, clutching his head, sobs, "It's all my fault! God, it's all my fault!" (513).

In the first version of the play, the doctor burst in at this point to threaten and accuse Ivanov. Chekhov wisely revised the act to end with Ivanov's own self-accusation. One of the points of the play is that Ivanov's own analysis of his personality and behavior is more true, and more damning, than any of the views of the people around him, particularly the doctor. While Dr. Lvov is morally correct in his opprobrium, he is himself a small-minded prig, incapable of understanding the depths of Ivanov's bitterness and despair.

Ivanov, like many a superfluous man in the nineteenth-century Russian tradition, compares himself to Hamlet, and indeed there is something Hamlet-like in the way his anguish seems to exceed any explicable cause. But Chekhov's explicit goal with the play was not simply to invoke, yet again, the superfluous man archetype, but finally to destroy it. In one of his many letters on the play – he wrote more about *Ivanov* than any other of his works – he asserts that to pigeonhole Ivanov as a superfluous man or a Hamlet is to misunderstand the play. An idealist who has burned himself out through misplaced enthusiasms, Ivanov will nonetheless not give himself the easy way out by assuming a literary pose. "Having fallen into such a situation, shallow and unconscientious people generally throw the whole blame on their environment, or characterize themselves as superfluous men and Hamlet and take comfort in that," Chekhov wrote to Suvorin.[5] Whereas Ivanov, who for all his faults is clearly Chekhov's hero, has the honesty to admit his moral bankruptcy and pass judgment on himself. On the stage, *Ivanov* became something of a *succès de scandale*, arousing both praise and condemnation, baffling critics through Chekhov's evident preference for the irresponsible Ivanov over the self-righteous Dr. Lvov. *Ivanov* made Chekhov's name as a playwright; and while it is conventional in structure compared to his later works, it shows off his dramatic craftsmanship, psychological acuity, and theatrical *chutzpah*.

The Wood Demon

While Chekhov's next play, *The Wood Demon*, was a significant failure for him – he had a hard time getting it produced, it received only a few performances, it was lambasted by the critics, and Chekhov declined to have it printed – it is a critical work in Chekhov's oeuvre for two reasons. It represented his first attempt at writing a new type of drama, centered not on a single charismatic protagonist but on the complex relations of a group of diverse characters. More importantly, it provided the raw material, through an extraordinary act of revision, for one of Chekhov's greatest plays, *Uncle Vanya*.

The Wood Demon, written in 1888–89, was originally envisioned as a collaboration between Chekhov and his friend, the publisher Suvorin. In an outline Chekhov wrote after they had discussed the project, the two central characters bear suspicious resemblance to the two collaborators: an older, self-made literary man with a young wife, and an idealistic younger man, "a poet, a landscape artist, with a terrific feel for nature."[6] The collaboration did not come off, perhaps because Suvorin saw himself in the unattractive character of the professor. Chekhov pushed on, though he recognized that his material was more suited to prose fiction: "I know very well that *The Wood Demon* is right for a novel," he conceded to Suvorin. "If I were to write a comedy *The Wood Demon*, my first concern would not be the actors or the stage, but literary qualities."[7] Chekhov's early difficulties with the project anticipated its later reception. The Literary-Theatrical Committee of Petersburg rejected it in part because of its unflattering depiction of a professor, a rank exalted in Russian society. The actor Lensky, to whose Maly Theatre Chekhov offered the play, advised him to stick to writing stories: "Your attitude to the stage and to dramatic form is too contemptuous, you respect them too little to write a drama."[8] And one of the play's reviews sums up the kinds of criticisms that would continue to bedevil Chekhov's work for the theatre:

> *There is no play* – because of the clumsily constructed scenes we see a tale
> or even a novel, *unfortunately*, squeezed into dramatic form. Everyone
> is fed up with banal conversations while eating and drinking either at
> home or with friends, and if you want to hear ten times people enquiring
> about others' health or quarrelling with each other then there's no need at
> all to go to the theatre and endure four acts of a "comedy."[9]

The Wood Demon is a clumsily constructed play, to be sure, but the problem is
not so much that Chekhov neglects the conventions of drama but that he has
not yet developed his own alternatives to them. There is indeed a backdrop of
eating and drinking and banal conversations, but the creakiest moments of the
play are the most conventionally theatrical. There are conveniently timed
entrances, incriminating or exonerating documents, hackneyed plot devices
and moralizing speeches throughout. It was by jettisoning all this, while keeping the sense of the humdrum daily life that "everyone is fed up with," that
Chekhov eventually turned the play into a masterpiece.

The central structure of *The Wood Demon* is that which survives into *Uncle
Vanya*. An aging professor has retired, with his young second wife Yelena, to a
country estate. Also living there is his daughter Sonya, together with her uncle
Voinitsky (the first wife's brother) and his mother. The uncle, whose first name
here is Yegor or *Georges* rather than Vanya, resents Professor Serebryakov and
covets his wife. There is also a neighboring doctor and environmentalist; in this
case he is named Khrushchov, and nicknamed *Leshy*, or the wood demon, for
his devotion to the forests. (Laurence Senelick translates *leshy* as "the wood
goblin," pointing out that the more traditional "wood demon" makes "too
diabolic an impression" for the impish sprite of the Russian forest.) A number
of other neighbors fill out the cast: the mill-owner "Waffles," the wealthy,
unromantic Zheltukhin and his hard-working sister Yulya, and the landowner
Orlovsky and his son, the dashing cad Fyodor. These last four characters were
removed when Chekhov revised the play into *Uncle Vanya*.

The first act introduces the characters and their relationships, including
Zheltukhin's pursuit of Sonya and Fyodor's of Yelena. It is rumored that she is
already the mistress of Voinitsky, but a conversation between them that
concludes the first act makes it clear that she is faithful to her husband, despite
her unhappiness. Act II – retained almost intact in *Uncle Vanya* – begins with
Yelena and the professor as they pass a fretful and stormy night. A series of
duet scenes reveal the tensions among the various characters, notably the
unacknowledged and misunderstood feelings between Khrushchov and
Sonya. In Act III, the various love intrigues are continued, and the action is
brought to a climax by the professor's plan to sell the estate. Voinitsky explodes
with rage and exits; meanwhile Khrushchov rushes in to implore the professor

not to sell his forests for timber. The melodramatic action culminates with Voinitsky shooting himself offstage.

Act IV of *The Wood Demon* startlingly, and rather ineptly, brings the play to a comic resolution. It is set in "*A forest and the house by the mill*"; here Waffles has provided a refuge for the runaway Yelena since the events of Act III. Rather implausibly, the professor and his entourage arrive for a tea party. Amid various recriminations, Dr. Khrushchov delivers himself of the high-minded sentiments of the play. He has discovered, though a convenient diary, how much he had misjudged Voinitsky and Yelena, and now he urges all present to adopt attitudes of honesty and forgiveness. Chekhov was conscious of criticisms that his work lacked a clear attitude to social problems, and was intrigued by Tolstoy's philosophy of universal love and moral renewal. Accordingly, he had Khrushchov address to the professor a speech that sums up the play's moral:

> For twenty-five years you've been a professor and served learning, I plant forests and practice medicine, but what's the point, who's it all for, if we don't show mercy to the ones we're working for? We say that we serve people, and at the same time we are inhumanly destroying each other. (658)

He concludes by saying that Russia needs heroes of a greater stature, and that at present "there are no real heroes, no geniuses, no people who could lead us out of this dark wood" (659). The sudden appearance of Yelena, and the discovery that the forest is ablaze, provide further emotional jolts, sufficient to prompt the various characters to sort out their personal problems. Yelena goes back to her husband, Sonya and Khrushchov declare their love for one another, and Fyodor determines to reform and marry Yulya. Amid "*laughter, kisses, noise,*" the pedantic Waffles declares, "This is fascinating! This is fascinating!" (667).

The incongruity of its happy ending with the melodrama of Voinitsky's suicide is only the most obvious of the structural problems of *The Wood Demon*, a play Chekhov later professed to "detest."[10] Some years after the play's failure, Chekhov turned back to it to undertake a large-scale revision. In December 1896, not long after the premiere of *The Seagull* in Petersburg, he wrote to Suvorin that in the collection of plays he was publishing, "two full-length plays remain to be set up in type: *The Seagull*, which you know, and *Uncle Vanya*, which no one on earth knows."[11] It is probable, but not certain, that the revisions took place after Chekhov had written *The Seagull*; *Uncle Vanya*'s greater economy and focus on indirect action suggest it is the later work. But much of what is great in *Uncle Vanya* comes from *The Wood Demon*, for all of the earlier play's problems. Chekhov's revisions were largely a matter of cutting and compressing. He enriched his characterizations by giving the remaining characters some of the traits and dialogue of those he eliminated. Dr. Astrov, in *Vanya*, has not only the idealism of Khrushchov but some of the rakishness of Fyodor. Sonya, taking on some of Yulya's estate-managing practicality, becomes a deeper and more poignant character – especially through Chekhov's decision to thwart her romance with the doctor. By cutting the happy unions and high-minded speeches of *The Wood Demon's* fourth act, Chekhov threw focus on the tense inner drama of Acts II and III. At its best, *The Wood Demon* reveals the quality that would define Chekhov's four mature plays: profound depths of feeling expressed through the apparently shallow lives of very fallible and human characters.

Later stories

Chekhov's name as an author of serious literary fiction was made with the longer stories he wrote for the "thick journals," beginning in the late 1880s. Having established himself with "The Steppe" (1888), he wrote fewer, more serious, and more ambitious stories over the next decade, before turning largely to playwriting for the last few years of his life. In the 1880s Chekhov published some four hundred stories; in the 1890s he published forty-seven; after 1900 he published four. While his later stories still have the Chekhovian hallmarks of economy, subtlety, and the impressionistic use of detail, they are more likely to consider the whole destiny of a character rather than a single telling incident. They often are broken into several chapters, each relating an episode that might have served the younger Chekhov for a complete story. While many of them have humorous moments, these stories are more uniformly sober and serious than Chekhov's earlier work. "Perhaps in the future it will be revealed to us in the fullest detail who Chekhov's tailor was," the philosopher Lev Shestov wrote shortly after Chekhov's death, "but we will never know what happened to Chekhov in the time that elapsed between the completion of 'The Steppe' and the appearance of 'A Boring Story.'"[1] There are a number of factors that could have contributed to the gloomier outlook of Chekhov's later works: the death of his brother Nikolai from tuberculosis, his own deterioration from the same disease, the moral and physical toll of the 1890 Sakhalin trip. There also may have been an impulse to answer the critics who accused him of lacking social commitment, and there was certainly a desire to engage with the ideas of Tolstoy, Russia's greatest writer. In any event, Chekhov took the literary values and techniques he had honed through hundreds of stories and turned them to profound and troubling questions about human life.

"A Boring Story"

"A Boring Story" (1889) marked the most sustained and relentless exploration Chekhov had yet undertaken of a character's inner world. It boldly announces its dreary subject matter in its title, and fully lives up to the depressing tone it establishes from the very beginning. Yet its portrayal of Nikolai Stepanovich, a dying professor of medicine, achieves poignant intimacy and heartbreaking weight. Chekhov wrote "A Boring Story" shortly after the death of his brother Nikolai, while he himself was wrestling with depression. While working on the story in Yalta, he wrote, "As a result of the heat and my wretched, melancholy mood, the story is turning out rather boring. But at least the subject is new, so perhaps people will find it interesting to read" (August 3, 1889). Chekhov resisted the identification of himself with the depressed, curmudgeonly narrator – "If I present you with the ideas of the professor," he wrote to Suvorin, "trust me and don't look for Chekhov's ideas in them" (October 17, 1889). In many cases, however, the old man expresses opinions that Chekhov had himself voiced elsewhere, from criticisms of the Russian theatre to concern over a lack of a purpose in life. The power of the story comes from the narrator's clear-sighted, objective analysis of his emotional state as he con-templates his life and its approaching end.

"A Boring Story" reveals Nikolai Stepanovich's alienation in the opening paragraphs: though the story is told in the first person (it is subtitled "From an Old Man's Notes"), it begins with a third-person account of a learned and decorated professor, known and revered through Russia and beyond, and friends with distinguished figures of the arts and sciences. Only in the final sentence of the paragraph does the narrator dryly observe that "this and many other things that might be said constitute what is known as my name."[2] Nikolai Stepanovich perceives a sour discrepancy between his "name" and himself: the one beautiful and brilliant, the other dull and ugly, with "bald head, false teeth and an incurable tic" (56). This estrangement from his reputation extends to all aspects of his life; in the pages that follow, Nikolai Stepanovich details how he has come to view his family, his colleagues and his daily routine with bafflement and revulsion.

The remainder of the story, told mainly in the present tense, documents and analyzes Nikolai's malaise, which might now be diagnosed as clinical depression associated with aging. His physical deterioration is dwelt on at length. Like the title character of Chekhov's early story "The Schoolmaster" (1886), Nikolai Stepanovich carries his illness about him like a cloud of ill omen: anyone who sees him, he feels, is struck by the thought that "this man will evidently die soon" (56). The chief manifestation of his depression – indeed, in his view, the chief fact of his existence – is insomnia. Chekhov conveys throughout the story how his hero's experience of time is changed by his approaching death, and his description of the miserable hours waiting for dawn is vivid and grim.

Chekhov's first-person narration conveys the acerbic bitterness of Nikolai Stepanovich while eliciting considerable sympathy for him. His attitude to his wife and children is poisoned by a contempt that he recognizes they do not deserve: his wife's petty worries over their debts, and his children's failure to make sacrifices to alleviate them, have left him cold and scarred. Chekhov makes Nikolai's alienation moving through the use of concrete details, such as his ritual of kissing his daughter's fingers as though they were different flavors of ice cream, a relic of her childhood that is now devoid of feeling. Of his wife, he can only marvel "that this old, very stout, ungainly woman with a dull expression of petty care … was once that same slender Varya" (58) he passionately loved.

Nikolai Stepanovich's inability to connect emotionally to people in his personal life is contrasted with his love for science and his dedication to his profession. In a long excursus, he details the fervent excitement of lecturing to an auditorium of medical students, when he could "give [him]self to passion and understand that inspiration is not an invention of the poets but exists in reality" (64). After describing the feelings of exhaustion and contentment the professor would feel at the end of a successful lecture, Chekhov abruptly pulls the rug from under the reader: "That was before" (65). In his weakened condition, Nikolai Stepanovich now finds lecturing a torment, so that he suddenly wants "to cry in a loud voice that fate has sentenced me, a famous man, to capital punishment, and that in six months or so another man will be master of this auditorium." Stunned and outraged by the loss of his powers, he finds himself poisoned by "thoughts such as I have never known" (66). As Michael Finke observes in *Seeing Chekhov*, the professor has gone from being subject to object of the analytic gaze: "the professional eye turned inward – upon himself and his family – proves paralyzing and self-destructive to the mortally ill professor of medicine … Where once he shone when all eyes and ears were on him in the lecture hall, now he reads in the mirrors of these eyes not his professional potency but his physical and emotional decomposition."[3]

After establishing the sterility of his habitual activities, and the emptiness of his relations with family, colleagues, and students, Chekhov introduces the one character who seems to matter to Nikolai, his ward Katya. The daughter of a deceased colleague, she came into the professor's house as a seven-year-old girl, and he was struck by her trusting nature, which seemed to express that "all that goes on in this world is beautiful and wise" (70). Now, after a disillusioning life as an actress – like Nina in *The Seagull*, she has had an illegitimate child who has died – she is as bitter as the professor. Together with another colleague, Mikhail Fyodorovich, Katya rails against the world in terms that even Nikolai sometimes finds too extreme in their cynicism.

The emotional strain the professor endures, and inflicts on those around him, comes to a head during a summer visit to a dacha in the countryside. On what is literally a dark night of the soul, Nikolai Stepanovich suddenly becomes stricken by a kind of blind panic and heartsickness that seems to transmit itself to his wife, his daughter, a howling dog outside, and even Katya, who is staying at a neighboring cottage. She comes to him and makes the gesture of selfless caring he had desired from his family, offering to give him her money in order to go away for a cure, but he refuses her – it is too late for him, physically and emotionally. The failure of Nikolai's relationship to Katya represents the final stage in his spiritual death and provides the culmination for the last episode of the story, his visit to Kharkov.

The professor goes to Kharkov to investigate his daughter's fiancé, an odious young man named Gnekker who seems to be out for the family's money. Sure enough, Gnekker's Kharkov connections turn out to be fabricated, and the professor gets a telegram from his wife that he and Liza have secretly married, so the whole mission is a failure. Nikolai Stepanovich receives the news with an indifference that he himself perceives not as stoical wisdom, but as a moral failing: "Indifference is a paralysis of the soul, a premature death" (104). Reflecting, he comes to see that something essential is missing from his whole being. "In all the thoughts, feelings, and conceptions I form about everything, something general is lacking that would unite it all into a single whole," he considers, describing this missing entity as "a general idea or the god of the living man" (105). He lived contentedly enough without this when he had a comfortable, rewarding life as a scientist; but now his approaching death has so shaken him that, with the loss of his scientific work and his ability to teach, he has no spiritual resources on which to draw to replace them.

This insight is merely a bemused reflection, not a blinding revelation. Unlike the hero of Tolstoy's novella *The Death of Ivan Ilych* (1886), to which "A Boring Story" has been compared since its publication, Nikolai Stepanovich undergoes no mystical transformation or deathbed epiphany. As Irina Kirk puts it, "Nikolai Stepanovich does not 'see the light' at the end, nor was he 'in the dark' from the beginning. Rather he is staring into a void throughout the story."[4] His spiritual impoverishment is underlined when, just as he has been dwelling on these existential meditations, Katya arrives to call on him for moral guidance. "I can't live like this any longer!" she cries. "For the love of God, tell me quickly, this very moment: what am I to do?" (106). The exact nature of her crisis is not addressed, though she seems to be having an affair with Nikolai's colleague Mikhail Fyodorovich – but the main thing is that Nikolai has no advice to give her. He can only feebly hint at his own approaching death, asking for her sympathy at the moment she most needs his. He is embarrassed and ashamed to realize that he is happier than she is: his nihilistic despair is relatively recent and will not last long, "but the soul of this poor thing has known and will know no refuge all her life, all her life!" (107).

Nikolai Stepanovich fails Katya at this crucial trial, yet he remains a sympathetic character to the end. Lev Shestov felt that Nikolai's very despair, and Katya's, enlists Chekhov's partiality: "While a person is settled to some work, while he has a future of some kind before him, Chekhov is utterly indifferent to him … But when he is entangled, and so entangled that he cannot be disentangled by any means, then Chekhov begins to wake up."[5] Shestov may be overstating the case here, but there is something heroic about the defeated and dying professor. There is an element of courage and integrity in his ruthless self-analysis, and his final moments with Katya, when he knows she has passed out of his reach, are heart-rending. With nothing to offer her, he feels he can ask nothing of her. As they exchange meaningless small talk and part, it seems that the one person he truly loves – as he perhaps only then realizes – is slipping away from him, along with his last few hours of life. But Chekhov does not dwell on these last moments: they pass rapidly in the breathless present-tense narration, which finally, in a last, defeated recognition, subsides into the past:

> I silently walk with her to the door … Now she has left my room and walks down the long corridor without looking back. She knows I'm following her with my eyes and will probably look back from the turn.
>
> No, she didn't look back. The black dress flashed a last time, the footsteps faded away … Farewell, my treasure! (107)

"The Grasshopper"

Chekhov's 1892 story *"Poprygunya"* – variously translated as "The Grasshopper," "the Butterfly," or, as by Pevear and Volokhonsky, "The Fidget" – returns to the theme of adultery that occupied many of his early stories. The title alludes to the Russian version of Aesop's fable of the Grasshopper and the Ant. In Ivan Krylov's 1808 poem, the leading character is actually a dragonfly, whose flightiness and singing during the summer leaves her hungry in the winter, while the industrious ants have stored up plenty of food. Chekhov's story uses the grasshopper/ant dichotomy to look at the contrast between the arts and the sciences, as well as the incompatible personalities of a dilettantish young wife and her dedicated doctor husband.

Chekhov's grasshopper is Olga Ivanovna, a vivacious young woman with artistic interests and a fascination with celebrity. The story opens with her marriage to Dymov, evidently a "simple, very ordinary and in no way remarkable man," who practices as a physician while working on his thesis. Olga surrounds herself with painters, actors, and musicians, and takes pains to live a very artistic life. Chekhov conveys Olga's sensibilities in his description of how the young bride decorates her new home:

> Olga Ivanovna hung all the walls of the drawing room with her own and other people's studies, framed and unframed, and around the grand piano and furniture she arranged a beautiful clutter of Chinese parasols, easels, colorful rags, daggers, little busts, photographs … In the dining room she covered the walls with folk prints, hung up bast shoes and sickles, put a scythe and a rake in the corner, and thus achieved a dining room in the Russian style.[6]

Chekhov is mocking Olga through a subtle use of free indirect discourse. The narrator does not comment critically on her aesthetic pretensions, instead letting her self-regard and enthusiasm creep into the narration, as in the report that "everything she did came out extraordinarily artistic, graceful, and pretty" (140). A. P. Chudakov, in *Chekhov's Poetics*, asserts that "the neutral exposition of the narrator assimilates the words and thoughts of the heroine from the very first lines of the story."[7] From time to time the narrative perspective shifts to a cooler, more critical tone, or into the consciousness of other characters, but Olga's is the dominant consciousness explored in the story.

Chekhov sets up the basic opposition of the story in a dinner-table conversation between Olga and Dymov. She tells him his one shortcoming is his lack of interest in art; he responds that "Your acquaintances don't know natural science and medicine, and yet you don't reproach them for it" (140).

The gulf of incomprehension between what C. P. Snow was to call "the two cultures" is an important theme in "The Grasshopper," and one that Chekhov, as a practitioner of both, felt keenly. Dymov's meek and pleasant nature causes him to indulge his wife and her friends, and his fair-mindedness prevents him from rejecting her artistic milieu. Though he does not himself understand landscape paintings or operas, he accepts that since intelligent people value them, they must have worth.

Dymov's indulgence receives its first serious challenge in a painful and funny episode set at their dacha, an episode in which the third-person narration takes on more of Dymov's perspective. Dymov, who has been working in town for two weeks, looks forward to visiting his wife in the countryside and brings along a parcel of delicacies to please her. Arriving at the dacha, he finds "canvases, brushes, greasy paper, and men's jackets and hats lying about on the chairs and windowsills" – the narration suggests his looking around the room in puzzlement – together with "three men he did not know" (143). Olga soon arrives and expresses unfeigned joy at seeing him; but then she sends him back to town for a dress she needs the next day for a "most original" outdoor wedding "in the style of the French Impressionists" (144). Chekhov communicates this interaction entirely through Olga's chatter and Dymov's silence; there is no editorial comment. Yet the narrator's indignation on Dymov's behalf is evident in the brief, bruising paragraph that ends the chapter:

> Dymov quickly drank a cup of tea, took a pretzel, and, smiling meekly, went to the station. And the caviar, cheese, and white salmon were eaten by the two dark-haired gentlemen and the fat actor. (144)

From this episode, Chekhov cuts immediately, and almost cinematically, to Olga onboard a riverboat on a moonlit night, on the point of beginning her affair with the painter Ryabovsky. His romantic rhetoric, the beautiful setting, and her own selfish desires for a life of art, fame, and passion cause Olga to rationalize betraying her husband: "'For him, a simple and ordinary man, the happiness he has already received is enough,' she thought, covering her face with her hands" (146). As she yields to Ryabovsky, Chekhov makes another jump-cut to a time, two months later, when their affair has already soured. Sitting in a squalid cottage by the Volga on a drizzly fall day, Olga longs for her husband's home in the city, not so much out of conscience as from a kind of aesthetic revulsion. In one of the story's most telling details, a peasant woman who is cooking their dinner carries a bowl of cabbage soup to Ryabovsky, "and Olga Ivanovna saw her thumbs dip into the soup. The dirty woman with her cross-tied belly, and the soup that Ryabovsky began eating so greedily, and the cottage, and that whole life, which she had liked so much at the beginning for its simplicity and artistic disorder, now seemed horrible to her" (149). The image of the peasant woman's dirty thumbs in the bowl of soup perfectly captures the physical and moral dirtiness that Olga finds suddenly unbearable.

She returns to the city, and though Dymov does learn of her adultery, he never confronts her about it. As Ryabovsky tires of her, she becomes desperate and imprudent in the manner of Flaubert's Emma Bovary (though Chekhov has reversed the sympathies accorded to the bored wife and her doctor husband). Olga's final resolve to quit Ryabovsky and begin a new life with Dymov comes too late: he has contracted diptheria, perhaps deliberately. Only in his death does Olga come to realize that he was a productive, dedicated scientist as well as a meek and tolerant husband; she "suddenly understood that he was indeed an extraordinary, rare man and, compared with those she knew, a great man" (159). But her reaction suggests that she has not really had a moral epiphany, but that she is merely reevaluating her husband according to the same shallow criteria she has always used. She recalls the praise her late father and his fellow doctors accorded Dymov, and realizes they might have seen him as a future celebrity: "The walls, the ceiling, the lamp, and the rug on the floor winked at her mockingly, as if wishing to say, 'You missed it! You missed it!'" (159). Chekhov offers up Dymov as a positive contrast to Olga, but there is little real evidence that he is a genius or a saint, as some commentators have found him; Chekhov is more concerned with Olga's inability to see beyond her own limited terms for valuation.

Chekhov based the characters in "The Grasshopper" on people and situations he knew personally, and the story reflects his ambivalence about the artistic world in which he was a sometime habitué. Chekhov's friend the painter Isaac Levitan was the clear model for the unscrupulous Ryabovsky; his mistress and her tolerant doctor husband became the Dymovs. Levitan was so offended by the story he wanted to challenge Chekhov to a duel; they did not speak for three years.

As a study of adultery, "The Grasshopper" looks back to earlier stories like "A Misfortune." Chekhov would continue to explore this territory in other stories titled after their female protagonists, "Anna on the Neck" and "Ariadne," both published in 1895, and "The Helpmate," of 1896. In the first of these, a naïve and timid young bride comes gradually to understand the power her sexuality gives her over her pompous husband and the men around her. The tone of the story is comic, and the sympathies are mainly with Anna. In "Ariadne," the heroine has more of the half-conscious sexual rapacity and manipulative deceit typical of Chekhov's negative depictions of women. The harshest of these stories is "The Helpmate," in which another deluded doctor recognizes his young wife's adultery and predation but is unable to free himself from her.

"The Grasshopper" is not only a picture of a marriage, however, but an examination of two incompatible worldviews. In contrasting Olga's art and Dymov's science, "The Grasshopper" is one of several stories of the early 1890s that build on this kind of binary structure. It is to the most famous of these that we will now turn.

"Ward No. 6"

Chekhov disliked tendentious fiction and avoided social or philosophical proclamations in his works, for which he received censure from liberal publications like *Russian Thought*, which insisted it was the duty of the writer to take a stand on social issues. But Chekhov did not shy away from the discussion of social ideas; he only refrained from producing conclusive solutions to social problems. In a letter to Suvorin, he declared that writers were not obliged to provide answers: "In demanding from an artist a conscious attitude toward his work you are right, but you are confusing two concepts: *the solution of a problem* and *the correct posing of a question*. Only the second is obligatory for an artist."[8] Accordingly, when focused on social concerns, Chekhov framed his stories as debates between opposed philosophical positions. Often the opposition was between activism and quietism: a struggle to alter the future versus an acceptance of things as they are. Philosophical debates on this order later turn up, in modified form, in Chekhov's major plays: Vershinin and Tusenbach (from *Three Sisters*) are the most obvious example, but one can think of other, similarly paired characters, such as Astrov/Vanya, Trofimov/Lopakhin, or Sorin/Dorn.

This framework, and the terms of these debates, have clear precursors in Russian literary history. The formula may stem from the contrast between the vigorous German Stolz and the inert title character of Ivan Goncharov's landmark 1859 novel *Oblomov*. In Chekhov's case, it probably had more to do with the ideas of Leo Tolstoy. "Ward No. 6" was Chekhov's sharpest, clearest rebuttal to Tolstoy's idea of non-resistance to evil. Chekhov had been much influenced by Tolstoy's philosophy, and his stories of the early 1890s often set up a polarization between a Tolstoyan position and its opposite. The stories are not simply intellectual debates, however; the competing perspectives arise naturally from the circumstances and personalities of the characters, and the questions raised by their conflicts are never fully answered. In "Gusev" (1890), written shortly after Chekhov's return by sea from Sakhalin, a gentle, peasant soldier and an angry firebrand react differently to their confinement in the sickbay of a military ship. Both nonetheless end up dying and being buried at sea, their contrasting perspectives subsumed in the serene immensity of nature. As Gusev's corpse sinks below the waves, "The sky turns a soft lilac. Seeing this magnificent, enchanting sky, the ocean frowns at first, but soon itself takes on such tender, joyful, passionate colors as human tongue can hardly name."[9] In "The Duel" (1891), the Darwinian scientist Van Koren and the bohemian idealist Layevsky come almost to a fatal conflict; Layevsky's dissipated indolence seems to the stern Van Koren deserving of extermination for the good of the species. "In Exile" (1892) tells of a gentleman, exiled to Siberia for fraud, who struggles unsuccessfully to create a sustainable life there for his family. He is contrasted with Semyon "the Explainer," an utterly self-reliant man, who, by renouncing all desires, has attained a kind of cruel satisfaction with the miseries of life. At the story's end, the young Tartar who provides the reader's window on the story reacts with revulsion to Semyon's life-denying cynicism:

> He good. … Good, and you – bad! You bad! Gentleman a good soul, excellent, and you a beast, you bad! Gentleman alive, and you dead … God created man for be alive, and be joy, and be sorrow, and be grief, and you want nothing, it means you not alive, you stone, clay! Stone want nothing, and you want nothing … you stone – and God not love you, but love gentleman.[10]

The most powerful of these stories, and the one dealing most overtly with Tolstoy's views, is "Ward No. 6," also from 1892. In it the Tolstoyan doctrine of passive acceptance is voiced by the torpid doctor, Andrey Yefimych Ragin, while a position of resistance and rebellion is taken by the articulate madman Gromov. As in "Gusev," the two men meet the same fate: locked in a mental ward under the heavy fists of the sadistic guard Nikita. Yet the benign, benedictory nature that appears in the sunset of "Gusev" is almost wholly absent from "Ward No. 6," one of the darkest stories Chekhov ever wrote.

   The central action of the story – a doctor gets locked in his own madhouse – has the stark symmetry of a parable, which is what many have taken "Ward No. 6" to be. Yet Chekhov arrives at this event by a slow and circuitous route, not introducing the doctor, Andrey Yefimych, until the fifth chapter, nearly a quarter of the way into the story. He begins instead with the madhouse itself, describing it, in present tense and first person, as though leading the reader on a tour: "let us go down the narrow path that leads to the annex and see what is going on inside."[11] The reader moves through the overgrown hospital yard and the squalid, cluttered entry into the large central room, where the narrator points out the soot and stench, the iron gratings, the beds screwed to the floor, and finally their inhabitants: "These are madmen" (172).

After briefly describing each of them, the narrator settles on one, Ivan Dmitrich Gromov, an educated and impoverished young man suffering from persecution mania. Only after relating his history in some detail does the narrator note that a "strange rumor" has begun circulating at the hospital: that "the doctor had started visiting Ward No. 6" (180). Chekhov lets pass without comment the rather heavy irony that it should be considered "strange" that a doctor should visit his patients. The remark is pertinent in the case of Dr. Ragin, who has become so convinced of the worthlessness of his profession that he rarely practices it. Chekhov shows some sympathy with Ragin's conviction that conditions are so bad at the hospital that his work makes no difference and actually helps sustain a morally bankrupt institution. When he gets to know Gromov, however, the doctor becomes reengaged. He finds Gromov a worthy interlocutor and starts hanging around the madhouse to speak to this "intelligent and interesting man" (196).

Their debates develop the quietist/activist theme, with Ragin arguing – citing the Stoics but also channeling Tolstoy and Schopenhauer – that suffering is inevitable and must simply be endured. Gromov rages against the system that has imprisoned him, and especially at what he sees as the indolent complicity of Ragin, who can assert that "There's no difference between a warm, cozy study and this ward" (197) precisely because he is not imprisoned in it. Ragin is charmed and fascinated by Gromov's critique of him but fails to take it to heart until, with tragic inevitability, circumstances place him in the madman's position.

The doctor's strange behavior in talking to the madman arouses comment, concern, and eventually a conspiracy to have him committed. Through this section of the story Chekhov develops sympathy for Ragin, especially when he has to endure a dreary trip to Moscow and Warsaw with his pompous postmaster friend. When he is finally tricked into Ward No. 6 by his unscrupulous assistant, Ragin has a simultaneous reversal of fortune and recognition of his plight that recalls Aristotle's definition of tragedy. Looking out through the barred windows at the nail-topped fence, the "cold crimson moon," and the "distant flames of the bone-burning factory" – images of horror and desolation – Ragin finally thinks "Here is reality!" (217). He and Gromov come into momentary accord, as both protest together against the injustice of the ward; but the brutal guard Nikita beats them into submission. Under the beating Ragin has a stroke, his sudden physical suffering yielding him a flash of awful insight:

> He bit his pillow in pain and clenched his teeth, and suddenly, amidst the chaos, a dreadful, unbearable thought flashed clearly in his head, that

exactly the same pain must have been felt day after day, for years, by these people who looked like black shadows in the moonlight. How could it happen that in the course of more than twenty years he had not known and had not wanted to know it? (219)

Just before dying, the doctor is granted a moment of grace, in a strange and lovely image that provides the only moment of beauty in this singularly bleak tale. As he lies on his bed in the ward, "A herd of deer, extraordinarily beautiful and graceful, which he had read about the day before, ran by him; then a peasant woman reached out to him with a certified letter …" (220). But this cathartic epiphany is only momentary; Ragin dies and is buried in the story's few remaining sentences.

Not surprisingly, Chekhov's readers took "Ward No. 6" as a political parable, with the ward as an emblem for a Russia corrupted by soulless bureaucracy and inhuman oppression. Among those who understood the story in this way was V. I. Lenin, who would overturn Russia's authoritarian structures only to create new ones of his own. Chekhov had more specific concerns in mind; he was appalled by the state of mental health care in Russia and the inadequacy of rural hospitals, and he had recently investigated and documented the ghastly living conditions of convicts imprisoned on Sakhalin island. And his allegory has existential, rather than narrowly political, dimensions. But whatever Chekhov's purposes, "Ward No. 6" provided Russia with an image of itself that remained potent throughout the following century. Donald Rayfield has pointed out that Alexander Solzhenitsyn's *Cancer Ward* is only one of many subsequent political allegories that build on Chekhov's story by recasting the state as an oppressive institution.[12] In 2009, Russia's submission to the Academy Awards' Best Foreign Film category was a new adaptation of "Ward No. 6" set in contemporary Russia, once again using the metaphor of the country as a madhouse.

"The Black Monk"

"Ward No. 6" showed Chekhov freeing himself from the influence of Tolstoy, as well as processing his experiences on the prison island of Sakhalin. His stories of the mid-1890s are less philosophical and social, and more concerned with personal relationships, art, and nature. In 1892, Chekhov bought his estate at Melikhovo, where he cultivated the gardens, spent time with his family, and embarked on one of the most produtive periods of his writing. "We are living on our very own estate," he wrote to his brother on March 21. "Like Cincinnatus, I spend my life in toil and eat my bread by the sweat of my brow." The influence of his surroundings is felt strongly in "The Black Monk," which uses a garden setting for a story that combines Chekhov's interests in horticulture and abnormal psychology with the trappings of gothic horror he had flirted with in the tales of his youth.

Insanity features in "The Black Monk" (1894) as it had in "Ward No. 6." In this case, it is the megalomania of the protagonist Kovrin, a scholar who believes himself one of an elect group striving for the good of humanity, and who thus destroys his own life and those of the people closest to him. His madness is manifested in his hallucinations of a black monk who convinces him of his unique status. Kovrin's vision is based on a dream Chekhov had while at Melikhovo, while the story's setting reflects his concern with tending his new home.

Much of the story takes place on a country estate, owned by a curmudgeonly and obsessive horticulturalist, Pesotsky, who was Kovrin's guardian in his youth. The estate combines a commercial orchard, romantic natural settings that "always made you want to sit down and write a ballad," and elaborate fairy-tale gardens containing Pesotsky's "whims, refined monstrosities, and mockeries of nature."[13] Kovrin visits the estate to recover from his strained nerves, and finds the setting and people pleasant and salubrious. In one memorable scene, he and Pesotsky's daughter Tanya spend a night-long vigil in the orchard when it is threatened with frost: "thick, black, pungent smoke covered the ground and, enveloping the trees, saved those thousands from the frost … Kovrin and Tanya walked among the rows, where fires of dung, straw, and assorted refuse smoldered, and occasionally met workers, who wandered through the smoke like shades" (225). In this strange and heightened atmosphere, Kovrin suddenly feels a patronizing tenderness toward "this small, weak, loquacious being" (226), and he begins to think of falling in love with her.

Kovrin's courtship of Tanya is encouraged by Pesotsky, who imagines that his son-in-law might maintain the orchard after his death. In the meantime, however, Kovrin has fallen under the spell of the black monk, who appears initially as a pillar of black smoke recalling the smoke in the orchard. The vision is called forth in Kovrin's mind by a performance of the "Angel's Serenade" by Gaetano Brata, in which "a girl with a morbid imagination heard some sort of mysterious sounds in the garden at night, so beautiful and strange that she could only take them for a sacred harmony, which the mortals were unable to understand and which therefore flew back to heaven" (229). This theme reappears in Kovrin's hallucination, which convinces him of his divinely chosen status through its heavenly messenger, the monk. He is described as an elderly man with grey hair, black clothes, and a gentle, sly, death-pale face, who appears and disappears across great distances with tremendous speed. He eventually speaks to Kovrin, telling him he is one of "the chosen of God" who will lead humanity "into the kingdom of eternal truth" (237) through his intellectual achievements. Acknowledging that Kovrin suffers from physical and mental illness, the monk reassures him that "only the ordinary herd people are healthy and normal" (238). The reference to the "herd" suggests the ideas of the German philosopher Friedrich Nietzsche, Chekhov's contemporary, who espoused the notion of an exceptional "superman" and who himself suffered from mental illness. The monk's flattering attentions invigorate Kovrin's work with new energy and pride.

Kovrin's elect status proves incommensurate with the normal life represented by Tanya. After their marriage, she becomes convinced of his mental illness and sends him for medical treatment, which cures him of his hallucinations but turns him into one of the "herd." "How lucky Buddha and Mohammed and Shakespeare were that their kind relations and doctors did not treat them for ecstasy and inspiration!" (246), Kovrin cries in frustration. Alienated from Tanya and her father, he takes up with another woman and travels to the Crimea for his health – like Chekhov, Kovrin is suffering from tuberculosis. There a letter from Tanya bitterly informs him that her father has died: "I owe that to you, because you killed him" (250). The orchard is perishing in the hands of strangers. The letter shocks him into anxious reflections, and for a moment, he seems to have insight into the banal misery of his life: "Kovrin clearly recognized now that he was a mediocrity, and he willingly accepted it" (251). Then, as Kovrin falls under the spell of nature and art, the monk returns.

The presence of the sea, which often evokes feelings of beauty and transcendence in Chekhov, arouses Kovrin's imagination, as the gardens had at the beginning of the story. "The bay, as if alive, looked at him with a multitude of blue, aquamarine, turquoise and fiery eyes and beckoned to him" (251). Standing on his hotel balcony, he hears from below the same Braga serenade that brought on his first hallucination. The monk appears like a tornado on the far shore of the bay and comes rushing into his room, where it convinces him, once again, of his elect status. He suffers a severe hemorrhage, but as the blood pours from his throat, he feels "an inexpressible, boundless happiness" and dies assured of his own genius, with "a blissful smile … frozen on his face" (252).

The story plainly condemns Kovrin's delusions of grandeur, and the sufferings they cause. But at the same time, Chekhov appears to have some sympathy with Kovrin's yearning for transcendence, and for freedom from the bourgeois banality of the "herd." The story takes most life around the episodes of the monk's appearances, when Kovrin's perceptions are heightened and his feeling for art and nature is most keen. If "The Black Monk," as a case study, warns of the dangers of megalomania, it also recognizes the value of idealism.

"The Student"

Chekhov declared "The Student" (1894) to be his favorite among all of his stories. This brief tale reflects Chekhov's consciousness of the spiritual power of art. Though Chekhov had found his religious upbringing oppressive, he was steeped in the beauty of many aspects of Russian Orthodox practice, and the illumination and consolation they offered. Several of Chekhov's stories use religious observance as an image of artistic creation. In "Art" (1886), a coarse and mangy peasant, Seryozhka, creates a beautiful, ephemeral structure of ice and wood for the celebration of an epiphany ritual. His inspired creation ennobles him in the eyes of the villagers: "they all feel that his art is not his personal affair but something that concerns them all, the whole people. One creates, the others help him."[14] Seryozhka in himself is a drunken wastrel, the people feel, but when at work on his art "he is at once something higher, a servant of God." In "Easter Night" (1886), it is the creation of "akathists," religious canticles, that represents the divine power of art. On his way to an Easter service, the narrator learns of a monk, recently dead, who "strewed his akathists with flowers, stars, and rays of sunlight," inspiring a deep love in the humble ferryman who now mourns for him.[15]

"The Student" is also set at Easter, the most important religious holiday in the Russian calendar. On Good Friday, a young seminary student, Ivan, is walking home through an icy meadow: "His fingers were numb, and his face was burned by the wind. It seemed to him that this sudden onset of cold violated the order and harmony of everything, that nature herself felt dismayed, and therefore the evening darkness fell more quickly than it should."[16] The dreary evening puts him in mind of the miseries of Russia's barbaric past, from the time of Rurik and Ivan the Terrible to the present – "the same savage poverty and hunger, the same leaky thatched roofs, ignorance and anguish" – and he feels that life would be no better even in another thousand years. Reflecting on this long span of suffering, Ivan encounters two poor peasant widows, mother and daughter, warming themselves by a fire. Falling into conversation with them, and thinking of the cold night on which Peter denied Jesus, he gives an impromptu retelling of the gospel story. Describing Peter's grief and shame, he notices that the mother is crying, and the daughter's face is flushed and strained "as in someone who is trying to suppress intense pain." As he walks on, he marvels that an event from nineteen centuries before still has a relation to the present. Ivan is humble enough to feel it was not the artistry of his telling that moved the woman to tears, but the power of the story itself:

> And joy suddenly stirred in his soul, and he even stopped for a moment to
> catch his breath. The past, he thought, is connected with the present in an

> unbroken chain of events flowing one out of the other. And it seemed to
> him that he had just seen both ends of that chain: he touched one end,
> and the other moved.

This realization lightens his mood, and "life seemed to him delightful, won-
drous, and filled with lofty meaning." There may be an element of gentle
skepticism in Chekhov's portrayal of the earnest young seminarian, but on
the whole the story seems to endorse his vision of the redemptive power of art
and the spiritual imagination. The idea that "the truth and beauty that guided
human life there in the garden and in the high priest's courtyard, went on
unbroken to this day" is one that even a presumed non-believer such as
Chekhov could entertain. In conversation with the young writer Ivan Bunin,
Chekhov offered "The Student" as evidence of his optimism to those who
viewed his outlook as despairing and gloomy.[17]

"The Student" is only a few pages long, but it is a story of extraordinary
economy, beauty, and power. The descriptions of nature suffering in winter's
grasp, the conception of Russian life as an unchanging desolation of darkness
and cold, the sudden insight connecting the two women to an event from
sacred history: all are conveyed briefly but with remarkable gravity and grace.
"The Student" not only describes the power of narrative to evoke spiritual
truth, it embodies it.

"The House with the Mezzanine"

Another story that asserts the spiritual value of art is "The House with the
Mezzanine" (1896), which Chekhov subtitled "An Artist's Story." The story is
narrated by an unnamed landscape painter, who is idling at the ramshackle
estate of an equally idle landowner. He makes the acquaintance of a mother
and her two daughters at a neighboring estate. The elder daughter, Lida, is
beautiful but has "a small stubborn mouth" and "a stern expression" indicative
of her determination and seriousness.[18] She is a *zemstvo* teacher, treats peasants in a clinic, and is very involved in local politics. The younger, Zhenya,
called "Missyus" after her English governess, has a childlike innocence, loves
reading, and finds a natural sympathy with the artist.

"The House with the Mezzanine" once again features an ethical and social
debate. Lida is a social activist, working tirelessly and rather grimly to improve
life for peasants in the district. She is contemptuous of the artist for his idleness;
when discussing her plans and programs, she tells him dismissively that "this
cannot be of interest to you." In the third chapter, the artist rises to the bait and
offers an opposing philosophy that helps to explain his apparent indolence. "In

my opinion, dispensaries, schools, libraries, first-aid kits, under the existing conditions, only serve enslavement," he explains. "The people are fettered by a great chain, and you don't cut the chain, you merely add new links to it" (290). As long as the majority of Russians toil under the burden of heavy physical labor, he argues, the minor ameliorations of literacy and medical care only make them unhappier, by increasing their needs without giving them time to develop their spiritual and creative faculties. The artist instead advocates a kind of utopian socialism whereby the labor will be evenly distributed among all Russians, and all Russians will thereby be able to devote themselves to the arts and sciences – not for narrow utilitarian reasons, but for the spiritual uplift of humanity. Under the present conditions, "an artist's life has no meaning, and the more talented he is, the more strange and incomprehensible his role" (293), since he is working for the amusement of a degraded humanity and supporting the existing order. Therefore the artist's idleness is, in a way, an act of revolt.

The structure of a debate between activism and quietism is one we recognize from other Chekhov works; and here, as elsewhere, the debate is complex and unresolved. Lida's harshness, her antagonism to the narrator, and the way she bullies her mother and sister suggest that Chekhov's sympathies do not lie with her. Yet the projects she undertakes – providing medical care to the peasants, establishing schools, raising funds for victims of catastrophes – are exactly those Chekhov performed himself. On the other hand, the artist's arguments, about superficial improvements only causing greater unhappiness, were also arguments Chekhov had advanced. The story seems to be another instance of Chekhov stating the problem without providing a solution, acknowledging the social ills of Russian society but refusing to accept easy or self-righteous positions with regard to them.

The other important dimension of the story is the love that develops between the artist and Zhenya. They share a feeling for nature, emotional vulnerability, aesthetic sensibilities. Irina Kirk points out that the artist's confrontations with Lida tend to take place indoors, whereas his idylls with Zhenya occur in the garden, the forest, or the moonlit field.[19] "I passionately wanted to paint for her alone," the narrator recalls, "and I dreamed of her as my little queen who, together with me, would one day possess these trees, fields, mists, the dawn, this nature" (295), in the midst of which the artist had previously felt himself isolated and useless. The artist's love for Zhenya has the potential to restore his purpose and productivity – a potential unrealized in the story.

The tone of much of the story is poetic and elegiac, with evocations of rural beauty and melancholy love that are the antithesis of Lida's stern utilitarianism. It is Lida who wins out, of course. On learning of her sister's love for the artist, she sends her and their mother away to a distant province, denying the lovers even a chance to say goodbye. Lida is last seen teaching the peasant children, dictating one of Krylov's fables in a loud, slow voice that turns literary artistry into grotesque absurdity: "To a crow somewhere … God sent a pie-e-ce of che-e-ese … Have you written that?" (296). The artist, too feeble to resist Lida's indomitable will, gives up and returns to Petersburg. Only in the final paragraph, while recognizing that he has begun to forget about the house with the mezzanine and what befell him there, does he express what the experience meant. "I suddenly recall, as if at random, now the green light in the window, now the sound of my own footsteps in the fields at night, as I, in love, made my way home, rubbing my hands from the cold." In the story's last words, the artist expresses the wan hope that "I, too, am remembered, waited for, and that we will meet … Missyus, where are you?" (297). The intensity of feeling in the story indicates that while Chekhov could respect the strong and practical, his sympathies were with the weak and beautiful. The gentle Missyus and the sensitive, hapless artist carry all of the story's emotional investment, whereas Lida, for all her good works, arouses fear and hatred.

"My Life"

"My Life" was the only other story Chekhov wrote in 1896, and it shares with "The House with the Mezzanine" a concern about how to live, as well as a hero who is a principled dropout. It is one of the longest and most personal of Chekhov's prose works, revisiting the provincial vulgarity of his upbringing.

Chekhov mixed longer and shorter pieces together throughout his career – his one full-length novel, *The Shooting Party*, appeared in 1884 – but in general his stories grew fewer and longer. In addition to "The Steppe" and "The Duel" (1888 and 1891), his longest works include three stories from the Melikhovo period: "The Story of an Unknown Man" (completed in 1893), "Three Years" (1895), and "My Life" (1896). The first of these, about a revolutionary working under cover as a servant, has a melodramatic, Dostoevskian feeling; it is the only one of Chekhov's major works to take place in Dostoevsky's usual setting of Petersburg. "Three Years" explores the world of Moscow's merchant classes, drawing on Chekhov's father's years working in a warehouse. "My Life" focuses on the dreary provinciality of a southern Russian city very like Chekhov's hometown of Taganrog. In their different milieus, all three stories ask, but don't clearly answer, questions about how Russians should live their lives. Interestingly, as Richard Pevear points out, all three stories end with the protagonist looking after a helpless orphaned girl, whose future must be provided for.[20] "The Story of an Unknown Man" ends thus: "Sonya was sitting on the table and looking at me attentively, without blinking, as if she knew her fate was being decided."[21] Evidently, in Chekhov's view, his characters' failures to find a better way of living do not free them from the obligation to do so.

Like "The House with the Mezzanine," "My Life" is narrated by its protagonist, a young man of noble birth with the unusual name of Misail (his sister is named Cleopatra). Their father, the local architect, is a petty despot, like Chekhov's own father and many fathers in his works. In the story's first episode, he beats Misail with an umbrella after the young man has lost his job for the ninth time. Unwilling to trade on his social position and take the fast track into a bureaucratic sinecure, Misail decides to work as a manual laborer, digging ditches, painting houses, assisting a butcher. Taking a high-minded Tolstoyan attitude, he declares that "Unwealthy and uneducated people earn their crust of bread by physical labor, and I see no reason why I should be an exception."[22] He finds this life honest and satisfying, and it awakens him to the plight of the working classes: in one of the more openly political statements in Chekhov, Misail observes that serfdom may have been abolished, but capitalism is taking its place.

Misail's status as a laborer creates an acute social embarrassment for his family and the town. Eventually he is summoned by the local governor, whom he visits after a day working in the slaughterhouse, reeking of meat and blood. Quizzing him about his subversive tendencies, the governor asks suspiciously, "Are you a vegetarian?" It is one of few comically satirical moments in a story that is mainly sober and serious in tone. The chief philosophical debates are between Misail and a military doctor named Blagovo, a forerunner of *Three Sisters'* Vershinin, who admires his friend's principled stand but argues that "if you expended this will power, this intensity, this whole potential on something else, for instance, so as to become in time a great scholar or artist" (466), the benefit to humanity would be greater. Misail argues for the moral law of being self-sufficient and not harming others; Blagovo trumpets the cause of progress, about which Misail is very skeptical. It occurs to the reader, long before it does to Misail, that Blagovo is merely philosophizing to kill time, and that his real interest is in Misail's sister Cleopatra. Blagovo's sister Anyuta likewise loves Misail but recoils from his social degradation.

Misail falls in love with Masha, the conservatory-educated daughter of a self-made engineer. Their first kiss is ominous: "Looking for a handkerchief to wipe her tears, she smiled; we were silent for a while, then I embraced and kissed her, getting a bloody scratch on my cheek as I did so from the pin that held her hat" (491). Masha is an amateur farmer and wants to create a rural idyll at one of the estates her father has bought. Misail marries her and goes along with the plan, although he finds that his Tolstoyan impulses do not extend to enjoying agricultural labor. The project is a disaster: the farming goes badly, the workers steal from them, their attempt to build a village school founders, and Masha finds the peasants frightening and repulsive. The picture of the peasantry in "My Life" is ambiguous, though Masha's disenchantment clearly reflects the shallowness of her social convictions.

Chekhov had mixed feelings about the peasants: he empathized with their troubles but never idealized them in the way Tolstoy did. The conflict between civic-minded gentry and suspicious, resentful peasants was a profound one in late nineteenth-century Russia, where idealistic Populists, or *narodniki*, tried to reach out to the peasants in a movement called "going to the people." It was a conflict Chekhov himself had experienced at Melikhovo, and a few years later he made it the subject of another whole story, "The New Villa." His account of the squalor and violence of rural life, "The Peasants," also dates from this period. In "My Life," the peasants, or muzhiks, are coarse and corrupt, but Misail still finds them morally superior to the intelligentsia:

> In fact, there was filth, and drunkenness, and stupidity, and deceit, but with all that you could feel, nevertheless, that the muzhiks' life was generally upheld by some strong, healthy core. However much the muzhik looks like a clumsy beast as he follows his plow, and however much he befuddles himself with vodka, still, on looking closer, you feel that there is in him something necessary and very important that is lacking, for instance, in Masha and the doctor – namely, he believes that the chief thing on earth is truth, and that his salvation and that of all people lies in truth alone, and therefore he loves justice more than anything else in the world. (509)

In the end, Masha leaves Misail to go abroad with her father, becoming an opera singer. She writes Misail that she has a ring like King David's, with the Hebrew inscription "Everything Passes," and that she takes comfort in it. He muses that he would inscribe his ring "Nothing Passes." Cleopatra is left pregnant by Blagovo, who returns to his wife and children, just as Vershinin will do in *Three Sisters*. Misail makes a final break with his father, raging at him and the town he represents in terms very similar to those Chekhov had used about Taganrog, and that Andrey will use about the provincial backwater in *Three Sisters*:

> You have to stupefy yourself with vodka, cards, gossip, you have to fawn, play the hypocrite, or spend decade after decade drawing plans, to ignore the horror hidden in these houses. Our town has existed for hundreds of years, and in all that time it hasn't given our motherland a single useful

man – not one! You've stifled in the womb everything that had the least bit of life or brightness! (535)

By closing, as it began, with a conflict between Misail and his father, the story has a kind of circularity, and there is a suggestion that things have not changed very much through Misail's revolt against convention. After Cleopatra's death in childbirth, Misail is left to care for her infant daughter. Anyuta Blagovo, who has supported him from a distance through little anonymous gifts, plays with the child at Cleopatra's grave, but still will not be seen in Misail's company. Misail himself, whose nickname is "Small Profit," seems reconciled to his lot, but while he has maintained a kind of integrity throughout the story, it is not clear that his life has added up to all that Chekhov believes a human life can be. At the end, Misail is gradually becoming more and more like the one man he seems to admire, a broken down old housepainter named "Radish," whose moralizing motto becomes a kind of epigraph for the story as a whole: "Worms eat grass, rust eats iron, and lying eats the soul."

"The Little Trilogy"

In 1898 Chekhov wrote three stories, unique in his career, that are linked together by a framing narrative and common themes. Published together in the journal *Russian Thought*, the stories came to be known as "The Little Trilogy." In fact, the stories are very different in tone and style, and each introduces a new setting and cast of characters. But all of them deal, in different ways, with withdrawal and insularity, with the condition of being "in a case," *futliar* in Russian. This condition of encasedness – "*futliarnost*" – is contrasted by the expansiveness of the framing narrative, in which three friends enjoy both thoughtful fellowship and the beauties of the Russian countryside.

The first story, "The Man in a Case," begins with the veterinarian Ivan Ivanych and the schoolteacher Burkin settling down for the night after a day's hunting (the format of the story recalls Turgenev's *Sportsman's Sketches*). Mavra, the wife of the man in whose hut they are sheltering, has become an obsessive solitary, going outside only at night. Her condition leads them to consider other antisocial people, including Burkin's late colleague Belikov, a teacher of Greek. The bulk of the story, narrated by Burkin, concerns Belikov's "constant and insuperable impulse to envelop himself, to create a case for himself, so to speak, that would isolate him, protect him from outside influ-ences."[23] As Burkin describes him, Belikov is a Gogolian grotesque, wearing overcoat and galoshes in all weathers, protecting his ears with cotton and his eyes with dark glasses, and keeping his umbrella, watch, and penknife in their own cases. More disturbingly, he is a life-denying force in the school, warning against even the slightest deviation from regulations lest "something may come of it." His attitude infects the whole community, so that, as Burkin puts it, "under the influence of people like Belikov, our town developed a fear of everything" (301).

Belikov's somewhat sinister influence, and his tendency to report all violations to the authorities, led Soviet critics to interpret the story as a parable of tsarist oppression and thought-policing. While he is clearly an object of satire, the teacher's fate is tragic. In the second half of the story, Belikov meets a vivacious Ukrainian woman named Varenka and her brother, a new teacher. A courtship ensues, promoted by the director's wife and the women faculty. But Belikov's obsession with propriety forestalls the marriage after a cartoon depicting "Anthropos in Love" circulates among the teachers. Belikov goes to remonstrate with the Ukrainian about his sister's riding a bicycle; the angry teacher throws Belikov down the stairs. At this moment Varenka enters with her friends, and her astonished laughter at the mishap literally kills Belikov. He takes to his bed and dies soon after, looking in his coffin "as if he were glad that he had finally been put in a case he would never have to leave" (309).

Belikov's fate recalls Chekhov's early story "The Death of a Clerk," in which anxiety about having sneezed on a government official leads to the death of the title character. Certainly, the narrator Burkin treats the episode as a mordant joke and observes that "burying people like Belikov is a great pleasure." Yet the slightly fantastic, exaggerated style of Burkin's narrative, unique in Chekhov's late prose, and the harshness of his tone cannot quite conceal the poignancy of Belikov's demise. Ivan Ivanych, responding to the story, notes how many aspects of their contemporary lives amount to "cases" of one kind or another. Even as Burkin goes to sleep, Ivan Ivanych reflects on the falsehood of their lives, which requires them "to endure insults, humiliations, not daring to say openly that you're on the side of honest, free people, and to have to lie yourself, to smile, and all that for a crust of bread, a warm corner, some little rank that's not worth a penny …" (310). His meditations are underscored by the eerie, unseen presence of the solitary Mavra, tapping her way down the silent, moonlit street.

The next story, "Gooseberries," finds Ivan Ivanych and Burkin again out hunting, this time caught by a downpour. They seek shelter at the house of a landowner, Alekhin, and in a lyrical interlude Ivan Ivanych swims in the millpond under the rain: "he made waves, and the white lilies swayed on the waves; he reached the middle of the pond and dove, and a moment later appeared in another place and swam further, and kept diving, trying to reach the bottom. 'Ah, my God …' he repeated delightedly. 'Ah, my God …'"[24] The feeling of blissful contentment is extended when the hunters sit with Alekhin "in silk dressing gowns and warm slippers" in his drawing room, with a beautiful servant girl, Pelgeya, "stepping noiselessly over the carpet and smiling softly" as she serves them tea and preserves. The story Ivan goes on to narrate, however, represents a challenge to notions of domestic satisfaction.

The central narrative of "Gooseberries" is Ivan's account of his younger brother Nikolai, a civil servant, who developed an obsession with having a country estate with gooseberry bushes. He lived a gray and frugal existence to save money for his dream, and even married an unloved widow to acquire her paltry fortune; she died from his neglect. On visiting him, Ivan finds him corpulent and piglike, giving himself the airs of a landowner, but, in his way, happy. Nikolai savors the gooseberries he has grown on his estate, though they are tough and sour. But seeing the meanness of his brother's pleasures, Ivan Ivanych is shocked into a realization about the hypocrisy of Russian life, in which people can lull themselves into happiness despite the squalor and suffering around them, since the miserable remain silent. Ivan launches into a tirade of protest that is as existential as it is political:

> At the door of every contented, happy man somebody should stand with a little hammer, constantly tapping, to remind him that unhappy people exist, that however happy he may be, sooner or later life will show him its claws, some calamity will befall him – illness, poverty, loss – and nobody will hear or see, just as he doesn't hear or see others now. (318)

Burkin and Alekhin are unsatisfied with Ivan's tale, which does not accord with their present feelings and surroundings: "With generals and ladies gazing from gilded frames, looking alive in the twilight, it was boring to hear a story about a wretched official who ate gooseberries" (319). Yet the effect of Ivan's tapping hammer is felt in the uneasy atmosphere at the story's close. Despite the fresh linens and comfortable beds, made up, as Chekhov notes, by the beautiful Pelageya, Burkin is unable to sleep, troubled by the stale tobacco of his friend's pipe, an odour he is strangely unable to identify. The final paragraph of the story, recalling the hammer, is terse and ominous: "Rain beat on the windows all night."

The final story, "About Love," is told the following day and is prompted by Alekhin's reference to an unhappy love affair between the brutish cook and the beautiful Pelageya ("*krasivaya Pelageya*" –the adjective attaches to her, like a Homeric epithet, almost every time she is mentioned). A discussion of love ensues, leading to Alekhin's account of his own unhappy love affair. At this point Chekhov's own narrative voice breaks in, noting that "people who lead a solitary existence always have something in their hearts which they are eager to talk about" – a comment that links the encasing *futliarnost* of the embedded narratives to the story-telling frame in a slightly cynical way.[25] Can it be that these three men, even in their apparent attempts to communicate, are still only locking themselves in cases?

Alekhin's own "case" is the conventional morality that prevented him from actively pursuing the love of his life. As a young man, he had become friends with a couple who become a kind of surrogate family for him. Anna Alexeyevna – like Tolstoy's Anna Karenina, of whom she is an obvious shadow – is married to a rather conservative, uninteresting older man, but she responds warmly to the young Alekhin. They begin a kind of unacknowledged, unconsummated love affair: "We talked a long time, and were silent, yet we did not confess our love to each other, but timidly and jealously concealed it. We were afraid of everything that might reveal our secret to ourselves" (298). Eventually Anna's health breaks under the strain, and she is sent off to the Crimea for treatment, after which she will join her husband at his new posting in a distant province. Only when she is finally leaving on the train do the lovers give way to their feelings:

> Kissing her face, her shoulders, her hands wet with tears – oh, how unhappy we were! – I confessed my love for her, and with a burning pain in my heart I realized how unnecessary, how petty, and how deceptive all that had hindered us from loving was. I understood that when you love you must either, in your reasonings about that love, start from what is highest, from what is more important than happiness or unhappiness, sin or virtue in their accepted meaning, or you must not reason at all. (301–2)

Chekhov sets off this passionate moment with a poignant reminder of the way the quotidian intrudes on the transcendent – during their parting the train has started, so Alekhin has to sit crying in an adjoining compartment until they reach the next station, and then walk all the way home.

The story seems to suggest that virtuous living can itself be a kind of "case," and comes close to condoning adultery as a moral act (an issue Chekhov took up again soon after in "The Lady with the Little Dog"). In any event, the three stories all focus on individuals circumscribing themselves, cutting themselves off from true freedom and what is best in nature and humanity. The things these encased characters are missing are evoked by lyrical passages in the frame narrative – the stillness of the cloud-cloaked fields, the childlike delight of Ivan's swim, the comforts of Alekhin's home, and the beautiful Pelageya. Near the end of "The Man in A Case," Chekhov addresses the reader directly with a kind of epiphany that lifts the perspective above limited human concerns to the plane of the eternal:

> When you see a wide village street on a moonlit night, with its cottages, haystacks, sleeping willows, your own soul becomes hushed, in that peace, hiding from toil, care, and grief in the shadows of the night, it turns meek, mournful, beautiful, and it seems the stars, too, look down on it tenderly and with feeling, and that there is no more evil on earth, and all is well. (310)

A yearning for the transcendent, for a plane above the messy squabble of human interactions, is a recurring theme in Chekhov's work. This eternal perspective appears from time to time in Chekhov's stories, especially his later ones, and especially near the end. It is often associated with the sky or the sea, as in "Gusev" and "The Black Monk." "The Little Trilogy" ends on a similar note, with the rain clearing and the millpond shining like a mirror in the sunlight, giving the conclusion a tone of hope, or at least of consolation.

"The Lady with the Little Dog"

The setting of human troubles against the background of sea and sky, the perspective *sub specie aeternitatis*, makes its definitive appearance in what is probably Chekhov's best-known story, "The Lady with the Little Dog" (1899). In this tale, what initially appears to be a rather sordid adultery between two inconsequential people takes on a kind of mystical aura, as it leads the characters toward profound self-realization. The first part of the story is set in the Crimean resort town of Yalta, where Chekhov spent his last years while suffering from tuberculosis. Here Gurov, an aging roué, smoothly seduces the unhappy young wife Anna Sergeyevna, in yet another echo of Tolstoy.[26] But while *Anna Karenina* ends in tragedy, the affair of Anna and Gurov leads to an uncertain future in which both characters for the first time come to be fully themselves.

Gurov, a married banker approaching forty, has become a serial adulterer and views women contemptuously as an "inferior race." His affairs have yielded him only passing satisfaction. The women he has known were either carefree sensualists, highly strung intellectuals like his wife, or cold and malevolent predators. Chekhov conveys Gurov's antipathy to this last group in an indelible image: "their beauty aroused hatred in him, and the lace of their underwear seemed to him like scales."[27] By contrast, Anna Sergeyevna's naiveté, awkwardness, and vulnerability attract him. Like the Anna of

"About Love," she is married to a provincial official and has come to the Crimea by herself. Anna and Gurov have various casual meetings, and then one evening, after they have watched a ship come into the harbor, he kisses her and they go to her hotel room. In a moment of post-coital guilt, with her hair hanging down in the candlelight, she appears posed, "like the sinful woman in an old painting." Bored and irritated, Gurov eats a slice of watermelon "unhurriedly" in a gesture of cool disdain (365). Finally, moved by her unfeigned sorrow, he kisses and comforts her, and takes her out for a drive.

They go to a seaside cliff at Oreanda, where Gurov has an epiphany that colors the remaining action of the story:

> The leaves of the trees did not stir, cicadas called, and the monotonous, dull noise of the seas, coming from below, spoke of the peace, of the eternal sleep that awaits us. So it had sounded below when neither Yalta nor Oreanda were there, so it sounded now and would go on sounding with the same dull indifference when we are no longer here. And in this constancy, in this utter indifference to the life and death of each of us, there perhaps lies hidden the pledge of our eternal salvation, the unceasing movement of life on earth, of unceasing perfection. Sitting beside the young woman, who looked so beautiful in the dawn, appeased and enchanted by the view of this magical décor – sea, mountains, clouds, the open sky – Gurov reflected that, essentially, if you thought of it, everything was beautiful in this world, everything except for what we ourselves think and do when we forget the higher goals of being and our human dignity. (366–67)

This lofty, compassionate perspective, contrasting human folly with natural beauty, mixing profound pity with serene detachment, recurs throughout Chekhov's work. Here it provides a turning point in the story, preventing the lovers from returning fully to the lives they knew before.

Initially, Gurov does his best to forget; when Anna returns to her gray provincial town of "S.," Gurov goes back to Moscow and tries to carry on with his accustomed life of restaurants and card parties. Yet her memory haunts him, to the degree that he wishes to talk about her, to share their secret with someone else. Leaving his club one night, he makes a tentative attempt to bring her up in conversation, but his companion, mishearing him, replies, "You were right earlier: the sturgeon was a bit off". It is a quintessentially Chekhovian exchange, mixing the transcendent and the grossly mundane. The remark puts Gurov on the defensive, perhaps unwilling to acknowledge a basely appetitive element, a spoiled fishiness, in his love affair: "These words, so very ordinary, for some reason suddenly made Gurov indignant, struck him as humiliating, impure" (370). He recognizes the emptiness of his Moscow life and goes to seek Anna in S., not quite knowing himself what he hopes to achieve.

The episode in S. is filled with details communicating the gray misery of the town. In Gurov's hotel room, "the whole floor was covered with gray army flannel and there was an inkstand on the table, gray with dust, with a horseback rider, who held his hat in his raised hand, but whose head was broken off" (370). The Russian émigré novelist Vladimir Nabokov particularly admired this inkstand, which he saw as emblematic of Chekhov's attention to minute but striking details: "It is nothing and it is everything in authentic literature."[28] Spying on Anna's house, which is fronted by a long, gray, spiked fence, Gurov "saw a beggar go in the gates and saw the dogs attack him" (371). S. is not only dreary but hostile, savage, soul-killing. When Gurov sits in his hotel room on the "cheap, gray, hospital-like blanket," he resembles Nikolai Stepanovich in "A Boring Story," waiting for death in Kharkov. Finally Gurov succeeds in meeting Anna at the theatre, kissing her in the stairwell in spite of two high-school boys who look on, smoking; he no longer cares about social appearances. Anna begins visiting him in Moscow, resuming their affair.

In Moscow, in the fourth and final section of the story, Gurov muses on the strange fact that he is only truly himself with Anna, in the secret world of their love:

> He had two lives: an apparent one, seen and known by all who needed it, filled with conventional truth and conventional deceit, which perfectly resembled the lives of his acquaintances and friends, and another that went on in secret. And by some strange coincidence, perhaps an accidental one, everything that he found important, interesting, necessary, in which he was sincere and did not deceive himself, which constituted the core of his life, occurred in secret from others, while everything that made up his lie, his shell … all this was in full view. (374)

Gurov's illicit love contains a greater truth than the outer world of social respectability, even, Chekhov suggests, than the obligations of family – his "apparent" life is sufficient for "all who needed it." Gurov and Anna go on meeting in secret, and their love grows stronger than ever, although his hair has now turned gray and her beauty is on the point of fading. Looking at himself and Anna in the mirror, Gurov reflects on the superficiality of his past affairs, and on their distance from the first real love he has ever felt. Throughout the story Chekhov has used free indirect discourse to convey, through third-person narration, the separate thoughts of Gurov and Anna. In the final paragraphs, he often speaks for both of them together: "it seemed to them that fate had destined them for each other, and they could not understand why he had a wife and she a husband; and it was as if they were two birds of passage, a male and a female, who had been caught and forced to live in separate cages" (376). The image of the caged migratory birds is full of pathos, but the story does not end on a despairing note. While not deluding themselves about the difficulties they will confront, Gurov and Anna face the future with hope:

> And it seemed that, just a little more – and the solution would be found, and then a new, beautiful life would begin; and it was clear to both of them that the end was still far, far off, and that the most complicated and difficult part was just beginning. (376)

Like many of Chekhov's stories, "The Lady with the Dog" ends with a beginning (quite literally – the last word is "*nachinaetsya*," "beginning"). The sense that a better future will be knowable in "just a little more" time is one that is often qualified in Chekhov; his three final plays all undermine such a hope in different degrees. But in "The Lady with the Little Dog," the acknowledgment of what is "complicated and difficult" in human life does not quite destroy the hope represented by the love of Anna and Gurov. As Nabokov noted, extending this observation to all of Chekhov's stories, "The story does not really end, for as long as people are alive, there is no possible and definite conclusion to their troubles or hopes or dreams."[29] Despite its sometimes mournful, elegiac tone, "The Lady with the Little Dog" is one of the most life-affirming of Chekhov's stories.

"In the Ravine"

By contrast, "In the Ravine," written shortly afterwards, in 1900, is one of Chekhov's bleakest works. It is the last of Chekhov's several studies of the peasantry; but unlike "Peasants," which exposed the poverty and squalor of peasant life, "In the Ravine" details the moral degeneracy of a family that is wealthy and prosperous. In this it closely resembles "Peasant Women," a story from 1891, in which the selfish, blind, or unprincipled behavior of peasant men leads to the criminality of their wives. "In the Ravine" features one of Chekhov's only portraits of unalloyed human evil in the daughter-in-law Aksinya. The story condemns not only Aksinya, however, but the whole social and physical environment in which she flourishes.

"In the Ravine" is set in a peasant village that is remembered only as the place "where the verger ate all the caviar at the funeral."[30] This reduction of spiritual values to gluttonous appetite is characteristic of the village as a whole.

The physical environment of the village, down in a ravine surrounded by factories that pollute the water, suggests its moral contamination by the bourgeois values of a grasping, heartless capitalism. The central family, the Tsybukins, are financially successful but morally bankrupt. The patriarch Grigory owns the village store. He is devoted to his family but cheats the peasants, selling rotten meat and bad vodka; Chekhov may be recalling his own father's shop in Taganrog. His elder son Anisim is a police inspector in another town, the younger, Stepan, is deaf and sickly. Stepan's wife Aksinya is the real power in the family, a shrewd businesswoman who is beautiful but malevolent. Chekhov gives her a green dress – a color he often associates with death – and a reptilian demeanor:

> Aksinya had gray, naïve eyes that seldom blinked, and a naïve smile constantly played over her face. And there was something snakelike in those unblinking eyes, and in that small head on its long neck, and in her shapely build; green with a yellow front, smiling, she gazed the way a viper in springtime, stretched out and head up, gazes from the young rye at someone going past. (395)

"In the Ravine" follows the fortunes of the Tsybukins through a series of significant events in their lives. Grigory, a widower, marries a kindly woman named Varvara, whose charity to the peasants functions "like a safety valve on an engine" (385) in the corrupt household. A marriage is arranged between Anisim and a poor, gentle girl named Lipa. She and her widowed mother Praskovya are intimidated by the Tsybukins and live like servants in their family compound. The scene of the wedding is grotesque and chaotic, emphasizing the materialism of the Tsybukins and the coarse vigor of the guests. The eating, drinking, and dancing go on for hours, occasionally interrupted by "some peasant woman in the yard" shouting "You've sucked enough of our blood, you Herods, a plague upon you!" (394). Anisim, drunk and preoccupied, never speaks to Lipa, who appears petrified. The consummation of the marriage is represented as a kind of hideous ritual enforced by the villagers on the unwilling participants. At the party, Anisim is drunkenly trying to arrest someone who stole a vest; "He ran outside, chasing after someone; they caught him, took him under the arms, brought him home, shoved him, drunk, flushed with anger, wet, into the room where the aunt was already undressing Lipa, and locked the door" (395).

Later in the story it emerges that Anisim, the policeman, is a counterfeiter. His crime is emblematic of the hypocrisy and corruption that poison the village. His arrest and imprisonment occur in the gap between two chapters; as in his plays, Chekhov focuses not so much on climactic actions as on their impact on his characters. Chekhov is likewise circumspect about the central action of the story, Aksinya's murder of Lipa's baby. Resentful of the fact that the infant Nikifor will inherit land that she covets, Aksinya throws boiling water from the laundry over him. Rather than describing the horror of this event directly, Chekhov abruptly changes perspective, moving the reader outside and concentrating on the result: "After that a cry was heard such as had never yet been heard in Ukleyevo, and it was hard to believe that such a small, weak being as Lipa could scream like that … And until the cook came back from the river, nobody dared go into the kitchen and see what had happened there" (411).

Aksinya goes unpunished and continues her takeover of the family; Lipa and her mother lose their place in the household and end up working in the brickyard. The last part of the story, however, strikes some positive chords. The evil of Ukleyevo is mostly in the background. Chekhov instead focuses on the natural world – represented by the mysterious, mournful call of a bittern, which seems to remind listeners that "life is given only once!" – and on the simple goodness of Lipa and her mother. The story's consolations are spiritual, but they are not those of organized religion. In a harshly satirical detail, Chekhov describes the gluttony at Nikifor's funeral feast, where "Lipa served at the table, and the priest, raising a fork with a pickled mushroom on it, said to her: 'Don't grieve over the baby. Of such is the Kingdom of Heaven'" (415). Yet Lipa is a Christlike figure in her suffering and her charity. At the end of the story, old Grigory has been thrown out of the house by Aksinya and roams the village half-mad and starving. In the story's final episode, he and Lipa meet in a subdued reconciliation that suggests a peasant Lear and Cordelia. Some village women are returning from their work at the brickyard, covered in red dust. "Ahead of them all went Lipa, and she sang in a high voice, pouring out her song as she looked up at the sky, as if celebrating and rejoicing that the day, thank God, was over and they could rest" (419). She and her mother encounter Grigory, greet him respectfully, and give him some of their food, bringing tears to his eyes. Then they walk on, "crossing themselves for a long time" (420).

Despite their suffering, Lipa and her mother remain strong, good, and generous. Chekhov suggests that something essential in the peasantry can survive the greed and cruelty of capitalism, the poisoning of the countryside, and the depredations of their lives. On the night Lipa is bringing her baby home from the hospital, she meets an old carter who tells her that "life is long, there'll be more of good and bad, there'll be everything. Mother Russia is vast!" (414). He concludes that, since he still wants to live, there must be more good than bad; and Chekhov, just barely, seems to agree with him.

Both Tolstoy and Gorky, who had originally suggested to Chekhov that he contribute a story to the left-wing periodical *Life*, praised "In the Ravine." Gorky wrote that "Chekhov has been reproached with having no philosophy. The reproach is absurd … Ever more often our ears can catch in his stories the melancholy but severe and deserved reproach that men do not know how to live, but at the same time, his sympathy with all men glows even brighter."[31] Chekhov confronts profound depths of suffering, and even evil, in "In the Ravine," but he perceives a rough gem of human goodness glinting through the dark, poisoned waters.

"The Bishop"

Chekhov wrote only two more stories after "In the Ravine," though he would live another four years. Much of his time was devoted to drama, to editing his collected works, and to his life with Olga Knipper, whom he married in 1901. Yet Chekhov was also gravely ill during this period, and these last two stories, "The Bishop" and "The Fiancée," deal directly with the coming of death. "The Bishop," written in 1902, covers the last few days in the life of Bishop Pyotr, within the context of Orthodox celebrations of Holy Week. The story is one of Chekhov's most audacious in its apparent formlessness; Virginia Woolf, in reviewing it, noted that it seemed that Chekhov made up his stories "in the way that a hen picks up grain," with no obvious governing principle, and yet with "the finest insight."[32] Such shape as the story has comes from the various liturgical observances and canonical hours that structure Pyotr's life. Like several of Chekhov's stories, "The Bishop" communicates the profound spiritual sensibility of its unreligious author.

"The Bishop" opens on the eve of Palm Sunday, when Pyotr, in a dreamlike sequence in church, sees an old woman who appears to be his mother, whom he has not seen in nine years. The vision moves him to tears, which in turn spread to the congregation, so that "the church was gradually filled with quiet weeping."[33] On returning to the monastery, Pyotr learns that it was indeed his mother, who has come to visit him, bringing a granddaughter for whom she hopes to procure Pyotr's financial help. Pyotr is happy to see her, and delighted by the young Katya, but he is disturbed by the deference his mother shows him. Pyotr is suffering from the strain and isolation of his office, uncomfortable in his authority, frustrated by the pettiness of his parishioners, and uncertain of his own identity. He is only at ease with a curmudgeonly old monk, Father Sisoy, the sole person not awed by his august position. Sisoy's grumblings and mutterings contribute a vein of comedy to the story, and with his homely ministrations to Pyotr's illness, he demonstrates care and affection.

Though it is heavy with disease and death, "The Bishop" is not a depressing story. C. J. G. Turner has commented on "the extraordinary fact that a story about a dying man, written by a dying man, is rendered credible without being either sentimental or pessimistic," being, indeed, "unexpectedly joyful."[34] The presence of his mother leads Pyotr to reflect back on many phases of his past, so that the story comes to encompass his entire life, not only his death. The eight-year-old Katya provides a reassuring image of the future, not only in her earnest youth but in her refusal to be intimidated by death. Speaking of her cousin, a medical student, she cheerfully tells the dying Pyotr that "Nikolasha cuts up dead people" (426), charming him with her frankness. Finally, the Easter celebration itself, with its associations of springtime and rebirth, places individual human suffering in a much broader temporal frame, as in "Easter Night" and "The Student." As Pyotr listens to the choir singing Holy Week hymns, he is "carried in his thoughts into the distant past, into his childhood and youth … and now that past appeared alive, beautiful, joyful, as it probably had never been" (430). The element of possible delusion is offset by Pyotr's spiritual uplift: "he was stirred by the same hope for the future that he had had in childhood, in the academy, and abroad. 'They're singing so well today!' he thought, listening to the choir. 'So well!'" (434).

Chekhov does not stint on the physical facts of Pyotr's dying, from typhoid fever and intestinal bleeding; yet Pyotr greets his sudden decline with the same words he had for the choir, "*Kak khorosho!*": "'How good!' he thought. 'How good!'" His illness breaks through the reserve of his mother, allowing her at last to treat him with intimate tenderness: "she no longer remembered that he was a bishop, and she kissed him like a child very near and dear to her." Death is a kind of liberation for Pyotr from the weight of his identity and position; he feels himself "a simple, ordinary man" who is "free as a bird" (435). The bishop's death is subsumed in the joyful ringing of Easter bells, the singing of birds, and the spring sunshine. There are ironic notes in the story's ending, as the bishop is quickly replaced and his earthly fame forgotten. Pyotr's mother can only speak timidly to her neighbors about her dead son who was a bishop, afraid they will not believe her; "And indeed," Chekhov concludes, "not everyone believed her." Yet this deflating ending does not erase the quiet dignity and sincere goodness with which the bishop faces his last days.

"The Fiancée"

Chekhov's final story likewise has a death by disease – by tuberculosis, indeed, of which Chekhov was in the late stages – but it also ends with a note of

ambiguous hope. The 23-year-old heroine Nadya is persuaded by her consumptive friend Sasha to abandon her provincial bourgeois life and idle
fiancé, in order to educate herself for a better future. The story was understood as a political statement when it was published in 1903, and it was later
embraced by Soviet critics. Sasha's diatribes against the unhealthy, overcrowded conditions in which the working classes lived are similar to those
voiced by Trofimov in *The Cherry Orchard*, and they reflect real social
problems of which Chekhov was keenly conscious. Yet Sasha, like
Trofimov, is a somewhat feeble and ineffectual character, one who will not
himself attain his utopian visions.

Sasha's criticisms of the idle, vulgar lifestyle of Nadya's family do take effect,
and she begins to reject her past and look to the future with hope. The story
gives a sense, however, that she is still somewhat unformed, that she acts not
from firm convictions but from a still-evolving sense of self. In describing her
impressions of her home and the people around her, Chekhov repeatedly uses
the phrase "for some reason" ("*pochemu-to*") as though her responses are
intuitive but only half-conscious: "for some reason her mother looked very
young"; "for some reason she wanted to cry."[35]

Nonetheless, her personal evolution moves her in a positive direction, as she
is able to see the injustice of her family's bourgeois luxury – always associated
with images of feeding and fatness – as well as its vulgarity, a quality, "*poshlost*,"
that Chekhov loathed. When her fiancé takes her on a tour of their prospective
future dwelling, she hates the showy furnishings and is "nauseated" by a
painted nude in a gilt frame, hinting at her sexual revulsion from the stout
Andrey. As they walk through the rooms, "in all of it she saw only banality
(*poshlost*), stupid, naïve, unbearable banality, and his arm that encircled her
waist seemed to her as hard and cold as an iron hoop." With Sasha's help, she
makes her escape, to the university in Petersburg.

Yet Nadya outgrows Sasha, just as she had her family. When she visits him in
Moscow after her first year at university, she finds him "gray, provincial" and
recoils from the squalor of his smoky, untidy room: "on the table, next to the
cold samovar, was a cracked plate with a piece of dark paper, and on the table
and the floor a multitude of dead flies" (454). Soon Sasha will be dead too, and
Nadya finds that this thought does not trouble her, "and her acquaintance with
Sasha now seemed to her something dear, but long, long past!" (454). On a visit
to her family, whose social position has been lost through her breaking of her
engagement, she learns of Sasha's death. Feeling nothing tying her to her
provincial roots, she prepares to leave. "She realized that her life had been
turned around, as Sasha wanted, that here she was lonely, alien, not needed,
and that she needed nothing here." The next day, "she said good-bye to her

family and, alive, cheerful, left town – as she thought, forever" (454).Whether Nadya will succeed in finding a new and better life in the bright, full world she dreams of is left open, but the qualifying "as she thought" allows for the possibility that she will not. The final stroke in Chekhov's career as a writer of fiction characteristically mixes warm-hearted hope with just a touch of weary skepticism.

Chapter 6

Later plays

The four plays Chekhov had produced at the Moscow Art Theatre between 1898 and 1904 represent, arguably, his greatest artistic achievement, as well as one of the most important contributions of any writer to world drama. *The Seagull, Uncle Vanya, Three Sisters*, and *The Cherry Orchard* are unrivalled in their combination of naturalistic detail, psychological insight, and poetic intensity. Chekhov's innovation, as Robert Brustein describes it, was "to achieve a synthesis between theatricality and reality, guiding events which seem to have no visible means of propulsion, and developing a form which seems to be no form at all."[1] The discussion that follows will proceed act by act through each of the plays, calling attention to key aspects of Chekhov's stagecraft as well as to interpretive cruxes that reveal the plays' complexity and ambiguity. Like the works of Shakespeare, Chekhov's plays lend themselves to multiple legitimate interpretations; as they unfold on the stage, subtle nuances of inflection, gesture, and characterization can send the plays off down myriad avenues of meaning. Yet any successful Chekhov production will highlight the qualities that make Chekhov's plays unique: a balance of interest among a large cast of characters, an attention to the subtleties of social interaction, and an awareness of the powerful submerged longings that animate even the most apparently mundane lives.

The Seagull

Critical studies of the *The Seagull* necessarily begin with the theatrical legend of the play's two premieres: its disastrous failure at the Aleksandrinsky Theatre in

St. Petersburg in 1896, and its equally spectacular success at Stanislavsky's Moscow Art Theatre (MAT) two years later. This account is something of an oversimplification, of course, but it provides an appropriate context for considering the play; not only because of the ongoing relationship of Chekhov and the MAT, but because *The Seagull* itself is so directly concerned with theatre. Its main characters are actors and writers, it contains a play within a play, it is filled with debates about drama and literature, and, perhaps self-consciously, it heeds its playwright-hero's call for "new forms" in the theatre. Indeed, its initial failure in Petersburg may have been inevitable, since it was written in part to subvert the conventions of the conservative imperial stage. Chekhov was conscious of the work's incongruity and felt that perhaps he should stick to fiction. But there is an element of defiant pride in his assertion, upon finishing *The Seagull*, that "I began it *forte* and finished it *pianissimo* – against all the rules of dramatic art."[2] It was only with Stanislavsky's MAT production in 1898 that Chekhov's experimental dramaturgy found a convincing expression onstage – even if it did not always convince Chekhov, whose relationship with the MAT was often contentious.

The Seagull represents a marked break from the well-made-play conventions that governed successful drama at Russia's imperial theatres, and a move toward the theatrical innovations of Chekhov's later works. Like Chekhov's other major plays, it concerns the relations of a large group of characters in a provincial household over an extended period of time. The play unfolds through four undivided acts; for the first time, Chekhov abandoned the structure of "French scenes" that marked his earlier plays, where each entrance and exit was discretely marked as a new unit of action. *The Seagull* nonetheless consists largely of dialogues between two characters at a time, and does not quite achieve the apparently formless, slice-of-life naturalism that distinguishes *Three Sisters* and *The Cherry Orchard*.

The play revolves ceaselessly around the twin themes of love and art. It is built, accordingly, on two primary structural devices: a daisy chain of unfulfilled desire, and a quartet of artistic characters, variously linked and vexed by generational, sexual, and aesthetic conflicts. The love-chain connects most of the play's characters at some stage: the schoolmaster Medvedenko loves the overseer's daughter Masha, who loves the young playwright Treplyov, who loves the would-be actress Nina, who comes to love the successful novelist Trigorin, who is involved with Treplyov's mother, the actress Arkadina.[3] Meanwhile Polina, the wife of the overseer Shamraev, is in love with Dr. Dorn; so that the only character who is not involved in a love-intrigue of some kind is the invalid Sorin, Arkadina's brother and the owner of the country estate where the action takes place. The idyllic lakeside setting and artistic milieu contribute to the atmosphere of frustrated longing.

The central characters are two male writers and two actresses, representing two generations and stages of success. The members of the older generation, Arkadina and Trigorin, are established and rather bored; they have fallen into patterns that the public has come to expect and are to some extent victims of their own success. The younger generation, Nina and Treplyov, have the fire and ambition of youth but have yet to find the fame or aesthetic achievement for which they yearn. Each generation envies and resents the other, and their artistic differences are exacerbated by their complex bonds of desire and jealousy. Treplyov's contempt for Trigorin's formulaic writing is fueled by jealousy of the man who takes both his mother's and his girlfriend's love. The affair between Trigorin and Nina is not only a matter of sexual passion: she longs for his fame, and he hopes her youth will reinvigorate his writing. When Arkadina sets out to recapture Trigorin as a lover, she does so primarily by flattering him as a writer. These four characters dominate the play, with each especially featured in one act: in sequence, Treplyov, Trigorin, Arkadina, and Nina. The other characters remain supporting figures in the background, characterized by one or two defining traits: Shamraev's coarseness and pedantic enthusiasm for the theatre, Medvedenko's money worries, Masha's heartsick drinking and snuff-taking, and so forth.

By making his central characters writers and actresses, Chekhov created an opportunity to hold forth on aesthetic questions of the day, yet he avoids making any one character his mouthpiece. Treplyov and Trigorin perceive themselves as rivals, yet there is something of Chekhov in each (as well as in the coolly detached Dorn). In inveighing against the banalities of the traditional theatre, Treplyov is expressing some of Chekhov's own views; but so is Trigorin, when he speaks of the compulsions and anxieties of a successful author. In Arkadina and Nina, Chekhov similarly juxtaposes accomplished triteness with blighted, unformed talent. The theatrical milieu also gives Chekhov license for stylistic experimentation and allusion. Treplyov's attempt to create "new forms" is expressed in a play-within-the-play, a Symbolist monologue that fails disastrously in the first act but returns with haunting force at the play's end. Further, the entire play can be seen as an echo of *Hamlet* – a keynote text in Russian intellectual life – to which there are several direct allusions. Treplyov is a melancholy role-player whose bitterness toward his mother and her lover poisons the atmosphere around him. He is frustrated by inaction and can express himself only through self-destruction. Nina similarly flirts with Ophelia-like madness in response to betrayal and loss. Yet Chekhov denies his characters the grandeur of tragedy, grounding them in a quotidian reality and qualifying theatrical suffering with astringent irony.

The first three acts move over the course of a single summer, establishing the rhythm that will be repeated in *Uncle Vanya* and *The Cherry Orchard*, as the characters play out their dramas in the country and then leave for town as winter nears. The final act, set two years later, looks back not only on the intervening action but on the play's opening, thus calling attention to the irrevocable distances the characters have traveled. Chekhov's originality lies in keeping the most dramatic events of the story offstage. Whereas his earlier full-length plays incorporated suicides, attempted murders, and adulterous affairs directly into the action, *The Seagull* mainly eschews melodrama and concentrates instead on the accumulated consequences of acts of passion. Though the play ends on a somewhat sensational note with Treplyov's suicide, it is mainly concerned with the day-to-day living of its characters, both in responding to the crises of their lives, and at moments that are apparently inconsequential. It was this psychological subtlety that the MAT production brought across so successfully, together with the detailed evocation of setting and mood.

A word should be said about the physical environment of the play. As Laurence Senelick has pointed out, the action moves inward, in stages, from an expansive natural environment to a cluttered interior: an action perhaps emblematic of the curtailing of Treplyov's aspirations.[4] All of Chekhov's major plays use both outdoor and indoor locations; and in all of the plays the movement between settings can be seen as exemplifying some oppression or dispossession of the characters. At the Moscow Art Theatre, these locations were rendered, as realistically as possible, in the sets of Victor Simov, a practice that occasionally necessitated some compromises. The MAT used the same set for Acts I and II of *The Seagull*, rather than moving, as Chekhov directed, from the lake to the more domesticated environment of a croquet lawn next to the house. Chekhov productions since the mid twentieth century have been more apt to opt for stylized, composite settings, in which indoor and outdoor elements are combined, birch trees coexisting with bookcases. In the case of *The Seagull*, this more abstract staging has tended to heighten the poetic and symbolic elements of the play.

Act I

Like many acts in Chekhov's major dramas, Act I is structured around a social gathering that doesn't come off as planned; in this case, Treplyov's play. Chekhov uses this device to bring on the various characters in overlapping scenes, often with just two or three people, and then assemble the entire dramatis personae for the central event. This event may be aborted, as here, not happen at all (the masquerade in *Three Sisters*), be a flop (the ball in *The Cherry Orchard*), or end in tears and gunfire (the family council in *Uncle Vanya*). The brief remainder of the act deals with the aftermath.

The opening lines of Act I set the tone of mordant humor that helps *The Seagull* live up to its subtitle as "A Comedy." Asked why she always wears black, Masha replies, "I'm in mourning for my life."[5] Whether it is meant sincerely or as a snappy rejoinder to her unwanted suitor Medvedenko, this line invariably gets a laugh in the theatre, and it perfectly captures the mood of self-indulgent and theatrical dissatisfaction that afflicts so many of the play's characters. The ensuing dialogue succinctly, indeed rather baldly, brings up the themes of art and love, as well as anticipating the central event of the act: "Miss Zarechnaya is going to act in a play written by Konstantin Gavrilovich. They're in love, and today their souls will merge in an attempt to present a joint artistic creation." Interestingly, all the non-artists in the play – Medvedenko, Sorin, Dorn, even Shamraev – envy and admire the artists (who for the most part find a singular lack of satisfaction in their profession). The old civil servant Sorin declares that he wanted two things in life: to get married and to be an author, "but I didn't manage to do either one." Disappointments in art and love pervade the play.

The dialogue of Sorin and Treplyov continues the exposition, establishing the latter's resentment of his mother and cool disdain for Trigorin. It also raises the critical issue of "new forms" in art, the banner under which Treplyov writes. His attack on dramatic convention seems an overt challenge to Chekhov's audience, and indeed to the imperial theatre that first presented the play in St. Petersburg: "When the curtain goes up on an artificially-lighted room with three walls, and these great talents, acolytes of the religion of art, act out how people eat, drink, make love, walk, wear their jackets; when they take cheap, vulgar plots and cheap, vulgar speeches and try to extract a moral. … I run out the exit and keep on running …" Treplyov's critique of outmoded forms is apt; but he has failed to find a suitable new form, as becomes evident when his play is enacted.

After two further misfiring love scenes (Treplyov/Nina, Polina/Dorn), the company arrives for Treplyov's play. There is a rather showy entrance by the charismatic grande dame Arkadina; Chekhov creates similar moments for Yelena in *Uncle Vanya* and Ranevskaya in *Cherry Orchard*, all roles played by Olga Knipper. The theatrical atmosphere is sustained, and the submerged tensions perhaps exposed, when Arkadina and Treplyov exchange lines from *Hamlet* about the Queen's guilty lovemaking with Hamlet's stepfather. The mother–son conflict explodes during the performance, causing Treplyov to bring down the curtain in fury. The performance is clearly a fiasco; but it is a matter of interpretation as to just how absurd Chekhov meant it to be.

It is hard, in performance, to take seriously Nina's monologue beginning "Humans, lions, eagles and partridges," and going on to describe the extinction of all living creatures and the conflation of their spirits into a single Universal Soul. In Russian, however, the repeated "-*y*" sound of the plural ending gives the catalogue of animals a more lilting, poetic, incantatory quality than it has in English, where it seems a rather flat and absurd list. Chekhov obviously did not choose to write his own plays as Symbolist monologues, so it is unlikely that he is endorsing Treplyov's technique; but he took an interest in the work of Maeterlinck, whose style he is to some extent quoting here. It seems contrary to Chekhov's intentions to make the play wholly ridiculous, as many modern productions do. Chekhov was mortified when audiences laughed at Nina in the Aleksandrinksy premiere. In the MAT production, there seems to have been a real attempt to give Nina's monologue some theatrical effect, as she is revealed silhouetted against the lake. Stanislavsky's production score specifies that "Her face is not visible, as the light is behind her. Only the contours of her figure can be seen, and this lends it a certain transparency … The lantern, which is alight in front of the stage, will to some extent interfere with the audience's view of Nina, and that, too, should heighten the dramatic effect of the scene."[6] Stanislavsky put considerable ingenuity into the theatrical effects of the will o' the wisps – mysterious moving lights appearing from among the foliage – and the red eyes of the devil.

The breakdown of the performance reveals Treplyov's combative insecurity, as well as Arkadina's defensiveness about her profession and her patronizing attitude toward her son. She accuses him of writing "avante-garde gibberish" in order "to teach us how to write and how to act." Surprisingly, Trigorin comes mildly to his defense, declaring, "Everyone writes the way he wants and the way he can." This is Trigorin's first line in the play, and one of only three he speaks in the act. His laconic presence – "I suppose there are a lot of fish in that lake" – works rather against expectations about a celebrated writer, but it ironically underscores his importance to the plot. His initial meeting with Nina, who is awed by his fame and glamour, sets in motion the principal dramatic action of the play, culminating in their destructive offstage affair.

It is noteworthy that the one person who seems truly moved by Treplyov's play is Dr. Dorn. He is a version of the stock character of the *raissoneur*, detached from the main action, a sympathetic and rational commentator, and one whose opinions the audience can conventionally trust. He recognizes that Treplyov's work shows talent, and more importantly, that this talent is a danger. In one of the conversations that closes the act, he tells Treplyov that "Every work of art ought to have a clear, well-defined idea. You ought to know what you're writing for; otherwise, if you travel this picturesque path without a well-defined goal, you'll go astray and your talent will destroy you." This seems to have been a view that Chekhov endorsed. In his notebooks, he states plainly that "Treplyov has no fixed goals, and that's what destroyed him. Talent destroyed him."

Act II

In terms of tone, the second act is the lightest in the play. The setting is a sunny croquet lawn, an intermediate space between the social order of the house and the free nature of the lake (both of which are visible in the setting, according to Chekhov's stage direction). Here Arkadina holds court, exerting her will over her younger rivals for her son's affection, as well as her brother and the household staff. The beginning of the act belongs to her, the end to Trigorin, whose musings about writing are buoyed up by the eager presence of Nina. The only dark note of the act comes in the middle, when Treplyov enters bearing the eponymous symbol of the play, the slain seagull.

Chekhov's portrait of the aging actress Arkadina is as close as Chekhov comes to pure social satire. She is vain, imperious, selfish and bored, and occasionally rather cruel. She teases the miserable Masha about having "let herself go" and declares that in spite of her age she is the younger of the two women. She makes herself rather ridiculous as *With her hands on her hips, [she] strides up and down the lawn"* and declares herself "Fit to play a girl of fifteen."[7] More seriously, she seems to have at least partially turned the head of Nina, feeding her dreams of fame and glamour, and further alienating her from Treplyov. When Masha asks her to recite from Treplyov's play, Nina replies, "It's so uninteresting!" This may well be her opinion, but in this instance it comes across as a betrayal, especially as Nina pointedly uses the same word, *neinteresno*, that Arkadina had used two speeches earlier with regard to Maupassant's *At Sea*. The Maupassant passage is a submerged jab at Arkadina: it deals with the destructive impact on a writer of a cosseting and predatory woman. Chekhov condemns Arkadina and implies that Nina may be becoming like her.

While Arkadina complains of "this darling rural boredom" and wishes she were in a hotel room learning her lines – "How wonderful! I know just what you mean," Nina declares *"rapturously"* – Dorn and Sorin engage in one of their philosophical disputes about life. Dorn's detachment is both funny and a little harsh; he feels Sorin should not bother with medical treatments at age sixty, though he does advise him to give up alcohol and tobacco. Sorin argues that he has not ever really lived, giving voice, as he often does, to the play's sense of unfulfilled desires; in Act IV he refers to himself as "The Man Who

Wanted To," a sobriquet that might apply to several Chekhovian characters. Sorin's illness and disappointment, partnered with Dorn's worldly, cynical pragmatism, provide a kind of choral background to the more theatrical passions of the principal characters throughout the play.

The most substantial event of the act is Shamraev's refusal to give Arkadina horses to go to town, which leads to a noisy contretemps, with the estate manager tendering his resignation and the actress announcing her intention to leave for Moscow immediately. This rather absurd fracas clears the stage for Nina's pivotal meetings with Treplyov and Trigorin.

Left alone on the stage, Nina reflects on the behavior of her hosts in one of the play's several soliloquies. "I thought that famous people were proud, inaccessible," she muses, continuing the play's consideration of fame and the artist. "But here they are crying, fishing, playing cards, laughing, and losing their tempers, just like anybody else." The list of five verbs recalls Treplyov's Act I criticism of the typical action of conventional society drama. Chekhov seems to imply that his play is truer to life, in that it depicts people fishing and playing cards instead of making love and shooting themselves; though both of those actions are yet to come in *The Seagull*.

Treplyov enters with the dead seagull and lays it at Nina's feet. Nina rightly observes that it is "a symbol of some kind" but claims she is too "ordinary" to understand it. The seagull is indeed a symbol, and a complex one, both within the play and in its relationship to theatrical culture. Its origins may lie in the woodcock Chekhov's friend Isaac Levitan shot but couldn't bring itself to kill, or in Levitan's own attempted suicide. Treplyov certainly implies that it represents himself: "Soon I shall kill myself in the same way." Later in the act, Trigorin turns it into "a subject for a short story," equating it to a young girl like Nina (who, at her entrance into the play in Act I, said she was drawn to the lake like a gull). In Trigorin's story, "by chance a man sees her and, having nothing better to do, destroys her." Something like this does indeed happen in the play, though Nina takes a more active role than Trigorin's story implies. In Act IV, we learn that Trigorin has asked for the bird to be stuffed, and it does appear onstage, though Tirgorin has no memory of the episode; the grief-maddened Nina has meanwhile taken to calling herself a seagull.

So the seagull means different things to different people throughout the play. Chekhov himself seemed to associate it primarily with Nina, usually referring to her character as "the seagull" in his letters. In the minds of critics, it was often linked with Ibsen's *Wild Duck*, another play in which a sacrificial heroine is associated with a hunted waterfowl. For the most part, these criticisms were unflattering to Chekhov, suggesting that he was both derivative and obvious in his symbolism; a famous cartoon after the Petersburg premiere shows

Chekhov, on the back of a seagull, being fired upon by his critics.[8] However, the success of the play at the Moscow Art Theatre led to the theatre taking the seagull as its emblem. To this day, a symbolic art nouveau seagull symbol appears on the MAT curtain and in its posters and publications.

Treplyov exits at the sight of Trigorin, who is jotting in a notebook and pacing "like Hamlet," though in fact it is Treplyov who is behaving in a Hamlet-like way (his scene with Nina recalls Hamlet's distracted behavior before Ophelia). After Treplyov's exit, Nina accosts Trigorin about what it is like to be a famous writer, leading him into a long disquisition about his worries and obsessions, many of which Chekhov shared: "I know no peace, and I feel that I'm devouring my own life, that to give away honey to somebody out there in space I'm robbing my finest flowers of their pollen, tearing up those flowers and trampling on their roots." Certainly, the unfavorable self-comparison Trigorin makes to Tolstoy and Turgenev was one of which Chekhov himself was conscious. Stanislavsky played Trigorin in the original production, making him a rather limp and spineless writer. Chekhov was never happy with the performance; he urged Nemirovich-Danchenko to refashion Stanislavsky's characterization: "Inject some sperm in him or something."[9] Chekhov's scene certainly allows for sexual chemistry between Trigorin and Nina, and the seagull story hints at their upcoming intimacy. Yet Trigorin, at this stage, makes no move to seduce her, and in many ways it is she who is more aggressive in her hunger for fame: "If I were a writer, like you, I would devote my whole life to the public, but I'd realize their only happiness lay in being brought up to my level, and they would be yoked to my chariot." When at the end of the act it transpires that Arkadina and Trigorin are staying, Nina is transported: "It's a dream!" In his production score for the play, Stanislavsky called for a final pause of ten seconds, and then suggested that the curtain on the stage platform should begin "swaying violently and flapping against the platform (as a hint of what is to be mentioned in Act IV)." It is unknown whether Nemirovich or Chekhov talked him out of this unscripted business, but Stanislavsky himself seems to have recognized that it might be going too far: "The danger is that it might produce a rather ridiculous effect."[10]

Act III

The third act is the shortest in the play, and the shortest in Chekhov's major drama. It contains some of the play's most volatile action and frank dialogue, as Arkadina and Treplyov quarrel over her affair with Trigorin, and she confronts Trigorin about his sexual attraction to Nina. The former scene, especially, caught the attention of the censor, who required several changes to which Chekhov acceded.

Like all of the acts, Act III begins with Masha, whose somewhat indulgent misery is a running theme throughout the play. Her formulaic self-description as one of unknown family who is living in the world for no known reason gives her suffering an existential tinge; Charlotta makes a similar statement in *The Cherry Orchard.* Chekhov's characters often perceive life's unhappiness with baffled bemusement, as though they are victims of some cruel cosmic prank.

The act's opening lines reveal that a major plot event has taken place: Treplyov has tried unsuccessfully to shoot himself. Much of the act concerns the causes and effects of this action, which Chekhov has characteristically chosen not to dramatize. Trigorin, mulling over Treplyov's "tactless" behavior in attempting suicide and then challenging him to a duel, can interpret it only as artistic resentment; poor Masha must point out that jealousy is also a factor. Nina enters on cue, disingenuously asking advice from Trigorin as to whether she should go on the stage. She also presents him with a medallion that alludes to a line from one of his works: "If ever you should have need of my life, come and take it."[11] The medallion episode is based on an event from Chekhov's own life, though sources disagree as to whether it was presented to him by the besotted Lydia Avilova or, rather implausibly, by the editors of *Russia Thought.*

Arkadina and Sorin discuss the motives for Treplyov's action, and when Sorin suggests that she might give him some money to get out of the house and make something of himself, she flies into a tizzy; Sorin has a fainting spell. Treplyov, after seeing Sorin from the room, subsequently asks Arkadina to give *him* some money. It is an amusing episode that highlights both Arkadina's parsimoniousness and the malaise of genteel poverty in which almost all of Chekhov's characters flounder.

The exchange about money begins one of the two duet scenes that anchor the act: passionate conversations between Arkadina and, respectively, her son and lover. Treplyov is affectionate at first, recalling episodes of Arkadina's kindness that she has herself forgotten. The emotions of the scene emerge through the business of Arkadina's changing Treplyov's bandage; in his notes, Stanislavsky specified that "the whole of this scene must be acted with Miss Arkadina and Konstantin kept busy all the time"; thus anticipating some tactics of his later acting "system."[12] The subject of Trigorin eventually leads to a violent quarrel, in which Treplyov's jealousy attaches itself to three distinct objects: his mother ("why do you give in to that man's influence?"), Nina ("he's somewhere in the drawing room or the garden, laughing at us, cultivating Nina"), and artistic success ("You want me to treat him like a genius … his writing makes me sick"). In a moment very characteristic of the play as a whole, psycho-sexual and aesthetic/political impulses form a potent chemical reaction that sets off an explosion of recrimination: "Go back to your darling theatre and act in your pathetic, third-rate plays," Treplyov shouts, while Arkadina reduces him to tears by calling him a decadent, a Kievian bourgeois, a parasite, and a nonentity.

After mother and son make up, she confronts Trigorin about Nina. He asks her to free him to pursue the younger woman, thus calling forth from Arkadina the performance of a lifetime. Her mixture of sexual and literary flattery, delivered in her most expressive melodramatic manner, is one of the most astonishing moments in the play:

> You're mine ... you're mine ... And this forehead is mine, and these eyes are mine, and this beautiful silky hair is mine too ... You're all mine. You're so talented, clever, our greatest living writer, you're Russia's only hope ... You've got so much sincerity, clarity, originality, wholesome humor ... With a single stroke you can pinpoint the most vital feature in a character or a landscape, your characters are so alive. Oh, no one can read you without going into ecstasy!

Trigorin's surrender is inevitable, if impermanent. Like the encounters with her brother and her son, the exchange with Trigorin reveals Arkadina's incontrovertible ability, through the deployment of her charismatic theatrical personality, to get her own way. At the successful conclusion of the perform-ance, she murmurs an aside – "Now he is mine" – that J. L. Styan calls "a gem of an alienation effect by which the old convention is completely transcended."[13] The theatrical flourish caps Arkadina's theatrical triumph.

Agreeing to leave, Trigorin looks bleakly into a future of "train compart-ments, stations, lunch counters, fried food, small talk"; Chekhov is again using the device of fivefold repetition to convey the dreariness of life among Russia's artistic classes.

The remainder of the act is taken up with preparations for departure. Each of Chekhov's major plays contains an elaborate departure scene; in the others it is in the final act, but basic pattern of *The Seagull*'s action is built over the first three acts, with the fourth as a kind of coda. *The Seagull*'s departure scene lightens the tone considerably with comic moments relating to the household staff and hangers-on. Shamraev lends comic relief with yet another tiresome story of incompetent provincial actors: Chekhov's ambivalence about the theatre emerges at some point in every act of *The Seagull*. Arkadina's meanness shows itself again in her gift of a ruble for the three servants, which she repeats twice for emphasis. She shares with Polina a moment of commiseration: "Time's running out for us!" "What can we do?" Medvedenko, as throughout the play, exhibits sad-sack devotion and is denied horses: "I'll go to the station on foot … I'm a fast walker." The trivial kindnesses and privations of ordinary life, rendered in fragmentary, prosaic diction, help to ground the histrionics of the previous scenes.

Chekhov clears the stage to give the act a false ending, a device he will repeat at the end of *The Cherry Orchard*. For good measure, he even sends the maid back to retrieve a basket of plums as the party leaves for the station. Finally Trigorin returns, either pretending to have forgotten his stick or actually having done so, for the hurried final encounter with Nina. Their "*prolonged kiss*" – Stanislavsky specifies ten seconds – gives the act a melodramatic curtain moment. For a play that ostensibly critiques and breaks from the conventions of well-made society dramas, *The Seagull* has a suspicious number of "strong curtains"; but in a way the overt theatricality is justified by the fact that these are, after all, theatrical people.

Act IV

"*Between Acts Three and Four, two years have elapsed.*"[14] So reads Chekhov's stage direction; but for an audience member who has not carefully studied the program, the clues to time's passing may be picked up only gradually. The autumnal weather – "*we can hear the trees rustling and the wind wailing in the chimney*" – communicates, at least, that we are in a different world from the summery one of the previous acts. Medvedenko's description of the ruined stage in the garden also suggests the ravages of time: "It stands there bare, unsightly, like a skeleton, and the scene curtain flaps in the wind." It soon becomes evident that he and Masha are now married and have a baby, and that any hopes of a harmonious union have been exhausted: "In the old days at least you used to talk philosophy, but now it's all baby, home," Masha complains.

The large gap of time is not unique in Chekhov – *Three Sisters* takes place over nearly four years – but it is unusual, and some critics have felt that this disruption of the unities deforms and unbalances the play.[15] However, it serves Chekhov in several ways. Most importantly, it allows him to keep the melodramatic action of Nina's seduction, single motherhood, and bereavement off the stage, concentrating instead on the long-term consequences of these actions. It also allows Chekhov to focus on the things that have and have not changed in the characters' lives during the lengthy interval. Masha still carries a torch for Treplyov, although she swears that soon she will tear her love out of her heart "by the roots" – precisely the same words she used at the beginning of the third act, two years earlier. On the other hand, Treplyov is evidently now a published author, and a surprisingly successful one. "Nobody had the slightest idea, Kostya, that you would turn into a real writer," Polina says rather tactlessly; but she speaks for the audience as well. Over the course of the act, however, it becomes clear that while the representatives of the younger generation may have achieved what they thought were their goals, things have not turned out as they had hoped; and the older generation are, more than ever, ensconced in their traditional ways and their established success.

The Seagull is subtitled a comedy, but it violates the norms of that genre in countless ways. It certainly has its share of humor, but it ends in death rather than marriage and can hardly be said to depict the regeneration of society. Most importantly, perhaps, it is a play where the old win out over the young, where hope and the impulse for change are crushed, in part through their own fragility and lack of conviction, but in part by the proficient ruthlessness of the seasoned old campaigners, their elders.

Change has come for the older generation too, of course. Dorn and Sorin maintain their pastime of philosophic bickering, but the former is in impecunious retirement and the latter is close to the point of death. "If you found it necessary to write for my sister to come here, it means I'm seriously ill," he says, and gets no reply. Arkadina, by contrast, is at the top of her game, having had a rapturous reception in Kharkov, and having thoroughly recaptured Trigorin. The motivating cause of the act's action is their return to Sorin's estate, apparently for the first time since Act III.

Before their arrival from the station, Treplyov provides the necessary exposition. The doctor, who has been on a long trip abroad, is the convenient interlocutor, but the device is still a little creaky. Treplyov's emotions about the history he recounts are barely repressed by a mask of callous detachment: "She had a baby. The baby died. Trigorin fell out of love with her and returned to his previous attachment, as might have been expected … Nina's private life has not been a roaring success." She has maintained a theatre career, but her acting is crude and tasteless, although, as Treplyov notes in a bitterly revealing detail, she has showed some talent for "screaming or dying." She has shown signs of madness, signing her letters "The Seagull"; and she has recently been seen in the vicinity. The audience may now recall Medvedenko's words, from the beginning of the act, that he thought he had heard someone crying on the dilapidated stage the previous night. The stage is set for the final, climactic encounter between Nina and Trigorin.

That encounter is placed in contrast to the irrepressible vitality of the play's survivors, who are enjoying a festive social evening. Arkadina makes a typically vivacious entrance, and Trigorin jovially greets the company. His overture to Treplyov is tentative, the latter's proffered handshake merely conventional. After Treplyov asks, rather curtly, whether Trigorin is staying long, the established writer responds with what is either callousness or veiled aggression. He enumerates his many ongoing projects, then makes a passing, seemingly offhand reference to Treplyov's failed play, the setting of which he is now adopting for one of his own stories. Trigorin may be intending a kind of man-to-man, writer-to-writer camaraderie in his exchange with Treplyov, but he could hardly twist the knife more effectively if it were his intention to do so.

The company passes the time with a game of lotto, driving Treplyov from the room. The Act IV set is a drawing room that has been converted to a study for Treplyov; Sorin has also had a bed made up in there, and the lotto players set up an additional table and chairs. As Laurence Senelick observes, "Treplyov has tried to set up a space of his own, only to have it overrun by a bustling form of life that expels him to the margins."[16] The lotto game is interspersed with casual dismissals of Treplyov's writing. Trigorin calls it "gibberish," noting, as Nina had in Act I, that there are no "living characters" in it; Arkadina confesses that she has never read it. Only Dorn defends it – "There's something there!" – but he repeats his previous criticism that Treplyov's work has no well-defined goals.

Treplyov himself subjects his work to critical scrutiny after the others have left the room. "I've talked so much about new forms, but now I feel as if I'm gradually slipping into a routine myself," he says, at the opening of the play's longest soliloquy. In comparing Trigorin's style to his own, he rejects the slick technique of the former (using an image from one of Chekhov's own stories as an example) but cannot get a handle on the latter. His new conviction that it is not old or new forms that matter, but "to write and not think about form, because it's pouring freely from your soul," represents a degree of artistic maturation, but it does not help him with the immediate problem of his work: nothing is pouring from his soul. At this point, Nina knocks at the window.

The scene between Nina and Treplyov is the longest sustained exchange between two characters in Chekhov's major plays. Coming in out of the stormy night to relate her story of betrayal and loss, Nina is a powerful theatrical presence. Critics have noted her similarity to a variety of cultural archetypes: Shakespeare's Ophelia; Rusalka, the seduced peasant girl who drowns herself and returns as a water sprite; Poor Liza, traditional figure of a fallen maiden in Russian literature. Chekhov's stories include numerous young actresses whose careers lead to disgrace and bereavement: Katya in "A Boring Story" and the daughter in "Panikhida" are two of the best known. Actresses living the kind of itinerant provincial life Nina describes were often reduced to poverty and prostitution, and Chekhov certainly knew such women. Yet for all of her sufferings, Nina resists being consigned to the status of a pathetic victim.

Donald Rayfield argues that viewing her as a defeated Ophelia is a mistake: "Nina, announcing her determination to continue the miserable life of a provincial actress, shows that she is in fact to be a second Arkadina, battling her way up from obscurity to fame."[17]

Nina's long speech seems to contain contradictory information about her situation, and indeed, it may be seen as a central interpretive problem of the play. Is she a determined survivor, or a defeated madwoman? Her wandering monologue, with its sudden abrupt assertions that she is a seagull – "no, that's wrong" – suggests the latter, but she also speaks enthusiastically about acting as a vocation, claiming she feels beautiful on the stage. Her summation is perhaps a more balanced perspective that could accommodate some of both:

> Now I know, understand, Kostya, that in our work – it doesn't matter whether we act or we write – the main thing isn't fame, glamour, the things I dreamed about, it's knowing how to endure. I know how to shoulder my cross and I have faith. I have faith and it's not so painful for me, and when I think about my calling, I'm not afraid of life.

All four of Chekhov's plays end with some such interpretive problem, with a character or characters voicing optimism in the face of what most would recognize as a clear and devastating defeat. How seriously does Chekhov want us to take their expressions of reassurance, that they "aren't afraid of life" (*Seagull*), that "we shall rest" (*Vanya*), that "just a little while longer and we shall learn why we're alive" (*Three Sisters*), or that the "new life" is just ahead (*Cherry Orchard*)? In the case of *The Seagull*, Richard Gilman argues that Nina's endurance is a strongly positive statement: "something essential has been saved out of the entire human substance of the play," and "the principle of relief from fatality that governs all comedy is now in place."[18]

Nina's endurance may be a victory for her, but it cannot save Treplyov; their meeting, and her continued love for Trigorin, may be what pushes him over the edge to suicide. Furthermore, she exits the play, not with her speech on endurance, but with the recitation of her monologue from Treplyov's play, with its emphasis on the extinction of all living things: "No longer does the meadow awake to the cries of cranes, and the mayflies are no longer to be heard in the linden groves." With these lines lingering in the air, Treplyov silently tears up his manuscripts "*over the course of two minutes.*" Few productions take this direction literally, but when they do (as in the 1991 Royal Shakespeare Company production with Simon Russell Beale as Treplyov), the effect can be shattering.

Treplyov's offstage suicide, and the delayed report of it, represents an advance on the melodramatic endings of *Platonov* and *Ivanov*, but it remains a moment that must be carefully judged in the theatre. At the Petersburg premiere, audiences laughed when Dorn reported that a bottle of ether had exploded in his medical bag. The ending is probably more effective if the audience, for a moment, shares Arkadina's relief, though there can be little doubt about what has happened. But by having Dorn relay only to Trigorin, *sotto voce*, that "Konstantin Gavrilovich has shot himself," Chekhov achieves a conventional strong curtain while also leaving the stage tensions unresolved. By concluding with a whispered aside rather than an outburst of grief and horror, Chekhov may have succeeded, as he put it, in ending his play "*pianissimo* – against every rule of dramatic art." While not as subtle as the conclusions of his later plays, the muted finale of *The Seagull* shows Chekhov experimenting with a dramatic version of the "zero ending" of many of his stories.

Uncle Vanya

Uncle Vanya (1897) is the shortest and most economical of Chekhov's major plays. It has the fewest dramatis personae, occupies the least time both in its onstage duration and its storyline, and has, strictly speaking, the least action. Apart from a flurry of quasi-farcical business in Act III (interrupted kiss, mad tirade, gunshots that miss), virtually nothing happens in *Uncle Vanya*. It is the only one of Chekhov's plays about which this trite statement can be made. This fact is the more remarkable given that *Uncle Vanya* is a working-over of the lengthy comic melodrama *The Wood Demon* (discussed in Chapter 4), which had half again as many characters and script pages, not to mention a suicide, multiple betrothals, and a forest fire. But *Uncle Vanya* is what David Magarshack has characterized as a "play of indirect action," in which the characters' passions and crises are revealed only gradually and obliquely; it was his mastery of this form that made Chekhov "one of the greatest innovators of modern drama."[19]

Things do happen in *Uncle Vanya*, of course, notably the final departure from the estate of the characters whose presence creates the dramatic situation; but many more things fail to happen. It is a play about disappointments and painful recognitions, about abandoning illusions and facing up to the true conditions of one's life. In a seminal 1946 essay, Eric Bentley summed up the impact of Chekhov's drama, and this play in particular, by comparing it to the classical model of tragedy, so dependent on dramatic reversals and recognitions. "In the Greeks, in much of French drama, and in Ibsen, recognition means the discovery of a secret which reveals that things are not what all these years they have seemed to be," Bentley wrote. "In *Uncle Vanya*, recognition means that what all these years seemed to be so, though one hesitated to believe it, really is so and will remain so."[20] For most of the characters, the principal action of the play is coming to terms with the reality of their wasted lives.

Like *The Seagull*, *Uncle Vanya* has a quartet of protagonists, two men and two women; and it also deals with unrequited love. Both Vanya and Dr. Astrov love the married Yelena; she is attracted to Astrov but loves no one. Vanya's niece Sonya, in turn, loves Astrov, but he does not recognize or return her affection. Indeed, though everyone in the play regards Sonya warmly, no one loves her "as a woman" (in Yelena's phrase) because she is "so unattractive" (in her own). But in a way, the desperate love-longings in *Vanya* lack conviction, as though these people are flinging themselves at impossible loves in the vain hope of giving some meaning to their lives. *Uncle Vanya* is not finally a play about love, but about the need for illusions, and the difficulty of living without them.

The central figures of the drama, Vanya and Astrov, are both failed idealists, "crackpots" (*chudaki*), as Astrov describes them. Vanya has lost his ideals through his disillusionment with his brother-in-law, the pompous Professor Serebryakov. Astrov is on the point of losing his, and squanders his energies on drinking and pursuing Yelena, the professor's wife. Near the end of the play, Astrov reflects on their failure to use their idealism to bring about a better life in their provincial backwater: "In the whole district there were only two decent, cultured men, you and I. But it took no more than ten years for humdrum life, despicable life, to drag us down; its pestilential fumes poisoned our blood, and we became just as vulgar as everybody else."[21]

The "pestilential fumes" of which Astrov speaks are not only metaphorical. The play repeatedly expresses concerns that we would now describe as environmentalist. Significantly, Chekhov subtitled *Uncle Vanya* "*Scenes from Country Life*" (a subtitle previously used by Chekhov's predecessor, Alexander Ostrovsky), and the rural setting is an important dimension of the play. The spoliation of the countryside, and the thoughtless destructiveness of human beings, is a central theme of *Uncle Vanya*. Through the conservationist Astrov, Chekhov details the deforestation, loss of wildlife habitat, pollution, and other environmental calamities that were affecting rural Russia with population growth and the rise of industrialization. "A person has to be an unreasoning barbarian to destroy what cannot be re-created," (829) he says. Yet *Uncle Vanya* does not romanticize rural life, repeatedly stressing the drudgery, isolation, and boredom of those who spend their lives away from Russia's cultural capitals.

Act I

The opening act is set in the garden of a country house; as in *The Seagull*, the action begins outdoors and moves, with each act, deeper into the heart of the household. The garden swing, abandoned guitar, and samovar on the table give a sense of listless leisure; Chekhov specifies that it is an overcast summer afternoon. The action begins gradually, with companionable small talk between Astrov and the old nanny Marina, "a corpulent, imperturbable old woman."[22] Louis Malle's brilliant film version, *Vanya on 42nd Street*, opens with idle chatter among actors preparing to rehearse *Uncle Vanya*, so that the scene begins without the audience being conscious that they are listening to Chekhov; so ordinary and inconsequential does this opening dialogue seem. Astrov and Marina reflect on the passage of time and the effects of age and drink, and Astrov expatiates on his becoming a "crackpot," and on the recent death of a patient. He gives voice, for the first time in Chekhov's plays, to the question with which so many of his protagonists concern themselves; the question of life one or two hundred years in the future. "Will they remember us, have a kind word for us?" Astrov asks; to which Marina can only reply that the people will not remember, but God will. Her simple rural piety is perhaps not a sufficient answer to the existential quandaries that plague the play's characters, but Chekhov does not dismiss it. This attitude of stoical faith and forbearance surfaces repeatedly throughout the play, and provides its final note in Sonya's heartbreaking "We shall rest" speech.

Vanya enters from a nap; the contrast between his rumpled clothes and fancy necktie (presumably worn for Yelena's benefit) says much about the way of life on the estate since the arrival of the professor and his wife. They have disrupted the order of things with their citified ways, late hours, odd demands, unhealthy lifestyle; and now the regular work of the estate is being neglected. This is the play's basic situation: the destructive presence of the Serebryakovs, perhaps linked metaphorically to man's destructive effect on the rural environment. Their passage across the stage, a moment later, highlights their incongruity and the threat they pose. The professor, insulating himself against the rural setting, wears overcoat, galoshes, and gloves, despite the hot weather; he is a variation on the "Man in a Case," a repressed schoolteacher in one of Chekhov's stories. He is obviously a killjoy, retreating to his study rather than staying for the tea party that has been delayed on his account. The young and vital Yelena Andreevna would seem to be a great contrast to her invalid husband, but in her way she is equally life-denying. She is a woman of great and destructive beauty, linked by her name to Helen of Troy. But she is also, as she attests, "inhibited," perhaps sexually repressed and socially ill-at-ease with her step-family.

Vanya's hatred of the professor, whose first wife was Vanya's beloved sister Vera Petrovna, is based on years of misplaced devotion. It was only after Serebryakov retired to the country that Vanya realized the essential hollowness of the man for whom he had been working diligently for years as estate manager. Vanya's tirade of resentment is interrupted as the company finally assembles, minus the professor, for tea. This scene reveals Chekhov's developing flair for revealing character and action through the banal conversations of everyday life. Vanya grumbles, his activist mother discusses pamphlets, the amiable, pock-marked hanger-on "Waffles" strums his guitar, Marina fusses around calling her chickens. Vanya expresses his exasperation with the stagnation of the intelligentsia: "For fifty years now we've been talking and talking, and reading pamphlets. It's high time we stopped." The scene captures the nerve-jangling boredom of an indolent, sultry afternoon. The only burst of positive energy comes from Sonya, as she launches into a love-fueled paean to Astrov's conservationist activities. She momentarily awakens the doctor's idealism, and he gives voice to his most earnest expression of his environmental vision:

> … when I walk through the peasants' forests that I saved from being chopped down, or when I hear the wind rustling in my stand of saplings, planted by my own hands, I realize that the climate is to some slight degree in my control, and if, a thousand years from now, humanity is happy, then I will be partially responsible …

Chekhov quickly and brutally undercuts this moment of elation, however, as Astrov goes off to attend an injured factory-worker after fortifying himself with a shot of vodka. Vanya awkwardly courts an exasperated Yelena, whose bitter rebuffs explicitly link the human stories of the play with its overarching ecological theme: "Why can't you look at a woman with indifference if she isn't yours? Because – that doctor's right – inside all of you there lurks a demon of destruction. You have no pity for forests or birds or women or one another." The characters in *Uncle Vanya* are wasting their environment just as they are wasting their lives.

Act II

A stifling night and a threatening storm provide the backdrop for emotional outbursts in Act II, which is retained, with only a few changes, from *The Wood Demon*. The act begins after midnight in an atmosphere of illness and exhaustion, with Serebryakov complaining of his ailments and everyone's nerves frayed raw. Yelena Andreevna repeatedly states that "there's something oppressive about this house," and the imagery of oppression and suffocation runs throughout the act.[23] The center of the tense atmosphere is Serebryakov, the invalid, whose illness is compounded by disgust, boredom, and irritation, qualities repeatedly alluded to and mirrored by the other characters. "You talk about your old age as if it was our fault you're old," his wife snaps. While clearly portraying the professor as despotic and demanding, Chekhov does not deny him all sympathy. His physical suffering seems to be real, though he is vain enough to compare his illness to Turgenev's. And he has features in common with the dying professor in "A Boring Story," whose sense of displacement at the waning of his academic career takes on tragic dimensions (Chekhov was writing "A Boring Story" at the same time as *The Wood Demon*, the source of *Vanya*). Finally, as Vladimir Kataev points out, Serebryakov has done nothing deliberate to deserve the hatred that Vanya, perhaps unjustly, bears toward him.[24] Chekhov's equanimity toward even such an unappealing character as Serebryakov is evident upon his exit. When everyone else has become thoroughly exasperated with his illness, the old nanny Marina shows him some simple kindness and is able to get him off to bed: "Old folks're like little ones, they want a body to feel sorry for 'em, but old folks got no one to feel sorry for 'em (*Kisses Serebryakov on the shoulder.*) Let's go, dearie, bedtime. …"

As in Act IV of *The Seagull*, Chekhov uses the storm outside to reflect the tempestuous emotions of the characters. In this he is flirting with what John Ruskin termed the "pathetic fallacy," a facile attribution of human feelings to inanimate nature. But Chekhov makes clear that the stifling night is partly the *cause* of the characters' oppression; and moreover, that they themselves are the ones assigning their feelings to the natural world. "Any moment now the rain will end, and everything in nature will be refreshed and breathe easy," Vanya reflects. "I'll be the only thing not refreshed by the storm." Left alone onstage, Vanya indulges in one of the play's several soliloquies, fantasizing about how he would experience the storm if he had married Yelena: "She'd be frightened by the thunder and I'd hold her in my arms and whisper, 'Don't be afraid, I'm here.'" His sexual jealousy fuels his hatred, as he rails about having been "cheated" by Serebryakov, who took advantage of his labor while at the same time acquiring the profession and wife that Vanya would have wanted for himself.

The latter half of the act is taken up with two long conversations, between Astrov and Sonya and between Sonya and Yelena. The former dialogue explores the drunken doctor's bitterness and disillusionment, using again the imagery of the forest: "When you walk through the forest on a dark night, if all the time in the distance there's a glimmer of light, you don't mind the fatigue or the dark or the prickly branches hitting you in the face," Astrov says, but for him "there's no light glimmering." Astrov sees the problem as both social and environmental: "A spontaneous, unpolluted, open relationship to nature and human beings no longer exists." But he is clearly also battling his own personal demons: while declaring himself unable to love, he hints at an attraction to Yelena, and he recalls for the second time a patient of his who died during surgery. Sonya uses the opportunity of this intimate conversation to make clumsy overtures to him, but Astrov is oblivious. After Astov's exit, she soliloquizes on how "it is an awful thing to be unattractive!"

Yelena enters, opening a window and commenting on the freshness of the air after the storm. Perhaps seizing on the metaphor, she attempts to clear the air with the resentful Sonya. The two share an emotional, sisterly scene, weeping, laughing, kissing one another, drinking together, and switching from the formal pronoun "*vy*" to the informal "*ty*." They gush about Astrov, Sonya guilelessly, Yelena hinting at a developing attraction. She admits to her lack of love for her husband, though she insists she married him in good faith. She recognizes that she has had only "a walk-on part" – *episodicheskoe litso* – in the dramas of her life. It is interesting that Yelena's expression of unhappiness is greeted with laughter and happiness by her stepdaughter; perhaps the saintly Sonya is not above a degree of *schadenfreude* at the discomfiture of the woman she must recognize as her rival. Yet the sisterly mood persists, with Yelena, a trained musician, offering to play the piano for Sonya. Sonya goes off to check with Serebryakov about whether this late-night concert will disturb him, as Yelena luxuriates in the emotional release to which the scene seems to be leading: "It's been such a long time since I played. I'll play and weep, weep like a fool." But Chekhov, in one of his most effective anti-climaxes, puts the kibosh on the moment with Sonya's return: "The answer's no." In Russian, it is a single word, "*Nelzya!*" – "It is not permitted!" – that comes down like a hammer of negation on the entire act, and any glimmers of hope it may have enkindled.

Act III

The third act, much of which is retained from *The Wood Demon*, drives into the open all of the submerged resentments, attractions, and animosities that have been seething throughout the play. While hanging around the parlor waiting for the professor's announcement, the four central characters expose the sexual desires they have to some degree heretofore concealed. When the announcement itself comes, it ignites Vanya's smoldering rage, leading to an explosion of violence and recrimination. The damage wrought throughout the act raises real questions about the value of confronting the truth, and the pain caused by stripping away comforting illusions.

Chekhov is very specific about the time in this act, as he often is when he wants to put pressure on events (as in the first act of *Seagull* or the last of *Three Sisters* and *Cherry Orchard*). It is 12:45; an important announcement will be made at one. Sonya and Vania are waiting, Yelena walks about "*with something on her mind.*"[25] She complains of boredom and Sonya urges work, stating flatly what has been apparent from Act I, that the presence of Yelena and the professor has brought the estate to a halt. She goes further, comparing Yelena to a witch whose seductive presence has put a spell on Vanya, herself, and Astrov, keeping them away from their duties. Vanya takes up the comparison, likening Yelena to a *rusalka* or water nymph, and openly urging her to adultery, if not with him, then with someone: "Satisfy your desires at least once in your life … take a nosedive into a whirlpool, so that Herr Professor and the rest of us throw up our hands in amazement!"

The emphasis on exposing concealed desires continues after Vanya leaves the stage to fetch Yelena a bouquet of "mournful" autumn roses. Sonya speaks with naked pain about her love for Astrov: "I love him more than my own mother … Even the servants know I love him." In response to Yelena's proposal to elicit Astrov's feelings, Sonya miserably speaks what might be the motto of the play: "Not knowing is better … then there's hope." Act III is an object lesson in the dangers of confronting the truth at all costs. Yelena, in soliloquy, begins to confront the truth of her own attraction to Astrov, and the very mixed motives from which she is proceeding: "I'm having an attack of conscience. … Any minute now I'll drop to my knees and beg Sonya's forgiveness, burst into tears."

Boldly, Chekhov delays the conversation about love until Astrov has delivered the longest speech in the play, his lecture, complete with maps, on the gradual degradation of the forests, wildlife, and population of the region. Chekhov plainly took these ideas seriously – he worked to prevent such decline in the district where he lived, a map of which was used in the MAT production – but it is likely that the audience found itself included in Astrov's sudden indictment, "I can see from your face that you find this uninteresting." The exchange that follows is subject to interpretation in performance: how much is Yelena speaking earnestly on Sonya's behalf, how much is she the "cunning vixen" Astrov perceives, using the interview to further ensnare him? "I'm a better, more decent person than you think," she protests with apparent conviction, and none of her lines imply a seductive purpose. However, desirable women in Chekhov's stories are often only half-conscious of their own motives as they embark on illicit affairs. Sofya Petrovna, the heroine of "A Misfortune," enacts her innocent virtue, even to herself, right up to the moment of her adultery. Chekhov does not allow us to find out what might happen between

Astrov and Yelena: at the moment of their kiss, Vanya enters with his roses, in a moment that turns from grand passion to absurd farce. Astrov comments on the weather and quickly retires; Yelena, unwilling to conceal the crisis, asks Vanya to arrange for their immediate departure. At this least opportune moment, Serebryakov enters to make his announcement.

Here again, Chekhov takes a moment that could be tragic or melodramatic and stages it as farcical. For all its atmosphere of boredom, apathy, and resentment, *Uncle Vanya* is a very funny play. Its humor is of a mordant kind; it anticipates Samuel Beckett's dictum that "Nothing is funnier than unhappiness."[26] Though Chekhov did not call it a comedy, the comic element is present throughout; if for no other reason than that the bitterest character, Vanya, is also the wittiest, and his discontent is vented with something of the incisiveness of a Shakespearean fool. His response to Serebryakov's proposal to sell the estate and move to Finland is a masterpiece of slow-burning sarcasm, as he pretends not to hear correctly – "my ears seem to be deceiving me" – and then responds with a mixture of feigned politeness and open hostility: "Obviously, up to now I didn't have a grain of common sense. Up to now I was stupid enough to think that this estate belongs to Sonya." Finally, Vanya explodes into a rage that is by turns ludicrous, self-aggrandizing, and infantile. He rails at Serebryakov that "You ruined my life!" says that he could have been a Schopenhauer or Dostoevsky, and ends up sobbing for his mother, who "*sternly*" rebukes him. Finally, he flings out of the room through the center stage door, declaring melodramatically, "You're going to remember me!"

In the succeeding pause, before Vanya returns with the revolver, there is an episode that reveals much about Chekhov's attitude to the dramatic action of his plays. Sonya kneels to her father and implores him to be charitable. According to an anecdote from Nadezhda Butova, Chekhov disagreed with the way the MAT's actress played the moment, tearfully kissing her father's hand. "She mustn't do that, that's not really drama," Chekhov purportedly said. "All the sense, all the drama of a human being is inward, and not expressed in outward manifestations. There was drama in Sonya's life up to that moment, there will be drama after that, but this is simply an incident," adding that the gunshots Vanya fires at Serebryakov are also only "an incident."[27] Chekhov subverts the melodramatic potential of the moment, just as he had by keeping the climactic events of *The Seagull* offstage. Vanya's gunshots are ridiculous, despite their lethal potential; this was one of Chekhov's most decisive changes from *The Wood Demon*, in which the equivalent moment culminated in the suicide of the unhappy uncle. Photos of the MAT production suggest that the original Vanya, Vishnevsky, played the episode farcically, with grotesque movements and expressions; and the text calls for

Vanya to shout out "Bang!" ("*Bats!*") as he fires. The incident exemplifies Vanya's existential predicament: he is denied even the momentary grandeur of a *crime passionnel.*

Act IV

The final act, the play's shortest, is all aftermath: its only action is the departure of Serebryakov, Yelena, and Astrov, the characters who have catalyzed the passions of the play. Unlike the lengthy resolution of *The Wood Demon*, with its dramatic forest fire, speeches of moral reformation, and happy pairings-off, the end of *Uncle Vanya* is a return to the status quo. Life on the estate will go on "as before," though Sonya and Vanya have had their illusions wrecked and must cling together amid the debris. Verbal echoes of Act I, and the suggestion of nature's rhythms as winter approaches, give a weary circularity to the play's vision of life. The bruising sense of anti-climax, as decisive actions are avoided, confrontations are dissipated, and life falls back into its patterns, has been compared by Donald Rayfield to the "zero endings" of many of Chekhov's stories.[28] *Uncle Vanya* ends, not with gunfire or sexual consummation, but with the chirping of crickets and the scratching of pens.

The crowded setting represents Vanya's bedroom, which is also Astrov's workroom and the estate office. Chekhov details the furnishings with greater specificity than in the other acts: there are ledgers and papers to suggest the work of the estate, paints and drawing instruments related to Astrov's conservation work, a caged starling symbolizing confinement, and even a mat for the peasants' muddy shoes. On the wall, mysteriously, is one of Chekhov's most famous properties, "*a map of Africa, apparently of no use to anyone here.*"[29]

The act begins with the humbler members of the household, Marina and Telegin, winding wool and reflecting on the Act III catastrophe, which has apparently had no consequences other than precipitating the departure of the Serebryakovs to Kharkov (the same dreary provincial town to which Lopakhin departs at the end of *The Cherry Orchard*, and where the old professor ends up in "A Boring Story"). They seem already to be enjoying some relief at the return to simpler ways; Marina sighs, "It's a long time, bless my soul, since I've had noodles." The presence of these benign, relatively untroubled characters helps muffle the sense of defeat in the play's close.

Vanya's theft of a bottle of morphine strikes an ominous note, but Astrov and Sonya soon persuade him to return it. His despair is articulated in terms of the painful process of simply facing the time in front of him: "Oh my God … I'm forty-seven, suppose I live to be sixty, I still have another thirteen years to get through! … What will I do, how will I fill them?" Astrov can offer little comfort, beyond a vague hope that life may be better in the future:

> Those who will live in a hundred, two hundred years from now and who will despise us because we lived our lives so stupidly and so gracelessly – they may find a way to be happy, but we … for you and me, there's only one hope. The hope that when we lie in our coffins, we'll be haunted by visions, maybe even pleasant ones.

Sonya urges patience and pity, and together she and Vanya hit on another kind of solution: work. The need for work is a cry heard frequently in Chekhov, and often it is mocked; in this play both Marina and the professor are heard pompously to declare "One must take action." But the productive work that Sonya and her uncle undertake here does seem to represent a positive step for them, and stands in contrast to the indolence, noted throughout the play, that has plagued the estate through the Serebryakovs' presence. Astrov, alone for the last time with Yelena, comments that "The two of you infected the rest of us with your idleness … wherever you and your husband set foot, destruction follows in your wake." His final attempt at seduction is rebuffed, though Yelena takes his pencil as a memento and *quickly conceals it*," the haste suggesting illicit pleasure or guilt. Her temptation is evident when, after he has given her a parting kiss on the cheek, she looks around her and says, "Whatever the cost, for once in my life!" and then *Embraces him impulsively, and both immediately and rapidly move away from one another.* The rest of the company assembles for the final partings.

Chekhov manages this last movement of the play in a way that is almost musical, with repeated phrases and sound effects setting up a new, subdued rhythm of life for those who remain. We hear the sound of harness bells, and then, one by one, Astrov, Marina, Sonya, and Vanya's mother enter with the single word "*Uekhali*," "They're gone." Astrov dawdles for a while, unwilling to leave, but Sonya and Vanya are absorbed in their work, and the dialogue becomes only fragmentary references to the estate accounts: "and carried over from the old debt two seventy-five …" Lingering for a few moments more, taking a shot of the vodka he forswore in Act II, Astrov suddenly comments, apropos of nothing, "I suppose there must be a heatwave over in Africa right now – something awful!"

Astrov's reference to the map of Africa is one of the most puzzling, profound, and celebrated moments of the play, and seems to exemplify the new dramatic technique Chekhov was achieving in the final moments of *Uncle Vanya*. Chekhov's attitude about it may be seen in a letter he wrote to Olga Knipper, complaining, as he often did, about Stanislavsky's performance.

Stanislavsky's Astrov had played the final interview with Yelena passionately, "clutch[ing] at his feeling like a drowning man at a straw." Chekhov asserted that this attitude was wrong:

> Astrov likes Yelena, she captivates him by her beauty; but in the last act he already knows that nothing will come of it, that Yelena is vanishing from him forever – and he talks to her in that scene in the same tone as about the heat of Africa, and kisses her quite casually, with nothing better to do. If Astrov carries on that scene tempestuously, the whole mood of the fourth act – quiet and despondent – will be lost.[30]

Chekhov evidently felt the Africa reference was a kind of throwaway; it is merely a passing mention of a vast, hot, distant continent, as far as possible from the confinement, oppression and encroaching Russian winter in which the characters of *Vanya* are doomed to carry on their lives. It conjures, very briefly, the sense of the exotic and unexplored, of the regions of life these characters will never know. The line's very strangeness heightens the poignancy of the moment; it is a key example of what Charles Timmer called "the bizarre element in Chekhov's art."[31] Astrov is on the point of his final departure, and having a hard time tearing himself away; but rather than voicing any of the feelings filling his heart, he comes up with the least relevant, most incongruous remark possible – which falls without a ripple into the despondent atmosphere of the scene. Whatever its intended meaning, the moment caught the imagination of Chekhov's contemporaries. The Futurist poet Mayakovsky saw the moment as evidence of Chekhov's innovative style: "When another writer would have needed to use a suicide to justify someone's parading around the stage, Chekhov gives the highest drama in the simple 'grey' words: Astrov: 'But the heat in that Africa there must be really terrific.'"[32] Maxim Gorky, soon to become a prominent playwright at the Moscow Art Theatre, also found the moment emblematic: "In the last act of *Vanya* when after a long pause, the doctor speaks of the heat of Africa, I trembled with admiration of your talent and with fear for people and for our colorless wretched life. How magnificently you struck at the heart of things here, and how much to the point!"[33] Astrov then departs, after putting a final nail in the coffin of Sonya's hopes by drinking the vodka he had promised her to give up in Act II. His exit reprises the musical motifs of the earlier departures: Vanya mutters about "twenty pounds vegetable oil," harness bells are heard offstage, and we get the twice-repeated "*uekhal*," "He's gone."

Sonya's final speech sounds a somewhat different note from the dismal tones that have preceded. "What can be done? We have to go on living." She preaches hard work and endurance, and looks forward to final rest, God's pity, and a heaven of diamonds. Her speech is another of the interpretive cruxes at the end of Chekhov's plays, a moment that could be hopeful or bitterly ironic, a glass half full or half empty. Is Sonya genuinely finding an unexpected strength, one that will allow her and Vanya to lead productive lives now that the veil of their illusions has been lifted? Or is she only deluding herself yet again, protesting too much – "I believe intensely, passionately" – about a heavenly future, when all she has to look forward to is drudgery and death? Her final, repeated refrain of "We shall rest" – "*My otdokhnyom*" – is soothing and musical, and merges with the tapping of the watchman, the strumming of Telegin's guitar, the scratching of Mariya Vasilyevna's pen, and the click of Marina's knitting needles in a soft *diminuendo* ending. Whether optimistic or defeated, the elegiac beauty of this conclusion exemplifies Chekhov's achievement in *Uncle Vanya*, in wringing the most profound feeling from the private, inner dramas of his characters.

Three Sisters

Three Sisters is the longest of Chekhov's four major plays, and perhaps the most technically innovative. Rather than centering the play on a particular individual or a clearly defined storyline, Chekhov distributes narrative interest among a large number of characters, and the action seems to proceed almost accidentally through the banal occurrences of everyday life. In place of conventional plot, there is a broad sweep of action, or non-action: the genteel Prozorov sisters yearn to leave their stale provincial life for Moscow, and fail to do so, while their vulgar sister-in-law gains ascendancy over their family home. This story is told in painstakingly realistic detail, with apparently aimless dialogue, random interactions, and trivial events; yet at the same time the whole work develops a broad and encompassing vision of human life. More than any other play of Chekhov's, *Three Sisters* seems to make universal claims: to say, not simply, that "this is what happened to these people," but "this is how life is." "Maybe it only seems to us that we exist, but as a matter of fact we don't," says Chebutykin, the old army doctor whose cynical nihilism permeates the play. "A time will come when everyone will realize why all this is, what these sufferings are for, there won't be any mysteries," Irina reflects in the play's final moments. "But in the meantime a person has to live."[34] *Three Sisters* confronts such basic existential questions in stark terms, making the play comparable to tragic masterpieces of the Western dramatic tradition, from *Oedipus the King* and *King Lear* to *Waiting for Godot*.

Three Sisters was the first play Chekhov wrote with the Moscow Art Theatre in mind, and this fact may have led him to take a more ambitious and experimental approach to the work. For all his quarrels with Stanislavsky, Chekhov recognized the originality and achievement of the MAT. In the letter to Nemirovich-Danchenko in which he announces that he has conceived the plot of *Three Sisters*, he declares that "The Art Theatre forms the best pages of that book which someday will be written about the contemporary Russian theatre" (November 24, 1899). In writing the play, Chekhov consciously played to the MAT's strengths of ensemble acting and meticulous *mises-en-scène*, though he worried that the result would be opaque and confusing: "I'm not writing a play but some kind of maze. Lots of characters – it may be that I shall lose my way and give up writing" (August 14, 1900). In other letters he worried that "there are a great many characters, it is crowded, I'm afraid it will turn out obscure or pallid," and declared the play "boring, slow-paced, awkward" with an atmosphere "gloomier than gloom" (September 5 and November 13, 1900). He labored over the text a good deal, making substantial revisions after the company had begun working on the play, and offering numerous suggestions about casting and staging.

Three Sisters was perhaps the most artistically successful of the collaborations between Chekhov and the Moscow Art Theatre, the instance where the aesthetic goals of his writing matched up most fully with the company's performance style. Certainly it was the only one of the MAT Chekhov productions about which the author himself was almost always enthusiastic: "*Three Sisters* is going splendidly, brilliantly, much better than the play text," he wrote to a friend in September 1901, though he added, "I took a slight hand in the directing, made a few author's suggestions, and the play, they say, now goes much better than last season." The play was a critical and commercial success, and became a mainstay of Moscow cultural life, to the extent that people attending the MAT spoke of "paying a call on the Prozorovs."[35]

Act I

The play's distinguishing characteristics, its mixture of surface realism, thematic depth, and an impressionistic interplay of words and images, are evident in the opening scene. The play begins with the eponymous heroines onstage together, in the first of several meaningful tableaux in which they will appear over the course of the play:

> *Olga, wearing the dark blue uniform of a teacher at a high school for girls, never stops correcting students' examination books, both standing still and*

on the move. Masha, in a black dress, her hat in her lap, sits reading a book. Irina, in a white dress, sits rapt in thought.[36]

Chekhov distinguishes the sisters carefully by their color-coded dresses, their actions, and their physical postures. He also calls attention to precise details of season, weather, date, and even time of day, in both the dialogue and the *mise-en-scène*. Olga's opening speech, dense with references to time (and interrupted by a clock striking twelve), lays out the sisters' situation: they moved to the provinces from Moscow eleven years before with their father, a general, and now, after his death, they long to return. Her speech is full of hope for a future where the sisters will recover their childhood happiness in the Moscow of their dreams. Yet Chekhov subtly undermines and qualifies this hope, partly through his manipulation of stage space and concurrent action. He specifies that the set is *"A drawing room with columns, behind which a large reception room can be seen."* While Olga is speaking to her sisters in the front room, three officers appear in the reception room behind. They are absorbed in their own conversation, but their laughter and cynical comments provide an ironic counterpoint to the sisters' longings. The first instance comes at the end of Olga's long and optimistic speech:

> … I woke up this morning, saw the light pouring in,
> the springtime, and joy began to quicken in my heart;
> I began to long passionately for my beloved home.

Chebutykin:	To hell with both of you!
Tusenbach:	You're right, it's ridiculous.

The lines bear no direct relation to the sisters' conversation, of which the officers are unconscious, but they have the effect of puncturing Olga's hopeful posture. Immediately after this, Chekhov notes that *"Masha, brooding over her book, quietly whistles a tune under her breath."* It is clear from Olga's hurt reaction that Masha's whistling, together with her rigid, static posture and her black dress, are also a kind of rejection of Olga's hopeful vision of their Moscow home.

In the exposition that follows, the hindrances to the sisters' dreams of Moscow gradually become evident. The family has become enmeshed in small-town provincial life: the brother Andrey is secretary of the County Council and has become involved with a local girl, Natasha, while Masha has married the schoolteacher Kulygin. Olga is a spinster schoolteacher, while the youngest, Irina, has vague plans to go to work. The Prozorovs feed their desire for culture by socializing with the officers of their late father's battery. As with Chekhov's other major plays, *Three Sisters* begins with an arrival and ends with a departure. The catalyst that sets the play's action in motion is the arrival, from Moscow, of a new battery commander, Lieutenant Colonel Vershinin. He seems to represent all that the sisters long for, and his philosophical speeches about the value of culture and education offer a kind of meaning to their lives: "In your wake, others like you will appear, maybe six, then twelve and so on, until at last the likes of you will be the majority." His conversation introduces a debate with the Baron Tusenbach that runs throughout the play, a debate about what human life will be like a few hundred years in the future. Vershinin's hopeful views mesh with the sisters' dreams, so that even the taciturn Masha decides to stay for lunch – indicating a developing attraction for Vershinin.

Apart from Vershinin's arrival, the first act contains little action: the characters greet each other, engage in conversation, and have a celebratory luncheon for Irina's name-day. Some of the dialogue is blatantly expository: as a newcomer, Vershinin needs to be introduced and caught up, so that the audience is filled in on the histories and relationships of the principal characters. Yet much of the conversation in Act I is apparently inconsequential: Solyony comments on how much weight he can lift with one or two hands, Chebutykin makes notes on a method for preventing hair loss, and Kulygin recommends storing rugs in naphthalene for the summer. Sometimes the characters' words are not their own: Masha quotes Pushkin's *Ruslan and Lyudmila*, while not herself understanding why; meanwhile Solyony utters a doggeral tag from Krylov's fables, Chebutykin sings operetta, and Kulygin quotes Horace and Juvenal in Latin. Occasionally, the utterances have no direct communicative value at all. Masha whistles as a way of shutting out her sisters, and Solyony makes cheeping noises to tease the Baron. The randomness of this dialogue creates the texture of lived reality, where much of social life consists of incomplete conversations, overheard phrases, and half-understood small talk. Yet these interactions reveal a complex network of relations among the characters and hint at simmering resentments and desires: Masha's unhappy marriage, Andrey's disappointments, Chebutykin's love for their late mother (now displaced onto Irina), and the rivalry of Tusenbach and Solyony. Chekhov's stagecraft intensifies the effect of fragmentary, accidental discoveries: he places the luncheon in the reception room upstage, sometimes focusing attention on the dining-table chatter, sometimes on more intimate conversations in the drawing room. The most important of these, which closes the act, is between Andrey and Natasha, and results in their engagement: the first step in her gradual takeover of the Prozorov household. Natasha is initially represented sympathetically, as the sisters snobbishly mock her manners and clothes; but by the beginning of the second act, her negative impact on the family is evident.

Act II

The hopes and expectations of Act I have dimmed by Act II, as the Prozorovs find themselves more deeply mired in provincial life, and Natasha begins to assert her will. Act II occurs some nineteen months after Act I; *Three Sisters* is the most temporally expansive of Chekhov's plays, taking up a total of three and a half years. Each act is carefully defined in terms of season and time of day, with the second act occurring on a Saturday evening in late winter, at carnival time, just before Lent. The initial conversation between Andrey and Natasha establishes that they are now married and have an infant son; moreover, it quickly becomes clear that she has assumed authority over the household and is on the point of evicting Irina from her room in order to turn it into a nursery. Andrey's dissatisfaction with his life emerges in a one-sided conversation with the old messenger Ferapont. In *The Seagull* and *Uncle Vanya* the characters sometimes expressed themselves, rather awkwardly, in soliloquy; in *Three Sisters* Chekhov always contrives a way for them to speak with at least one other character present. Ferapont is deaf, and Andrey admits that "If your hearing was good, I probably wouldn't be talking to you."[37] Nonetheless, the old man's tales of fatal pancake feasts and mysterious ropes stretched across Moscow provide an absurd, incongruous counterpoint to Andrey's longings for an academic life in the capital.

The act is structured, like acts in several Chekhov plays, around a festive occasion that goes awry; in this case, an evening of carnival masquerade. The sisters and officers are all, in various ways, tired and frustrated at the end of a long day. They look forward to the evening, with its promise of fellowship and relaxation; all will have their hopes disappointed. The dialogue between Masha and Vershinin establishes their growing attraction and their marital dissatisfactions. Vershinin articulates a kind of universal malaise among the provincial gentry: "If you listen to any educated man in this town, civilian or military, he's sick and tired of his wife, sick and tired of his home, sick and tired of his estate, sick and tired of his horses …" The repeated *zamuchilsya* – the verb is etymologically linked to death by torture – sums up the intolerable boredom and frustration under which the characters languish, as well as Vershinin's own exasperation with its pettiness. His complaints about his wife lead directly to seductive advances, which Masha both rebuffs and encourages: "Don't say it again, please don't … (*In an undertone.*) Go on, do talk, it doesn't matter to me." The phrase "it doesn't matter" ("*vsyo ravno*") is a leitmotif that runs through the whole play, providing its penultimate line.

Irina also complains of exhaustion as she returns from her job. The telegraph office has not given her what she longed for from work, but only

"Drudgery without poetry," summed up in her anecdote about being rude to a grieving mother who could not remember her brother's address. Real financial worries creep into the conversation – Andrey has been losing money gambling, Chebutykin does not pay his rent – but gradually, as the company assembles, the mood begins to improve. Vershinin and Tusenbach embark on their most protracted bout of philosophizing, debating the nature of life two hundred years in the future. Vershinin, the idealist, declares that future generations will enjoy a happiness for which the present must work and suffer; Tusenbach, the pragmatist, finds the possibility of happiness in the present but argues that life itself is unchanging, hard, and inscrutable, with no knowable meaning. He expresses his views through one of the play's dominant images, that of migrating birds:

> Not just two hundred or three hundred, but even a million years from now, life will be the same as it's always been; it won't change, it will stay constant, governed by its own laws, which are none of our business or, at least, which we'll never figure out. Birds of passage, cranes, for instance, fly on and on, and whatever thoughts, sublime or trivial, may drift through their heads, they'll keep on flying and never know what for or where to.

Masha resists this notion – "Either you know why you live or else it's all senseless" – but the metaphor of blindly flying birds, beautiful and direction-less, continues to hang over the sisters throughout the play.

The party scene in *Three Sisters* is perhaps Chekhov's supreme achievement in an innovative, apparently unstructured realism. Characters pass the time over the course of the evening, coming and going through the same two-room set used in Act I. The stage is filled with ongoing simultaneous actions, over-lapping conversations, and a range of background noise and chatter. Through the apparent randomness of these activities, Chekhov develops and reveals his characters and advances several of their storylines. He also creates evocative associations between seemingly unrelated ideas and images, so that the tech-nique of the act is not merely slice-of-life realism, but a kind of poetic impressionism. Maurice Valency, commenting on this scene, notes that "the subtle play of associations keeps us continually aware of the hidden currents of thought and feeling which work below the surface of the visible action, and give it another dimension, the nature of which is intimated but the full extent of which can only be surmised."[38]

In the most distinctive such moment, Chebutykin, who has been silently reading his newspaper in the upstage reception room, suddenly comments, "Balzac was married in Berdichev." Deciding to jot this curious fact in his notebook, he repeats it, as Irina, sitting nearby at the table playing solitaire, sings quietly to herself. A moment later, laying out her next game, she also murmurs, "*pensively*," "Balzac was married in Berdichev." Nothing further comes of this; the next spoken line, from the drawing room downstage, is Baron Tusenbach announcing to Masha that "The die is cast," and he is resigning from the army.

What are the meanings of this strange, seemingly inconsequential stage moment? What does it reveal about the people involved? At the simplest level, it continues their characterization, for their words are consistent with their culture and education. The odd fact that a famous French writer was married in an obscure Ukrainian town might catch the interest of members of the Westernized Russian intelligentsia; and a philosophically minded officer might well use a famous phrase of Julius Caesar's (on crossing the Rubicon) to express his having taken a decisive action. But the meanings go beyond this level. Irina is herself stuck in a provincial town, and thinking of marriage; we learn later that her hopes of finding the man of her dreams all hinge on getting away to Moscow. Balzac's marriage may have personal resonances for her, as she lays out the cards of her game of solitaire. Tusenbach has resigned his commission partly in hopes of marrying Irina; he wishes for them to settle together into civilian life and pursue their dreams of productive work. Irina's line and Tusenbach's have no direct relation – the characters are in separate rooms and do not obviously hear each other – but both touch on the same storyline. And the die is indeed cast by Tusenbach's resignation to court Irina, for his action precipitates the quarrel with Solyony that leads to the Baron's death in Act IV. (There is a double irony in Tusenbach's quoting the world's most famous general in order to leave military service, and thus setting in motion events that will end in his death by gunshot.) The moment's meanings go beyond character and plot, however, to the subtle evocation of mood. Irina's quiet singing, the softly alliterative *b* and *v* sounds of "*Balzac venchalsya v Berdicheve*," the lonely associations of solitaire, called in Russian by its English name "patience": all feed into the poignant atmosphere of deferred hopes that shrouds the act like a fog.

The second act of *Three Sisters* is filled with such moments, apparently unconnected to the plot, and often quirky or bizarre. Important plot points, like the Baron's resignation and Vershinin's wife's attempted suicide, are mentioned in passing or as whispered asides; they seem secondary to the overall texture of the act. The conversation ranges in all directions (though it often circles back on the sisters' desire to go to Moscow). The characters busy themselves with tea, cards, music; they quote from Gogol, Pushkin, and Griboedev. In a quintessentially incongruous moment, the extraneous

Lieutenant Fedotik explains that his new jackknife has a tool for cleaning one's ears. Chebutykin reports that smallpox is raging in Tsitsikar, while Solyony provokes meaningless arguments about ethnic food and the number of universities in Moscow. Erratic and clownish, Solyony contributes significantly to the randomness of the act. Early on, when Natasha is cooing about her beloved little Bobik, Solyony abruptly announces, "If that baby were mine, I'd fry him in a skillet and eat him." As the action proceeds, he becomes more confrontational and threatening, but his provocations serve mainly to set off the group's growing high spirits as the time for the masquerade performance approaches. Andrey, Tusenbach, and Chebutykin dance and sing. Tusenbach sits at the piano, laughing, and plays a waltz, to which Masha dances by herself, singing, "Baron's drunk, baron's drunk, baron's drunk!"

Just as the party has roused itself to its Mardi Gras celebration, Lent arrives early in the person of Natasha. Her concern for Bobik's health forestalls the festivities, making evident her power over the household. All are disappointed, but only the embittered Masha is explicit in her resentment, referring to Natasha as a "*meshchanka*," a slur at her lower-class origins (Senelick's translation is "Small-town slut!"). The community that had formed breaks down into dispirited pairings, as Andrey and Chebutykin sneak out to gamble, Solyony makes unwelcome protestations to Irina, and Kulygin and Olga return exhausted from a staff meeting. Natasha's killjoy status is given an ironic twist when, after canceling the party, she herself elects to go out for a troika ride with Protopopov, the local bigwig who becomes her lover. In a 2003 National Theatre production, director Katie Mitchell took literally Chekhov's stage direction that Natasha walks through the reception room "*Wearing a fur coat and hat*." Just before she exited to meet Protopopov, Natasha's coat fell open to reveal that she was wearing little else; she evidently anticipated a sexual liaison in the troika. Chekhov is not so explicit, but the implication is that Natasha's affair with Protopopov begins on this particular night. With her exit, the stage is left dark and quiet; Chekhov specifies that the servants have extinguished the lights. Evocative sounds are heard from offstage – a concertina in the street, the nursemaid's lullaby – as Irina, alone in the dark, voices her yearning: "To Moscow! To Moscow! To Moscow!"

Act III

Chekhov uses the setting, action, and *mise-en-scène* of the third act to reflect a crisis in the lives of the characters. A fire in the town creates an atmosphere of panic and exhaustion, which precipitates confrontations and confessions as the Prozorovs see their hopes going up in flames. Though their house is not damaged, it is overrun by those fighting or fleeing the fire. The setting is the cramped bedroom shared by Irina and Olga, through which all of the dramatis personae tramp during the course of the act; the Prozorovs have no privacy and no secrets. The time is between two and three in the morning. Chekhov specified that the feeling of weariness should outweigh even the commotion of the fire: "the noise is only in the distance, backstage, a muffled noise, faint, but here onstage everyone is worn out, almost asleep."[39] Chekhov took pains over the sound effects in this act, working with the MAT company to get the sound of the alarm bell right, pulling Stanislavsky back from overdoing the offstage noises, and specifying particular moments when the sounds of the fire highlight the dramatic action. The fire sometimes recedes to the background as characters fall asleep or exchange whispered confidences; sometimes it assumes almost apocalyptic power, as in the following speech of Vershinin, which Chekhov sets off with the alarm bell:

> … when my little girls were standing on the doorstep in nothing but their underwear, barefoot, and the street was red with flame, and there was a terrible racket, it occurred to me that things like that used to happen many years ago when there'd be a sudden enemy invasion, looting and burning …[40]

For Vershinin, this glimpse of Russia's barbaric past serves to highlight his hopes for the future, but for the sisters the night of the fire corresponds to the destruction of their dreams: "I've aged ten years tonight," Olga says.

The crowded setting is both a metaphorical and a literal indication of the sisters' loss of their home to their rapacious sister-in-law. Natasha's mention of an infant daughter, perhaps the child of Protopopov, indicates the passage of a year or so since the previous act. In the interim, Natasha has succeeded in taking over Irina's room for Bobik and forcing the sisters in together. Natasha is not necessarily a villainess: she is energetic and pragmatic compared to the ineffectual Prozorovs, and lacks the murderous malice of Aksinya, her equivalent in Chekhov's story "In the Ravine." But in this scene Chekhov shows her at her worst, as she flies into a rage at the old nanny Anfisa for sitting in her presence. J. L. Styan notes that "In this scene Chekhov is in some danger of making Natasha a figure of loathing," as Olga's weak attempt to defend Anfisa provokes an explosive outburst.[41] Chekhov captures Natasha's bossy petulance by separating out her syllables as she stamps her foot and insists she knows what she-is-talking-about ("*ya znayu, chto go-vo-ryu*"). She concludes, "Honestly, if you don't move downstairs we'll always be quarreling" – laying claim to this room as well. Natasha appears only once again in the act, walking through silently with a candle, "as if she were the one who'd set the fire," in

Masha's words. Stanislavsky originally had her play the moment naturalisti-cally, with a lot of stage business, putting out lights and looking under the furniture for burglars; Chekhov wrote that "it would be better to have her walk across the stage in a straight line, without a glance at anyone or anything, à la Lady Macbeth, with a candle – something a bit tighter and more frightening."[42] The shy and awkward town girl on whom the sisters looked down in Act I has become a baleful, almost inhuman specter heralding their destruction.

The possibility that the Prozorovs' plight is not specific to them, but represents some broader condition of decline and decay, is raised by Chebutykin, the drunken, nihilistic doctor. Like Astrov in *Uncle Vanya*, he drinks to anesthetize his guilt over losing a patient, a situation Chekhov had experienced personally, and one that had a devastating psychological impact on him.[43] But Chebutykin's cynicism goes beyond Astrov's to a kind of universal despair that anticipates the absurdist vision of Samuel Beckett: "My head's empty, my soul's frozen. Maybe I'm not even a human being, but just seem to have arms and legs … and a head; maybe I don't even exist at all, but it only seems to me I walk, eat, sleep. (*Weeps.*) Oh, if only I didn't exist!" Later in the act, Chebutykin drops a porcelain clock that had belonged to the Prozorovs' mother, his lost love. The moment is dense with meaning: the smashing of past dreams, the shattering of time into a perpetual present of deferred hopes. Chebutykin drops the clock just after Vershinin mentions, in passing, the key event of the play – that the brigade will be transferred and the soldiers will abandon the town for Poland or Siberia. Irina says hopefully, "And we shall go away!" but the smashing clock seems to contradict her aspirations. For Chebutykin, the clock exemplifies the unreality of all of their lives: "Could be I didn't break it, it only seems like I broke it. Maybe it only seems to us that we exist, but as a matter of fact we don't. I don't know anything, nobody knows anything." In this episode, Chekhov makes the crisis of his characters an emblem for the universal condition of humanity.

Chekhov ends the act by bringing the three sisters together, alone onstage, for the first time since the play's opening. Their despair takes on an edge of hysteria, as they see the culture and education in which they have placed such value ebbing away into the vulgarity that is taking over their lives: "Where has it all gone?" Irina sobs. "I can't remember the Italian for window, or, uh, ceiling … I forget everything, every day I forget, and life goes on and won't ever, ever come back, we'll never get to Moscow …" In extremis, the sisters lay themselves open emotionally. Olga laments her spinster existence and urges Irina to marry the Baron, which she eventually agrees to do. Masha confesses her love for Vershinin and exits to consummate it. In one of Chekhov's distinctive non-verbal moments, Vershinin hums part of a Tchaikovsky aria from offstage, and Masha answers: "Trom-tom-tom!" "Tra-ta-ta!" Andrey confesses that he has mortgaged the house to pay his gambling debts, and tries to defend Natasha, but the sisters flee behind their screens and he retreats in despair. Kulygin looks in briefly, seeking Masha, and then exits. There follows one of Chekhov's strangest and most haunting stage directions: "*Alarm bell; the stage is empty.*" The action of the play has been completely suspended: the juxtaposition of cacophonous noise and total stasis is a bleak representation of what the Prozorovs' world has become. Irina, peering from behind her screen, voices one last wish for Moscow, and the act is over.

Act IV

The exterior setting of the final act provides a clear visual expression of its essential action: the eviction of the sisters from their home. While the departure of the brigade takes up much of the dialogue, it is the final image of the sisters, bereft and dispossessed, in the shadow of the house that is no longer theirs, which makes the play's climactic statement. In one of the most famous modern productions, the Berlin *Drei Schwestern* of 1984, director Peter Stein used the two back-to-back stages of the Schaubühne to create an immense open space, 150 feet deep, which contrasted shockingly with the crowded interiors of the previous acts. Into this vast wasteland the sisters were expelled like Beckettian migrants.

Presiding over the farewells and departures is Chebutykin, whose weary cynicism has hardened into a kind of armor plating against life. He is "in an affable mood that stays with him throughout the act"; his singing of the vaudeville song "Tarara boom-de-ay," and his repetition of his mantra "it doesn't matter," become the choric background to the other characters' painful partings.[44] He is even indifferent to the possibility, hinted at throughout the act and realized in its final moments, that Baron Tusenbach will be killed by Solyony in a duel: "The Baron's all right, but one Baron more or less – does it really matter?" The Baron's death takes on a kind of inevitability over the course of the act, as most of the characters seem to know about the duel but none does anything to prevent it. Even Irina, when she learns of it, responds "I knew it, I knew it," and soon turns her thoughts back to her original dream of a life of productive work.

The scene of Irina's parting from Tusenbach, as he goes to his death, is one of the most poignant in Chekhov. He knows she does not love him – as she puts it, her heart is like a locked piano with a lost key – but he wants desperately for her to give him some sign of affection. He speaks of seeing the trees for the first time in his life, recalling Vershinin's story from Act II of a convicted politician who only noticed the flight of birds from the window of his prison. He imagines himself continuing to take part in life, like a dead tree swaying in the breeze with the others. He tells her where papers she gave him are, in his desk. He starts to leave, then turns back, wanting some final, meaningful exchange with her. After a painful pause, all he can manage to say is, "I haven't had any coffee today. Ask them to make me some." This episode is quintessentially Chekhovian, as the most profound moment in a man's life is subsumed under the most mundane of daily activities.

The principal characters all seem weighed down with a sense of failure and loss. Masha speaks of how her unhappiness has coarsened her; she inquires after her departing lover Vershinin in the same way "our cook Marfa used to refer to her policeman." Her disappointment in Andrey and the hopes of the family is memorably expressed in the image of a great bell cast for a village church: "Thousands of people were hoisting a bell, a lot of energy and money was expended, and all of a sudden it fell to the ground and smashed." Andrey himself is equally disillusioned, acknowledging, for the first time, the unhappiness of his marriage. "A wife is a wife," he says of Natasha. "She's honest, decent, oh and kind, but for all that there's something in her that reduces her to a petty, blind sort of bristly animal. In any case, she's not human." He sees Natasha's grasping vulgarity and bestial, instinct-driven mode of living as having infected himself, the whole town, and by implication all of Russia. "Our town has existed for two hundred years, it contains a hundred thousand inhabitants, and not one who isn't exactly like the others, not one dedicated person, past or present," he cries. "All they do is eat, drink, sleep, then die … others are born and they too eat, drink, sleep and, to keep from being stultified by boredom, vary their lives with vicious gossip, cards, vodka, crooked deals, and the wives cheat on the husbands while the husbands lie, pretend to notice nothing. …" This passionate monologue, Andrey's longest speech in the play, expresses thoughts very similar to Chekhov's own words in letters about his hometown of Taganrog. He obviously felt it was an important speech, and a direct challenge to the life of contemporary Russia; he said the actor of Andrey "should almost threaten the audience with his fists!"[45] For those who, like Gorky, believed Chekhov was a crusading reformer who wished to tell his fellows how bad their lives were, this speech could serve as a central text.

Vershinin expresses similar views in his final burst of philosophizing, though characteristically he puts a more positive spin on them. Though life seems hard and hopeless, humanity needs something better and will one day find it: "if only hard work were supplemented by education, and education by hard work." Chekhov may have shared Vershinin's sentiments, but here they rather lack conviction, as he is only killing time while waiting to say farewell to

Masha. Their parting is hurried and painful, with Olga looking on as an awkward chaperone. The desolate Masha is left muttering a confused version of the Pushkin poem she was quoting at the beginning of the play: "On the curved seashore a green oak stands, a golden chain wound round that oak … A green cat stands … a green oak stands …" The cuckolded husband Kulygin, who may have witnessed his wife's parting from her lover, is left to try to cheer her up by putting on a false beard he has confiscated from one of his students. Amazingly, it works, if only for a moment. In a scene characteristically mixing deep pathos and vaudevillian comic timing, Kulygin notes that the disguise makes him look like the German teacher, and Masha, momentarily distracted, responds:

> **Masha:** Actually, it does look like your German.
> **Olga:** *(Laughs)* Yes.
> *(Masha weeps)*
> **Irina:** That's enough, Masha!
> **Kulygin:** A lot like him …

At this point, Natasha enters and sets everything in order in her new domain. Her behavior in the last scene – assigning child-care responsibilities, cattily commenting on Irina's dress, shouting at a maid about a mislaid fork – has a comic dimension. Yet Robert Brustein's assessment, though extreme, is suggestive: "her final triumph, no matter how Chekhov tries to disguise it, is the triumph of pure evil."[46]

As Natasha exits, Chebutykin arrives with the news of the Baron's death. The sisters come together for their final tableau, flanked by the complaisant Kulygin, Andrey with his baby carriage, and Chebutykin with his paper. As the military music plays in the background, the sisters cling together and try to rally their spirits. Olga sounds the final note of endurance and hope: "Oh, dear sisters, this life of ours is not over yet. Let's go on living! The music plays so gaily, so cheerfully, and it seems as if, just a little while longer and we shall learn why we're alive, why we suffer … if we only knew, if we only knew!" The stirring music and her hopeful words are counterpointed, however, by Chebutykin's vulgar song "Tara … ra … boom-de-ay", and his muttered, nihilistic refrain, "Doesn't matter! Doesn't matter!"

Richard Gilman is one of many critics who have compared the world of *Three Sisters* to that of Samuel Beckett; the sisters' dreams of Moscow are as illusory as the tramps' hopes for Godot. Gilman compares the ending of *Three Sisters* to the final phrases in Beckett's novel *Molloy*: "I can't go on, I'll go on." For the sisters, "They can't, they do. It's unendurable, they endure … In the midst of successive losses they survive, in part through goodwill that leaps periodically over the worst of the conditions – *the* condition – to issue in camaraderie and affection."[47] With regard to the play's final juxtaposition – Olga's wish to know the meaning of their sufferings, and Chebutykin's assertion that it makes no difference – Gilman provides an apt summing up of Chekhov's ethos: "She and the doctor both have it wrong: they can't know and it does make a difference."[48] Like all of Chekhov's endings, the final tableau of *Three Sisters* is open to a range of interpretations; but the image of the sisters, sheltering together amid the ruins of their lives, provides at least a glimmer of human warmth in the wasteland.

The Cherry Orchard

Of all Chekhov's major plays, *The Cherry Orchard* is the one that has been subject to the widest range of interpretation. Chekhov called it "a comedy, in places even a farce," [49] but Stanislavsky read it – and played it – as a tragedy. The MAT production was considered an icon of naturalistic theatre, yet theatrical innovators like Meyerhold viewed the play as symbolic and abstract. Soviet ideologues hailed *The Cherry Orchard* as a portent of the Revolution, citing Trofimov's hopeful cry that "All Russia is our orchard," while many in the West viewed the play as a mournful lament for a doomed culture. These three axes of interpretation, on questions of genre, style, and politics, have governed responses to the play in the century since its premiere. All these interpretive cruxes are built into the play, which looks both forward and backward, laughing and crying, in Chekhov's final attempt to represent the life of his times on the stage.[50]

When *The Cherry Orchard* first appeared at the Moscow Art Theatre in 1904, it served as an obituary for the nineteenth century and a harbinger of the twentieth. The loss of the Ranevsky orchard was a powerful metaphor for the decline of the Russian gentry in the face of inexorable historical pressures. At the same time, the MAT *Cherry Orchard* represented the culmination of a theatrical tradition that had reached its limits. The eerie sound effect of a breaking string that concludes the play represents not only a social and political rupture, but an aesthetic one. The naturalism pioneered by the MAT was giving way to the explosive theatrical experimentation of the early twentieth century. The subsequent history of the play has drawn on the tensions between past and future built into the structure of the play itself. A century of productions and interpretations have explored its mixture of tradition and innovation, nostalgic longing and revolutionary change. The discussion that follows will try to sketch out how the play's multiple and often contradictory meanings are latent in the interpretive decisions it demands as it unfolds, moment by moment, in the theatre. Whatever the final meaning of any given production, *The Cherry Orchard* remains a poignant, potent myth of wasted opportunities, frustrated dreams, and fragile hopes.

Act I

The Cherry Orchard, like *Three Sisters*, tells the story of a family losing its home. In the opening act, the widow Lyubov Andreevna Ranevskaya, together with her daughter Anya, returns to her estate, which is encumbered by debt and threatened with foreclosure. The situation is laid out clearly by the former serf, Lopakhin, who warns of the impending catastrophe, and urges Ranevskaya and her brother Gaev to cut down the cherry orchard, subdivide the land, and lease it for summer cottages. Their inability to entertain this plan, or any other solution to the crisis, provides the essential action, or non-action, of the play.

Chekhov's opening stage directions for *The Cherry Orchard* are detailed and evocative:

> *A room, which is still known as the nursery. One of the doors opens into Anya's bedroom. Dawn, soon the sun will be up. It is already May, the cherry trees are in bloom, but it is chilly in the orchard, there is an early morning frost.*[51]

The fact that the room is "still known" as the nursery suggests that the Ranevskys are somehow dwelling in the past, or in a state of retarded infancy. Perhaps there is a reminder of Ranevskaya's dead son Grisha, who would have been the last to occupy this room. The MAT production had miniature tables and chairs, at which the characters sat like overgrown children. Modern productions often include a rocking horse or a toy train to complete the effect. The stage directions suggest that the orchard, with cherry trees in blossom, is visible outside the windows of the house. This visual impression seems to have been important to Chekhov: he wrote to Stanislavksy, "It's called *The Cherry Orchard*, it has four acts and in Act One cherry trees can be seen in bloom through the windows, the whole orchard a mass of white."[52]

The opening dialogue provides necessary exposition about the return of Lyubov Andreevna, who has been abroad for five years. Lopakhin, a peasant-turned-businessman in white waistcoat and tan shoes, remembers her with a complex mixture of emotions. He recalls as a boy being beaten by his drunken father, and Lyubov Andreevna bringing him into the nursery to wash his bleeding face. This memory of her may include a tinge of desire for the slender young lady, as well as class anxiety or resentment. The young Lyubov's kindly meant admonishment – "Don't cry, my little peasant, you'll live long enough to get married" – sets up the terms of their relationship and also hints at the coming questions about Lopakhin's marriage to Varya. Lopakhin is clearly self-conscious about his transition from serf to gentleman – he is still, in his colorful simile, like a pig in a pastry shop.

Chekhov had used an empty stage with vivid offstage sound effects at the climax of *Three Sisters*, during the Act III fire. Here he uses a similar technique to introduce Ranevskaya and her train. During this brief passage across the stage, Chekhov provides a range of character information, both essential and irrelevant: that this room was Ranevskaya's nursery, that her brother Gaev likes to complain, that Varya dresses like a nun – and that Charlotta's dog can eat nuts. Vladimir Kataev points out how these exchanges point up an important theme of the play: that, as Ranevskaya says of both Varya and Gaev, "You're just the same as ever" – that the characters are trapped in a kind of personal immobility while time rushes forward around them.[53]

Varya, the adopted daughter, learns from Anya about their mother's life in Paris. Their conversation ends with the recognition that the interest on their estate has not been paid, and the estate will be sold in August. At this moment of high emotional tension, Lopakhin suddenly sticks his head in the door and bleats like a calf or sheep. One of Chekhov's characteristic intrusions of the bizarre, this may be a comic non sequitur revealing Lopakhin's oafishness with regard to Varya, or perhaps it is Lopakhin's way of commenting on the women's anxieties about a problem he believes he has solved. At any rate, the episode gives the audience a first picture of the Lopakhin/Varya relationship, with its elements of surface teasing, repressed emotion, and painful absurdity.

Soon afterwards, Ranevskaya appears in her Parisian clothes, with her circle of admirers fussing around her. In response to Lopakhin's declaration that he loves her "more than my own kin," Ranevskaya ignores him, and gets up to start kissing the bookcase and the table. Is she deliberately avoiding an intimate conversation, or is she oblivious of Lopakhin's ardor, or does she simply take his devotion for granted? The change in tone brings Lopakhin back to practical matters, and, checking his watch as he does repeatedly throughout the play, he introduces the subject of the cherry orchard and his plan to cut it down and divide the estate into lots for summer cottages. Ranevskaya and Gaev scoff at the plan, revealing for the first, but not the last, time their inability to take action to save the estate.

At this point Varya interrupts to give Ranevskaya two telegrams from Paris. She receives these, from her wayward lover, in every act, and each time she reacts differently. Here she tears them up with apparent indifference. Gaev pointedly changes the subject by addressing the hundred-year-old bookcase in terms of veneration. This splendidly absurd speech can be played as a natural effusion of Gaev's loquacious and sentimental spirit, or as a deliberate attempt to distract Ranevskaya from her thoughts of Paris. Chekhov says Gaev speaks *"through tears"* by the end, and he is *"somewhat embarrassed"* afterwards, as he returns to his imaginary billiard-playing. Ranevskaya and Gaev open the windows and look out into the orchard, remembering their childhoods. Suddenly Ranevskaya seems to see their mother. She *"laughs with joy,"* though her emotions have also been stirred by painful memories of the past. This highly charged moment sets up the entry of Trofimov, her dead son's tutor, who appears at the point in the act when Chekhov has wound things up to their most intense emotional pitch. Like Ibsen, Chekhov had learned from melodramas the power of the long-delayed entrance of the ominous visitor. Trofimov is a surprising and probably disturbing presence in his shabby student's uniform and spectacles, with his thinning hair and mangy beard. Ranevskaya dissolves in tears upon seeing him, but she almost immediately begins commenting on his appearance: "Well now, Petya? Why have you become so homely? Why have you got old?" Whether her response to him is a comic non sequitur, or a way of continuing to mourn the past, or an attempt to put him in his place, depends on the choices of the individual actors and the general tenor of the scene.

After Ranevskaya's exit, Varya comments on her spendthrift ways and Gaev on her sexual morals. Anya's entry turns the focus to Gaev's impulsive and irresponsible urge to talk. Though his nieces chide him, their attitudes soon turn to admiration as he spins out his three-pronged attack on the cherry orchard problem. Whether Gaev, or the women, believes any of his schemes is up to the actors, but his planning lifts the final mood of the scene. Trofimov is given another memorable entrance, standing silently as he watches the sleeping Anya being led away, then bursting into an effusion of happiness: "My sunshine! My springtime!"

By the end of the first act, Chekhov has introduced all of the principal characters and set up the main relationships: the youthful idealism linking Anya and Trofimov; the hypothetical betrothal of Lopakhin and Varya, with its attendant teasings and frustrations; the below-stairs triangle of the servants; the web of relationships – of desire, duty, and dependence – centering on the magnetic Ranevskaya; and finally the bond of brother and sister to each other and to their ancestral home. The plot has been set in motion as well, and the clock is ticking toward the inevitable auction.

Act II

Act II is the only exterior scene of the play; Chekhov wrote to Nemirovich-Danchenko, "you must give me proper green fields and a road, and a sense of distance unusual for the stage."[54] Chekhov's description of the scene, like the play as a whole, looks both into the past and the future. The "*old, long abandoned shrine*" stands next to "*large slabs that were once, apparently, tombstones.*"[55] In the background, however, a row of telegraph poles represent the technologies of the twentieth century and suggest the presence of the railway line Lopakhin so often mentions. (Stanislavsky wanted to show the train passing across the back of the stage, but Chekhov talked him out of it.) A large town is just visible on the horizon, suggesting urbanization and industrialization, and the city-dwellers who might one day occupy the cottages Lopakhin wants to build.

It is evening, and four of the household servants are onstage, all, Chekhov specifies, "*rapt in thought.*" The maid Dunyasha and the caddish valet Yasha sit on an old bench, while the clumsy bookkeeper Yepikhodov sets the tone with his plaintive guitar. The act begins with an autobiographical monologue by Charlotta, the governess, an isolated quasi-soliloquy of existential implications. "I haven't got a valid passport … where I'm from and who I am – I don't know." Charlotta's speech can be played for incongruous comedy – she cuts a strange figure with her peaked cap and gun, eating a cucumber while she talks of her early life as a circus-girl. But her rootlessness, and her odd self-questionings delivered to the baffled or bored servants, give her lines disturbing power: "All alone, alone, I've got no one and … who I am, why I am, I don't know."

The scene that follows uses the traditional device of servants aping the manners of their masters, with Dunyasha powdering her nose and giving herself the airs of a lady. The singing of Yepikhodov and Yasha breaks the mood of Charlotta's speech – she says that they howl like jackals. The melancholy Yepikhodov, failing to get attention from Dunyasha, produces a revolver and mutters about suicide. This prop calls to mind one of Chekhov's tongue-in-cheek maxims – that a gun shown onstage must be fired by the last act – a principle Chekhov seems here determined to violate. He wrote proudly that "there's not a single pistol shot in the whole play."[56]

Ranevskaya, Lopakhin, and Gaev arrive, in the midst of a heated discussion about the cherry orchard question. Lopakhin tries to make them realize the immediacy of the sale by naming the potential buyer, the wealthy Deriganov – one of the play's many important offstage figures, along with the lover in Paris, the great-aunt in Yaroslavl, Pishchik's daughter Dashenka, and Yasha's peasant mother. As his summer cottage proposal is once again rejected as "vulgar,"

Lopakhin turns to go, but Ranevskaya stops him, *"frightened."* She says she keeps waiting for something to happen, "as if the house were about to collapse on top of us." Her mood of dread leads her to think about her life and her "sins," and she finally gives the back story of her drunken husband, drowned child, and faithless lover. As in Act I, she tears up a telegram from him; how do the two gestures compare?

As he does in each act, the ancient servant Firs chides Gaev like a boy for wearing the wrong clothing. Firs's presence brings in some of the more serious material of the act, as he mentions the Emancipation of the Serfs, a sweeping historical change that hangs over the whole play. "I didn't go along with the freedom then, I stayed with the masters," he recalls. Lopakhin also comments on the past, presumably with bitter irony: in those good old days you could at least get flogged. These lines raise the theme, prevalent throughout the play, of the different responses throughout the social hierarchy to the huge changes affecting Russian society in the late nineteenth century. The political dimension of the play now becomes central, as Trofimov enters with Anya and Varya, and the conversation turns to the present state of affairs in Russia.

Lopakhin and Trofimov immediately begin quarreling. Trofimov launches into a diatribe against the Russian intelligentsia and their failure to ameliorate the social conditions of the poor. Some of Trofimov's attacks are on target, to the extent that Chekhov was forced by the censor to change them: "anybody can see that the working class is abominably fed, sleeps without pillows, thirty or forty to a room, everywhere bedbugs, stench, damp, moral pollution." While Trofimov's tirade has force and reflects some of Chekhov's own views, it also comes from a questionable source. Just as in *Three Sisters* the exhortation to work rings false when coming from the idle Irina and Tusenbach, so Trofimov's speeches mark him as the kind of prating intellectual he has been condemning. When Lopakhin, who actually does work, takes up Trofimov's themes, his speech has more impact. In an unusually reflective mood, he also comments on the poor state of Russia: "Sometimes, when I can't sleep, I think: 'Lord, you gave us vast forests, boundless fields, the widest horizons, and living here, we really and truly ought to be giants.'" The juxtaposition of these two men and their attitudes to their country recurs throughout the play and is one of the key places where productions develop their political messages.

The scene is now set for one of the most extraordinary moments in Chekhov's drama. Yepikhodov strolls past playing his guitar, and the meditative tone is set by one of Chekhov's quasi-musical repetitions:

> **Ranevskaya:**   (*dreamily*). There goes Yepikhodov …
> **Anya:**   (*dreamily*). There goes Yepikhodov …

It is sunset; Gaev makes a brief speech on Nature as the giver and destroyer of life but is quickly hushed by his nieces.

> *Everyone sits, absorbed in thought. The only sound is FIRS, softly muttering. Suddenly a distant sound is heard, as if from the sky, the sound of a breaking string, dying away, mournfully.*

This, along with its reprise at the play's end, is arguably the most significant sound effect in world drama; in few other works does an offstage sound have such symbolic power. For the MAT production, Stanislavsky used three piano strings of different weights, strung from the flies behind the scenes, with a rumble of thunder on a drum to set the sound in relief. The characters comment on the sound in various ways that help to define them and also suggest the expressive range of the sound itself. Lopakhin, the practical man, guesses that a cable has snapped in a mine-shaft. Gaev suggests a heron, Trofimov an owl: birds consistent with their personalities. Ranevskaya, still in a foreboding mood, merely comments that it was "unpleasant anyhow." Firs reads it as a political portent, foreboding a catastrophe such as the Emancipation was to him: "Before the troubles, it was the same: the screech owl hooted and the samovar never stopped humming."

Lopakhin's is the "correct" explanation, probably. The same sound occurs in Chekhov's 1887 story "Happiness," and there is no doubt as to its source: a bucket falling in a mine-shaft. Chekhov had heard the sound in his youth and refers to it in his letters. Yet its evocative power clearly extends beyond any single explanation, whether a snapped cable, a broken string on Yepikhodov's guitar, or a numinous portent from the underworld. Whatever meanings may be attributed to it, the sound of the breaking string creates a compelling theatrical effect, stopping the play for a moment with the assembled cast onstage, giving the audience an opportunity to reflect on the characters' situation and their varied responses to it.

Immediately after the ominous sound, an ominous figure appears: the drunken vagrant, who quotes revolutionary poetry and asks for money. In performance, this character can range from a comic stage drunk to a spectral herald of doom. Regardless, in his rootlessness and poverty he calls attention to the social disorder invoked by the speeches of Trofimov, Lopakhin, and Firs. His snatches of poems by Nadson and Nekrasov speak of a tired "suffering brother" and the weary moans of Volga workers. His presence frightens Varya and provokes another display of fiscal irresponsibility from Ranevskaya: startled and perhaps guilty, she gives him a gold coin.

As the other characters leave the stage, Anya and Trofimov are left alone on what promises to be a romantic moonlit evening. Trofimov, however, almost immediately declares that they are "above love," and speaks as though to a student rally: "Forward! No dropping behind, friends!" Any production must determine how much this scene is a comic one, of an eager young woman and a distracted would-be revolutionary, or a serious reflection on property and oppression. The scene contains some of Trofimov's silliest rhetoric, but also some of his strongest. When Anya observes that Trofimov's revolutionary ideals have caused her not to love the cherry orchard as she used to, he replies, "All Russia is our orchard." The censor took the scene seriously, and Chekhov had to remove the lines in which Trofimov indicts the Ranevsky family for having owned serfs: "They owned living souls – it's corrupted all of you, honestly, those who lived before and those living now."

The act ends on an upbeat note, with the moon rising, and Trofimov's premonition of happiness. Chekhov's original ending was lower key, so much so that Stanislavsky persuaded him to change it. Chekhov had ended the act with Firs and Charlotta discussing their past lives: she recalling her circus youth and her dead parents, he thinking of a murder committed sixty years before. The present ending, with its focus on youth, idealism, and dreams of the future, may give the audience a fragile hope to carry beyond the end of the play; or it may merely set us up for the catastrophe that befalls the family in Act III.

Act III

Act III begins with a burst of sound and movement: the "*grand-rond*" of the ball at the Ranevsky estate. The party is in full swing, and the company dances through in pairs. The dancing makes a powerful theatrical statement, and it is hard not to read it metaphorically. The Russian Symbolist writer Andrey Bely called it "a crystallization of Chekhov's devices: in the foreground room a domestic drama is taking place, while at the back, candle-lit, the masks of terror are dancing rapturously."[57] Avant-garde director Vsevolod Meyerhold likewise found Act III a *danse macabre* representative of the entire play. "As in a nightmare," Meyerhold wrote, the characters "whirl around in a tedious dance without amusement, or fervor, or grace, or even lust, not knowing that the earth on which they are standing will be sold from under their feet."[58]

The stage itself is divided, as in the first act of *Three Sisters*, into upstage and downstage rooms, which Chekhov uses for effects of irony and contrast. As in *Three Sisters*, the public event takes place upstage, farthest from the audience, whereas more private encounters occur in the drawing room downstage. While Ranevskaya is agonizing over the fate of the orchard, Chekhov specifies that "*In the ballroom a figure in a gray top hat and checked trousers waves its arms and jumps up and down.*"[59] This clownish figure, the governess Charlotta, becomes a kind of presiding deity for the act, as she performs magic tricks, ventril-oquizes, and leads the atmosphere of grotesque gaiety.

After the dancing, the sense of anxiety is established through Varya's concern about paying the musicians, Pishchik's momentary panic over losing his money, and Ranevskaya's explicit fears about the auction. When Ranevskaya is left alone with Trofimov, she reveals the depth of her concern for the estate: "I love this house, without the cherry orchard I couldn't make sense of my life, and if it really has to be sold, then sell me along with the orchard." This statement is Ranevskaya's most passionate expression of her love for the orchard, her identification with it as a symbol of all that is best in her life. Yet the conviction of even this outcry can be questioned. In the introduction to his adaptation of the play, American playwright David Mamet argues that "nobody in the play gives a damn about the cherry orchard."[60] Mamet sees the play as centered on a network of frustrated or distorted sexual relationships. For him, Ranevskaya's primary concern is her lover in Paris. There is plenty of evidence in the play for this view. As Ranevskaya weeps over the orchard and her drowned son, a telegram from Paris falls out of her handbag onto the floor; and it is an argument over the lover that brings the scene to its highest emotional pitch.

Ranevskaya's scene with Trofimov is the longest two-person exchange in the play, and perhaps the most emotional. It ranges across the deepest concerns of both of their lives: Trofimov's relationship with Anya and his professions of being "above love"; his idealistic vision of the future, contrasted with Ranevskaya's concern for the past, and her desire to flee to Paris to look after her invalid lover. When Trofimov challenges her – "he robbed you blind … he's a petty scoundrel, a nobody" – Ranevskaya responds with unprecedented venom, attacking Trofimov's masculinity: "You should act like a man … you're simply a puritan, a funny crackpot, a freak." The scene ends with Trofimov storming off in a rage. Immediately there is a loud offstage crash, and Anya laughingly reports, "Petya fell down the stairs!" This is probably the most extreme example in *The Cherry Orchard* of Chekhov undermining the quasi-tragic tone of the play with an injection of pure farce. Trofimov has made a deliberately grand and theatrical exit ("All is over between us!") and Chekhov literally pulls the rug out from under him. There is a similarly farcical moment shortly afterwards, when Varya accidentally strikes the entering Lopakhin with Firs's stick.

Lopakhin's return sets up the climax of the play, which is expressed in dialogue of tremendous economy and power:

Ranevskaya: *Prodan Vishnyovy Sad?*
Lopakhin: *Prodan.*

Ranevskaya:	*Kto Kupil?*
Lopakhin:	*Ya Kupil.*
Ranevskaya:	Is the cherry orchard sold?
Lopakhin:	Sold.
Ranevskaya:	Who bought it?
Lopakhin:	I bought it.

Ranevskaya slumps against her chair; Varya throws down her keys and goes out. Lopakhin now enters into the long speech that is the apex of his role: a mixture of triumph, shame, sympathy, and rage. "My God, Lord, the cherry orchard's mine!" Exactly what this means to Lopakhin is complex and uncertain, although the element of triumph is unmistakable: "I bought the estate where my grandfather and father were slaves, where they weren't even allowed in the kitchen." The purchase is partly a victory for Lopakhin over his class origins, partly, perhaps, an attempt to raise himself above his brutal peasant father. It is unquestionably a shrewd business move. But it is likely also to be a decisive shift in the complex and sublimated relationship between Lopakhin and Ranevskaya, whom he has perhaps loved since she was a slender young lady washing his bleeding face. Since Lopakhin is convinced, because of his class status, that he can never have her, then perhaps despoiling her beloved orchard will yield him some measure of satisfaction: "Come on everybody, see how Yermolay Lopakhin will swing an axe in the cherry orchard, how the trees'll come tumbling to the ground!"

Almost as soon as he says these words, Lopakhin regrets them. When he addresses Ranevskaya he seems to long for some way beyond their current impossible situation. Chekhov specifies that he speaks through tears: "Oh, if only this were all over quickly, if somehow our ungainly, unhappy life could be changed quickly." Harvey Pitcher argues that these lines are central to the play:

> On a personal level, Lopakhin is trying to reach out to Ranevskaya emotionally, trying very belatedly to bridge the gap between them by looking ahead to a future where this kind of situation could never arise. But the remark is also striking because it is the only occasion in *The Cherry Orchard* where one of the characters manages very briefly to place himself outside the situation in which they all find themselves. [61]

Like Vershinin in *Three Sisters*, and with more conviction than Trofimov, Lopakhin tries to imagine a better life that would redeem their present suffering. But that life will come too late for them; Lopakhin knows it, so he resumes his attitude of triumph, now shot through with self-mocking irony. He orders the musicians to play:

> Let everything be the way I want it! (*Ironically*) Here comes the new
> landlord, the owner of the cherry orchard! (*Accidentally bumps into a
> small table and almost knocks over the candelabrum.*) I can pay for
> everything!

It is Anya alone who can express hope for the future with conviction; she kneels
by her mother and talks of a better life, of planting a new orchard, of the
possibility of joy. Whether Ranevskaya or the audience can share that hope is
one of the major interpretive questions of the play.

Act IV

The setting for the final act makes a powerful visual impression that highlights
the arrival/departure format of the play and the fate that has befallen the
household. The set is the same as in Act I, but it is empty, stripped to the
walls. Chekhov specifies that there are no curtains, no pictures, "*a feeling of
emptiness.*"[62] The act is the shortest in the play; its playing time is just about the
twenty minutes that Lopakhin says they have before the departure to the
station. Concern for catching the train places pressure on the scene and its
few events: the packing, the farewells, the possible engagement of Varya and
Lopakhin, and the final departure.

The first substantial scene of Act IV is a long conversation between
Lopakhin and Trofimov. The two men needle each other in familiar ways
but also seem to show some genuine affection and mutual respect. Though
Trofimov warns Lopakhin that his hopeful plans for the orchard are merely a
form of "arm-waving," he expresses real regard for the peasant-turned-
businessman: "Anyhow, I can't help liking you. You've got delicate, gentle
fingers, like an artist, you've got a delicate, gentle heart." Lopakhin seems to live
up to Trofimov's regard when he comments on his poppy crop; on the one
hand, it made him a lot of money, but its beauty seems to be what he valued
most: "when my poppies bloomed, it was like a picture!" If a production wants
to get the audience to believe in an optimistic ending for *The Cherry Orchard*,
this scene is one place to do it, as the two men of the future, in opposition to
each other throughout the play, grope toward some kind of understanding.
Donald Rayfield calls this exchange "the only prolonged affectionate inter-
change between two characters in all of Chekhov's work."[63] Yet there is still
much cause for doubt; and the conversation is interrupted by the shocking
sound of axes striking the cherry trees. Anya enters, on Ranevskaya's behalf, to
ask Lopakhin to wait to cut down the orchard until they have gone.

The brief exchanges that follow return the play to a mood of haste and
expectation. Surprisingly perhaps, the characters seem to be in a good mood.

Anya is radiant, looking forward to a "new life," and Gaev observes that they have all "cheered up" now that the question of the cherry orchard has been finally settled. Suddenly Pishchik charges in, full of excitement and elation – some Englishmen have found "some kind of white clay" on his land, and he is now rich enough to pay back all his debts. This ironic stroke of fortune keeps the mood elevated until Pishchik realizes they are leaving, and then his boisterous comic persona is subdued to deep emotion.

Ranevskaya again reminds the audience of the time – there are five minutes remaining – and raises the question of whether Firs has been taken to the hospital. Hurrying everyone else out of the room, she makes a final attempt to arrange the Lopakhin/Varya marriage. Lopakhin is left alone, and after stifled laughter and whispering outside the door, Varya enters. In one of Chekhov's most justly famous scenes, Lopakhin and Varya exchange a dozen lines of inconsequential small talk that determines the future direction of their lives.

Varya pretends to look for something in a trunk; they talk about their immediate plans, about the end of life in the house, finally about the weather.

> **Lopakhin:**   Last year by this time it was already snowing, if you remember, but now it's mild, sunny. Except that it's cold … About three degrees of frost.
>
> **Varya:**   I haven't noticed. *Pause.* And besides our thermometer is broken …

Somehow the moment has passed, and when a voice calls for Lopakhin from outside, he hastily leaves, "*as if expecting this call for a long time.*" Lopakhin and Varya will not be married; she sinks to the floor, lays her head on a bundle of clothing, and sobs. Ranevskaya comes in, assesses the situation, and says simply, "We've got to go."

This little scene is an example of Chekhov's intuitive use of the Stanislavskian notion of subtext: there is nothing whatever in the words themselves to indicate the weight of emotion and intention behind them. Indeed, it remains up to the actors to determine at what points Lopakhin might be beginning a tentative overture, at what point he gets cold feet, at what point Varya finally gives up hope (although "our thermometer is broken" has an irresistible sadness about it). Further, the emotional motivations behind the scene are left obscure. How exactly does Varya feel about Lopakhin? Why is he unable to propose? Is it unacknowledged love for Ranevskaya, guilt over having ruined Varya's family, or simply that he finds her unattractive? Chekhov does not tell us, and it is possible that Varya and Lopakhin do not know themselves. In any event, the halting rhythms and impoverished dialogue of the scene, together with its climactic placement in the final act, give it devastating emotional impact.

By now it is time to leave, and the last few moments of the play are a series of farewells to the house. Ranevskaya, taking a last moment to look around the room, seems to see the walls and ceilings for the first time, just as Tusenbach, going to his death in *Three Sisters*, saw the trees as he had never seen them before. Gaev is prevented by his nieces from making a farewell speech, but he produces, in its place, a vivid and affecting memory: "I remember when I was six, on Trinity Sunday I sat in this window and watched my father driving to church." Chekhov leavens this potentially lachrymose moment with insistent and repeated comic touches. Yepikhodov has another misfortune, choking on a glass of water; Varya seems once again about to strike Lopakhin, accidentally; Trofimov finally finds his galoshes; and Gaev goes through his billiards routine. Finally they leave the house.

Harvey Pitcher points out that the characters exit in inverse order of their attachment to the estate.[64] Anya and Trofimov go first, eager to get to the new life. Varya takes a last look around the room and goes out without haste. Lopakhin hurries the others along. Finally Gaev and Ranevskaya are left alone together. These exits are interspersed with a repeated verbal motif, like the choric "They're gone" at the end of *Uncle Vanya*. In this case the repeated phrase is "Let's go," spoken by several characters. Gaev and Ranevskaya share their final, tearful moment in the house but are summoned by Anya and Trofimov's eager cries. They go out, and as far as the audience knows, the play is over.

The stage remains empty as sound effects convey the exodus: doors are locked, carriages leave, an axe is heard on the cherry trees. Then footsteps come from offstage, and Firs shuffles in, looking ill. He tries the door handle – "Locked … Forgot about me" – and after his characteristic worries about Gaev's clothes, he sits and reflects on his existence: "This life's gone by like I ain't lived." As he lies down on the couch, he chides himself with the untranslatable word he has used throughout the play on all those who met with his disapproval: "*Nyedotyopa!*" This word, apparently Chekhov's coinage though its source is debated, has been rendered in English as "good for nothing," "duffer," "nincompoop," and in Senelick's version, "half-baked bungler." With its suggestions of incompetence and incompleteness, it is an appropriate choice for the closing word of the play. It is not, however, the last thing the audience hears before the curtain falls on Chekhov's final work:

> *We hear the distant sound, as if from the sky, the sound of a breaking string, dying away mournfully. Silence ensues, and all we hear far away in the orchard is the thud of an axe on a tree.*

The eerie sound effect of the breaking string is even more charged with meaning than its predecessor in Act II. Heard inside the house, it cannot be ascribed to any natural source. It encompasses the death of Firs, the loss of the Ranevsky estate, the passing away of a whole historical order. It also suggests a final break with the realistic stagecraft of the Moscow Art Theatre, and the nineteenth-century performance tradition within which Chekhov had created his masterpieces. It is hard not to hear in the breaking string, as in Prospero's breaking of his staff at the end of Shakespeare's *The Tempest*, a note of artistic valediction.

Chapter 7

Reception

By the end of his life, Chekhov was recognized as one of Russia's greatest writers of both fiction and drama; in the century following his death, he became one of the most influential figures in world literature. Following the shape of his own career, his international reputation was established first as a writer of fiction, and subsequently as a dramatist; in the past few decades the latter may have eclipsed the former. Chekhov made indelible marks on both literary and dramatic history: the modern short story and the contemporary theatre would not be the same without him.

Because of the nature of Chekhov's work and the history of the twentieth century, the story of Chekhov's reception must be a kind of Cartesian graph, with axes dividing fiction from drama, and East from West; time would add a third dimension. Chekhov's impact as a fiction writer in Britain in the 1930s was very different from his stature as a playwright in Soviet Russia in the same period, and each had changed a generation later. The discussion that follows will try to plot a few points in each quadrant, but it will be necessarily brief and incomplete. Chekhov's influence continues to be felt in new ways in the global literary worlds of the new millennium.

Chekhov in his lifetime

Chekhov was a celebrated writer from the time of his youth. The established fiction writers Dmitri Grigorovich and Nikolai Leskov recognized his gifts early. Grigorovich wrote him encouraging him to take his talent seriously, and Leskov, on a drunken cab ride with Chekhov and his brother, seemed to single out Chekhov as his literary heir, saying, "I shall anoint you with oil as Samuel did David … Write."[1] The Pushkin Prize of 1888 secured his reputation, but his work was not without detractors. The critical orthodoxy in Russian literature, dating from the progressive criticism of Vissarion Belinsky in the 1840s and the populist idealism of the 1860s, was for social activism. Writers were expected to take stands on political issues, exalting the people, resisting oppression, and providing a positive program for Russia's social advancement. Liberal critics found Chekhov's work insufficiently committed; at the same time, critics on the Right condemned him for pessimism. The Populist critic Nikolai Mikhailovsky in 1890 recognized Chekhov's talent but felt he squandered it on formless, apparently unfinished work like "The Steppe"; he also condemned Chekhov's apparent lack of ideals. The same year Chekhov was chastised in *Russian Thought* as a "high priest … of unprincipled writing" (April 10, 1890), provoking him to write an uncharacteristic rebuke to the editor, Vukol Lavrov. Chekhov won this round; in future years Lavrov would publish many of Chekhov's important stories in *Russian Thought*.

As mentioned in Chapter 2, two of Russia's greatest writers, Tolstoy and Gorky, were friends and supporters of Chekhov, though each willfully misread him according to his own outlook. Tolstoy's essay on Chekhov's "The Darling" (1898) is a case in point. "The Darling" is a humorous, gently satirical story about a young woman named Olenka whose malleable personality accommodates itself completely to the various men in her life. While married to a theatre manager, she throws herself into the entertainment world; with her second husband, a lumber merchant, she becomes very interested in wood; after his death, she takes up with a veterinarian and is always making proclamations about the health of horses. Tolstoy wrote that Chekhov, while meaning to ridicule Olenka for her shallowness, actually revealed the loving qualities of what Tolstoy saw as an ideally feminine woman: "He, like Balaam, intended to curse, but the god of poetry forbade him, and commanded him to bless."[2] At other times, Tolstoy found fault with Chekhov for his amoral attitudes toward sexual love, which Tolstoy had renounced as degrading. Tolstoy condemned the lovers in "The Lady with the Little Dog" as Nietzschian and bestial.

Maxim Gorky admired Chekhov greatly, and the two met and corresponded often during Chekhov's later years. Gorky was much more of a politically committed, activist writer than Chekhov, but he sought the elder author's literary advice and praised his works highly. Writing to Chekhov after reading

"The Lady with the Little Dog," Gorky said that Chekhov was "killing realism." He evidently meant this both as praise for Chekhov's talent and as eagerness to dispense with what he saw as an outmoded technique:

> That form has outlived its time. It's a fact! No one after you can go any further on that path; no one can write so simply about simple things as you can. After reading the most insignificant of your stories everything else seems coarse, written not with a pen but with a fence post.[3]

Gorky wrote reminiscences of Chekhov that recalled him as a gentle and tolerant soul, but also invested him with some of Gorky's own hatred of bourgeois idleness. Gorky imagined a parade of Chekhov's characters, describing them in harsher terms than Chekhov himself ever did: "slaves of their love, of their stupidity and idleness, of their greed for the good things in life."[4] To this "dreary, gray crowd of helpless people," Gorky imagined Chekhov appearing, "a great, wise and observant man":

> With a sad smile, with a tone of gentle but deep reproach, with anguish in his face and in his heart, in a beautiful and sincere voice, he said to them: "You live badly, my friends. It is a shame to live like that."

While Chekhov may not have shared Gorky's political fervor, he clearly liked and respected the younger writer. When, in 1902, Gorky was removed from the Russian Academy of Sciences for political reasons, Chekhov resigned in protest.

After his death in 1904, Chekhov was lionized as a great Russian writer, but the misunderstandings and criticisms continued. The Symbolist writer Dmitri Merezhkovsky felt that Chekhov's works expressed the bankruptcy of the intelligentsia and a gloomily static view of ordinary Russian life, or "*byt*": "Chekhovian *byt* is the bare present, without past or future, only a frozen, motionless moment, a dead stop in contemporary Russian life, without any link to world history or world culture."[5] Lev Shestov, an important Russian philosopher of Existentialism, similarly called Chekhov the "poet of hopelessness." In a fascinating and provocative essay entitled "Creation from the Void," Shestov interpreted Chekhov as a morbid, despairing author who "during all the years of his literary activity … was doing one thing alone: by one means or another he was killing human hopes."[6] In Shestov's view, Chekhov always puts his characters "in such a situation that only one thing is left for them – to fall down and beat their heads against the floor." Shestov's essay focuses on "A Boring Story," "The Duel," *Ivanov*, and *Uncle Vanya* and makes illuminating remarks about all of them, but he fails to come to terms with the full range of Chekhov's work, notably his comic sensibility, spiritual resilience, and feeling for the natural world. In casting him as a philosopher of despair, Shestov, like many subsequent critics, to some degree remade Chekhov in his own image.

Chekhov's emergence abroad

Less than a decade after Chekhov's death, his plays were performed in translation in various Western countries, though it was only with the Moscow Art Theatre tours of the 1920s that his reputation as a playwright was secured. The most important early translations of Chekhov into English were by George Calderon, who, as an introduction, wrote a sensitive appreciation of Chekhov's dramatic technique. Calderon recognized that Chekhov's style was markedly different from the drama familiar to English playgoers; and indeed, this unfamiliarity led to the failure of the first several English-language productions. In trying to characterize Chekhov's style of playwriting, Calderon described it as "centrifugal," focusing our minds not so much on the characters and their actions as outward, on "the larger process of the world which those events illuminate." For Calderon, the resulting experience is both more distanced and more profound than identification with individual characters:

> … the sentiments to be aroused by the doings and sufferings of the personages on his stage are not so much hope and fear for their individual fortunes as pity and amusement at the importance which they set on them, and consolation for their particular tragedies in the spectacle of the general comedy of Life in which they are all merged.[7]

Calderon recognized that the nature of Chekhov's dramaturgy, with its emphasis on the ensemble rather than a few lead characters, would require a new style of acting. The English stage, still governed by the Victorian tradition of star actor-managers, to whose declamations the bit players would necessarily defer, was unprepared for the very different texture of Chekhov's drama: "His disjunctive manner is defeated of its purpose unless the whole company keep continuously alive; and each line is so unmistakably colored with the character of its speaker that there is no need for the rest to hold their breath and 'point' that we may know who utters it."[8] It would take several years for the London theatre to make this adjustment, though eventually Chekhov became a staple of the British stage.

Initially, Chekhov's biggest influence abroad came as a prose writer. The publication of Constance Garnett's translations, in thirteen volumes beginning in 1916, brought Chekhov's fiction to the reading public in Britain. Virginia Woolf's response summarized the difficulties readers had with Chekhov, as well as the value many came to see in his subtle stories. "Our first impressions of Chekhov are not of simplicity but of bewilderment. What is the point of it, and why does he make a story out of this? we ask as we read story after story."[9] She dwelt in particular on Chekhov's endings, which the reader may be tempted to dismiss as "inconclusive" but which, in Woolf's view, are therefore truer to the flux of experience. "We need a very daring and alert sense of literature to make us hear the tune, and in particular those last notes which complete the harmony."[10] Completing her musical metaphor, which she often employed with Chekhov, Woolf predicted that while he might have a hard time finding a readership in Britain, those who made the effort would be well rewarded:

> This may not be the way to catch the ear of the public; after all, they are used to louder music, fiercer measures; but as the tune sounded so he has written it. In consequence, as we read these little stories about nothing at all, the horizon widens; the soul gains an astonishing sense of freedom.[11]

Woolf's own work bears Chekhov's influence clearly, and she became one of his most enthusiastic advocates in the anglophone world. In *Virginia Woolf and the Russian Point of View*, Roberta Rubenstein argues that "As she taught herself how to read Chekhov, Woolf educated readers who were bewildered by the absence of expected narrative cues in his fiction."[12] One of her most important literary essays, "Modern Novels" – later retitled "Modern Fiction," perhaps, Rubenstein suggests, because of the importance Woolf accorded the non-novelist Chekhov – features a discussion of Chekhov's unique style in the story "Gusev." Woolf focuses on the absence of traditional plot in the story, as well as Chekhov's use of the surprising and significant point of emphasis, the telling detail, which became a feature of her own fiction as well:

> The emphasis is laid in such unexpected places that at first it seems as if there were no emphasis at all; and then, as the eyes accustom themselves to twilight and discern the shapes of things in a room, we see how complete the story is, how profound, and how truly in obedience to his vision Chekhov has chosen this, that and the other, and placed them together to compose something new. But it is impossible to say that this is humorous or tragic, or even that it is proper to call the whole a short story, since the writer seems careless of brevity and intensity, and leaves us with the suggestion that the strange chords he has struck sound on and on.[13]

Other British writers who praised Chekhov or showed his influence were E. M. Forster, John Middleton Murry, and especially Katherine Mansfield, who paid him the compliment of virtual plagiarism with some of her stories, notably

"The Child-Who-Was-Tired," which is a reworking of "Sleepy." James Joyce's stories are often compared to Chekhov's, though Joyce claimed not to have read Chekhov when he wrote *Dubliners*.[14] The stories in *Dubliners* are certainly analogous to those of Chekhov, in their evocation of characters' lives through apparently mundane incidents that contain moments of spiritual illumination. Gabriel Conroy's climactic realization, in "The Dead," of "how poor a part he had played" in his wife's life recalls the recognitions in Chekhov stories such as "Sorrow" and "Rothschild's Fiddle," and Joyce's characteristic conflation of the everyday and the epiphanic is similar to Chekhov's.

The MAT tours of the 1920s helped establish Chekhov's drama outside Russia, playing in Berlin, Paris, and New York. A number of Russian émigré actors and theatre artists helped create successful productions of Chekhov in translation in various Western capitals. Georges Pitoëff in Paris, Theodore Kommisarjevsky in London, and Peter Sharoff in Milan all staged Chekhov's plays, influencing not only contemporary tastes in the theatre but a generation of new writers who responded to Chekhov's understated naturalism and subtle poetry. The impact was particularly great in the United States. American Method acting flourished as an outgrowth of Stanislavsky's productions, nourished by Russian exiles who became successful actors and teachers, such as Richard Boleslavsky and Chekhov's nephew Michael Chekhov. Writers like Tennessee Williams and Arthur Miller incorporated Chekhov's influence into their poignant family dramas. Homegrown productions soon became popular, and by the mid twentieth century Chekhov was established in the international dramatic repertoire.

The Soviet era

Despite the tremendous political and cultural upheavals of the early twentieth century, Chekhov never really lost his central place in Russian literature and drama. The balance, complexity, and ambiguity of his art – stating problems without solving them, concentrating on the suggestive detail rather than the sweeping statement – left his work open to varying interpretations; and this openness helped ensure its survival during the storms of revolution and repression. In the realm of drama, for instance, the Moscow Art Theatre developed more optimistic productions of Chekhov's plays after the 1917 October Revolution, stressing the positive messages about the future expressed by characters like Vershinin, Trofimov, and Lopakhin. Other theatres, finding the MAT staid and retrograde in the heady years of theatrical experimentation that followed the Revolution, took a more radical approach to Chekhov's work.

The Leningrad Comedy Theatre experimented with a farcical *Cherry Orchard* in 1926; Andrey Lobanov directed the same play a few years later as a vicious, cartoonish satire on the doomed bourgeoisie. The greatest avant-garde directors of the time, Yevgeny Vakhtangov and Vsevolod Meyerhold, turned to Chekhov's vaudevilles as the most effective material for their dynamic and politicized theatre. Meyerhold directed a famous production combining *The Jubilee*, *The Bear*, and *The Proposal* into an evening entitled *33 Swoons*, exaggerating the neurasthenic paralysis of Chekhov's self-centered vaudeville protagonists. In Chekhov's day Meyerhold had been a young star of the MAT, creating the roles of Treplyov and Tusenbach, but he came to feel that Stanislavky's style was too conservative and old-fashioned for the times; he called instead for "an October Revolution in the Theatre." Ironically, with the rise of Stalin and the establishment of "Socialist Realism" as the official policy of Soviet art, it was Stanislavsky's approach, rather than Meyerhold's, that won out. Lenin and Stalin were both fans of the MAT and its Chekhov productions. Stanislavsky was named a People's Artist of the USSR and given a state funeral at his death in 1938, while Meyerhold, falling foul of the authorities, was arrested and executed.

Soviet literary critics looked for the proto-revolutionary in Chekhov. While some continued to find fault with his lack of social activism or derided him as a relic of the bourgeois intelligentsia, many rehabilitated him as a prophet of the Revolution. Progressive social messages, like Misail's critique of capitalism in "My Life" or Sasha's concern for the working class in "The Fiancée," were duly noted. Mikhail Koltsov, in 1928, called Chekhov "a socially conscious writer of the highest order, a bold and merciless satirist of the epoch preceding ours."[15] Not all Soviet critics concentrated on the political dimensions of Chekhov, however. The Russian Formalists, critics more concerned with poetic language and literary structure than social context, also valued Chekhov and provided some important analysis of his fiction. Viktor Shklovsky, in his landmark 1925 volume *Theory of Prose*, details Chekhov's innovative techniques of construction, focusing especially on the early stories, which previous critics had tended to dismiss for their lack of seriousness. Shklovsky wrote, "It is high time for Chekhov not only to be republished but reexamined as well. Everyone who does so will surely admit that his most popular stories are also the most formally perfect."[16] With reference to the anti-climactic, inconclusive endings frequently used by Maupassant and Chekhov, Shklovsky borrowed from linguistics the term "zero ending," which has since been a regular feature of discussions of Chekhov's prose.

Another critic who examined the formal features of Chekhov's fiction was Avram Derman. In a book published in 1929, Derman was critical of Chekhov's

detachment and the apparent formlessness of his stories, reading these ideologi-
cally as responses to the pre-revolutionary world in which he lived. In subsequent
decades, however, Derman undertook a more sustained structural analysis
of Chekhov's prose, published posthumously in 1959 as *On Chekhov's
Craftsmanship.* Derman pointed out the increasing severity with which
Chekhov cut unneeded exposition from the beginning of his stories, depending
on "the active reader" to "reconstruct what was most important in the hero's past
life" through "a skillfully depicted present."[17] The second structural element
Derman explored was the economical development of a theme through the
selection of specific "signposts," as in the story "Ionych," in which the doctor-
hero's worldly prosperity and moral decline are charted through references to his
means of transport: first walking on house-calls, then acquiring horses, a coach-
man, a troika, and so forth. Derman paid particular attention to the endings of
Chekhov's stories, and his movement from the surprise ending of his early works
toward more open-ended conclusions. Building on the work of A. G. Gornfeld,
Derman pointed out how many of the later stories end when the protagonist has
begun to reflect in response to the events of the story: "the thoughts and reflections
of the hero are a projection of the presumed thoughts of the reader."[18] The heroes
of "The Student," "The Lady with the Dog," and "The Fiancée" are among those
Derman cited as "beginning to think" at the ends of their stories.

A similarly Formalist study, entitled *Chekhov's Art: A Stylistic Analysis,* was
published in Bulgaria by Peter Bitsilli in 1942, though it probably had its
greatest influence outside the Soviet Union, after the publication of a
German translation in 1966. Bitsilli eschewed the historical/sociological tendency of Soviet criticism, focusing instead on the stylistic and structural
elements of impressionism, laconicism, and musicality. Bitsilli particularly
noted the impersonal way in which impressions of the world seem to take
hold of the Chekhovian protagonist. Defending Chekhov against the usual
charges of not having a "worldview," Bitsilli asserted that Chekhov's worldview
is contained in his impressionistic style:

> Something flashes by, enters our field of vision, image after image, and
> then slides away; these flashes and disappearances, which arouse anxiety
> and spiritual tension, are followed by a catharsis – a resolution through
> the fusion "of all this" into something whole which points to ("it seemed")
> an inexpressible truth, to a fulfillment and completion in a another plane
> of reality.[19]

The epiphanic moments in stories like "The Bishop," with the spiritual regeneration that accompanies the Bishop's release into death, correspond clearly to
Bitsilli's analysis.

A. P. Chudakov's important study *Chekhov's Poetics* was published in 1971. Using a statistical analysis, Chudakov divided Chekhov's stories into three periods, each with a distinctive approach to narration. In the early period, up to 1887, there tends to be either a first-person narrator or a subjective narrative voice that intervenes in the story to comment and make value judgments. In the second period, 1888–94, the narrator is objective, but the story is often suffused, though free indirect discourse, with the thoughts and speech-patterns of a protagonist, such as Olga in "The Grasshopper" or the Doctor in "Ward No. 6." The stories of the final phase, such as "In the Ravine," tend to have an interplay of subjective and objective elements. The perceptions of a character like Lipa are included, but not in the terms she would be capable of articulating. The subjective narrative voice returns more strongly in these stories, sometimes speaking on behalf of the characters. Further, the narrative voice is less likely to be associated with a single hero, but rather to encompass a range of perspectives while still maintaining its own independent stance.

The range and sophistication of approaches like those of Derman, Bitsilli, and Chudakov make evident that there was no single, monolithic "Soviet" manner of interpreting Chekhov, and that in spite of ideological pressures, Russian readers continued to engage with his works in evolving ways throughout the twentieth century.

Chekhov on the world stage

By the mid twentieth century Chekhov's plays were recognized as classics of world drama and were consequently opened up to a range of new theatrical interpretations. While the decades following Chekhov's death were dominated by the performances of Stanislavsky's Moscow Art Theatre, which defined Chekhov's theatrical identity both in Russia and the West, the years after World War II showed the world a new Chekhov. The rise of the director as *auteur* led to innovative and contemporary reworkings of Chekhov's plays, along with those of other "classic" authors like Shakespeare, Molière, and the Greeks. The development of a vigorous new non-naturalistic drama helped theatres and audiences to find in Chekhov elements other than the meticulous depictions of pre-revolutionary life that Stanislavsky's productions had provided. In the theatre of Brecht, Beckett, Pirandello, and Pinter, many new Chekhovs were suddenly possible.

One such production was Jean-Louis Barrault's of *The Cherry Orchard* in Paris in 1954. Barrault's understanding of the play as chiefly concerned with the process of time gave the production an unusual rhythm and a quality of universality. The chief theatrical exponent of the spiritual verse-dramas of Paul Claudel, Barrault found in *The Cherry Orchard* a poignant philosophy that transcended the historical contingencies of its composition. Barrault declared *The Cherry Orchard* Chekhov's masterpiece because of all his plays, "this is the one which comes closest to universality and to generalizations which embrace all men."[20] He observed that "It is a play about the passing of time; therefore whether the characters are Russian or Japanese does not matter. Like some plays of Shakespeare and Molière it is a play which has universal value and which belongs to all mankind."[21] Using stylized settings, evocative lighting, and delicately shaded performances, Barrault created a *Cherry Orchard* that spoke to a French public still wrestling with the existential aftermath of the war. Barrault's wife Madeleine Renaud played Madame Ranevskaya as an emblem of universal humanity, weak but generous, fallen but still full of love. Gaev, Lopakhin, and Trofimov were representatives of, respectively, the past, present, and future. Barrault himself played Trofimov, in an essentially optimistic production that recognized the necessity of breaking with the past.

Another landmark *Cherry Orchard* came from the Italian director Giorgio Strehler in Milan in 1974. For this production, Strehler and his designer came up with a revolutionary setting that eschewed realism in favor of an abstract setting of breathtaking beauty. The orchard was evoked by an almost entirely white design, with a steeply raked platform over which was suspended a gauzy and voluminous white veil filled with thousands of paper petals, which swayed and drifted and occasionally fluttered down onto actors and audience – like snow, falling blossoms or autumn leaves, depending on the act and season. Strehler's production, bearing influences as diverse as Brecht, Pirandello, and *commedia dell'arte*, was complex and multilayered. Strehler saw the play as existing simultaneously at three levels, which he defined as reality, history, and life itself. While the performers' interactions carefully evoked the play's emotional nuances and social relations, Strehler also included theatrical flourishes that placed the action in a more timeless, symbolic perspective. At the play's end, all of the characters, at the same moment, swept dark cloaks and overcoats over their white costumes, "as if angels of death had flung their black wings over the living," and then moved slowly off the stage.[22] The white veil descended, scattering the paper petals like dead leaves over Firs, the stage, and the audience. While at the level of history Strehler acknowledged the necessary passing of the Ranevskys' world, at the level of life he mourned the inevitable vanquishing of beauty by time.

Theatrical reevaluations of Chekhov were not limited to the West. In Soviet countries, directors were also eager to shake off the dominance of the Stanislavsky productions, which in some cases ran for decades with the original sets and some of the original actors (Olga Knipper played Ranevskaya for nearly forty years, until she was in her seventies). Three key productions of *Three Sisters* illustrate changing Russian approaches to the play.

In 1940, Nemirovich-Danchenko, at the age of eighty-three, re-directed the play for the Moscow Art Theatre. In accordance with Soviet values, the production was optimistic, built around the notion of "yearning for life," and ending with a positive image of the sisters facing the future: Chebutykin's caustic cynicism was cut from the finale. Yet the production was not simply socialist propaganda, but a thorough reinvention that infused the play with life; Laurence Senelick has said it "may well have been the greatest staging of a Chekhov play in the history of the Art Theatre."[23] The Prozorovs, and especially the soldiers, were not enervated idlers but heroic idealists thwarted by circumstance, played by an outstanding ensemble of actors. Their energy and sensitivity was matched in the set, which used soaring vertical elements – windows and birch trees – and radiant lighting to lift the spirits of wartime audiences. The production blew the cobwebs and gloom off the play and filled it with air and light.

Twenty-five years later, at the tail end of the Krushchev "thaw," Georgy Tovstonogov directed another reevaluation of *Three Sisters* at Leningrad's Gorky Theatre. This production took a more critical look at the characters. As Tovstonogov put it, in the 1940 Nemirovich production "fine and noble people were victimized by the times and the social order," whereas for him it was important "to assert that it is not something or someone from the outside that destroys, but that the Chekhovian characters themselves – intelligent, subtle, suffering people – destroy one another by their own passivity and irresolution."[24] His production was accordingly complex and shifting in tone, employing a stagecraft that allowed both sympathy with the characters and moments of Brechtian critical distance. Tostonogov achieved this by enlisting the devices of the cinema, using lighting, mobile scenic elements, and monochromatic designs to create the effects of close-ups and wide-angle shots at different points during the play. Convinced that "today's Chekhov will not tolerate one stage second wasted on the reproduction of everyday detail,"[25] Tostonogov created an epic production that called the play's characters to account.

As the thaw gave way to stagnation under Brezhnev, Anatoly Efros, an *enfant terrible* of the Russian theatre, produced a very different *Three Sisters* in Moscow. The bitterness of its concept was evident in its barren set, dominated by a lifeless metal tree with gilt leaves. The production reversed the usual sympathies, making the Prozorovs nasty, selfish, and petty while Natasha and Solyony were polite and intelligent. The Baron's longing for work was made absurdly ironic. The cynical Chebutykin was the presiding genius of the production. His Act III monologue was preceded by a grotesque and clownish dance: "Jerking and writhing like a marionette plugged into an electric socket, he expressed the *intelligent*'s despair and self-contempt at being unable to improve anything or break through the circle of lies."[26] The production touched a nerve with the frustrated Moscow public and became an immediate sensation, but the Soviet authorities quickly moved to shut it down.

Postmodern Chekhov

In the final decades of the twentieth century and the first of the new millennium, Chekhov's impact worldwide continued to spread. With the breakup of the Soviet Union in 1991, Chekhov's star waned briefly in the Russian theatre, while directors eagerly performed glasnost-era playwrights like Alexander Galin and Lyudmila Petrushevskaya, or writers like Mikhail Bulgakov who had been previously banned. Soon, however, theatres in Russia and the former Soviet states began to reclaim Chekhov, often in radical new stagings. One of the most celebrated theatre artists of the post-Soviet period, Kama Ginkas, has created exuberant, expressionist versions of Chekhov stories, including "The Black Monk," "Rothschild's Fiddle," and "The Lady with the Little Dog." While filled with theatrical vitality, these productions embody a reading of Chekhov that is essentially tragic. "In each of these productions Ginkas stripped away the clichés that cling to Chekhov and bared the working mechanisms of art and humanity both," wrote John Freedman in the *Moscow Times*. "Each of these pieces was in its own way a gauntlet thrown at God."[27] Ginkas's performances contain Chekhovian narrative and dialogue mixed with dynamic and sometimes incongruous stage action. In "The Lady with the Little Dog," for instance, the lovers are accompanied by two Beckettian clowns in old-style bathing suits who stand in for the Yalta populace and help create the physical action of the story. Ginkas's productions have been seen all over the world, both in Russian and translation, and have challenged the distinction between Chekhovian fiction and drama.

  Chekhov production worldwide has created an unprecedented array of stagings, making Chekhov one of the most frequently revived authors in world theatre and placing his works in new and surprising cultural and performance contexts. *The Seagull* has been reset in rural Ireland by Thomas Kilroy; *The Cherry Orchard* was adapted by Janet Suzman to post-apartheid South Africa. In New York, *Three Sisters* was deconstructed by The Wooster Group into *Brace Up!*, a collage mixing live performance and various electronic media. Among the numerous movie versions of Chekhov, *Uncle Vanya* has been filmed in settings as diverse as Wales (*August*), Australia (*Country Life*) and a run-down theatre off Times Square (*Vanya on 42nd Street*). In the late 1980s in Japan, Suzuki Tadashi combined Chekhov's last three plays into a ninety-minute performance entitled *The Chekhov* that incorporated conventions of Noh drama and Beckettian absurdism. Like Shakespeare, Chekhov has become a kind of touchstone against which divergent cultures can test their perceptions and preoccupations. The extraordinary range of performances Chekhov's work has inspired has been documented in recent criticism focusing on production, most notably in Laurence Senelick's landmark overview *The Chekhov Theatre: A Century of the Plays in Performance*.

Chekhov's impact on the writing of short fiction is probably unparalleled. Modern masters of the short story like Eudora Welty, John Cheever, William Trevor, and Alice Munro plainly reveal Chekhov's influence; Welty and Cheever both wrote essays on their relation to Chekhov's work. Modern authors have often engaged directly with their debt to Chekhov through their own writing. Joyce Carol Oates's story "The Lady with the Pet Dog" riffs on Chekhov's story of adultery from a modern feminist perspective. Raymond Carver, often considered one of the most "Chekhovian" of modern writers, paid Chekhov an eerie act of literary acknowledgment. His final story, "Errand," written just months before the end of his life, is a fictionalized account of Chekhov's death.

The fragmentation of any single, unitary view of Chekhov, a characteristic response of postmodernism to any canonical author, was hastened by the 1991 breakup of the Soviet Union and the accessibility of previously restricted archives. The publication of Donald Rayfield's biography *Anton Chekhov* in 1997, and Rosamund Bartlett's collection of unexpurgated letters in 2004, gave English-language readers new perspectives on many dimensions of Chekhov's life. The Rayfield biography in particular, with its emphasis on Chekhov's affairs with women and his sometimes callous behavior toward them, challenged the saintly view of the writer that previous biographers, and Soviet publicists, had promulgated. But the more complex and conflicted Chekhov that emerges from these new sources remains a remarkable if elusive personality.

Among the wealth of recent books on Chekhov, Michael Finke's psychoanalytic study *Seeing Chekhov: Life and Art* (2005) is one of the most significant, using biographical materials to explore the mind of the writer. Finke traces the notions of seeing and being seen – both literally and metaphorically – in Chekhov's life and works. He examines how Chekhov's medical background affected both his perspective as a writer and his own reluctance to acknowledge his tuberculosis. Finke notes the importance of seeing in many Chekhov works, as well as the author's ambivalence toward his status as a public figure. *Seeing Chekhov* helps account for the elusiveness of Chekhov while illuminating many aspects of his work.

Other recent studies of Chekhov have used a wide range of critical approaches. Robert Louis Jackson's collection *Reading Chekhov's Text* provides readings by several contemporary scholars of fourteen of Chekhov's short stories.[28] Julie de Sherbinin, in *Chekhov and Russian Religious Culture* (1997), examines the paradigm of the two Marys – the saintly virgin mother and the repentant harlot – as expressed across various Chekhov works. Other religious or archetypal elements that have been identified in Chekhov's works include the St. George myth and the classical journey to the underworld. Vladimir Kataev's *If Only We Could Know!*, condensed by Harvey Pitcher from a number of works by this influential Russian critic, explores Chekhov's stories (and plays) of discovery, in which central characters have to radically shift their perceptions of the world. Cathy Popkin's *The Pragmatics of Insignificance* places Chekhov's emphasis on the trivialities of life within a literary context encompassing his forebear Gogol and his follower Mikhail Zoshchenko.[29] Donald Rayfield's comprehensive *Understanding Chekhov* traces the many links between Chekhov's fiction and his drama.

Among recent studies of Chekhov's plays, *The Cambridge Companion to Chekhov*, edited by Vera Gottlieb and Paul Allain, incorporates a range of important perspectives, including those of actors and directors involved with Chekhov production. David Allen's *Performing Chekhov* and Peta Tait's *Performing Emotions* both explore the relationship of Chekhov's texts to their theatrical interpreters.[30] John Tulloch, in *Shakespeare and Chekhov in Production and Reception*, considers the cultural meanings that surround recent Chekhov performances.[31] A number of older studies of Chekhov's drama remain valuable touchstones. Robert Brustein's *The Theatre of Revolt* puts Chekhov in the context of other revolutionary modern dramatists like Ibsen, Brecht, and Pirandello.[32] The studies of the major plays by David Magarshack, Maurice Valency, Harvey Pitcher, Richard Peace, and Richard Gilman all provide valuable insights into Chekhov's dramatic technique.[33]

Notes

Preface

1. "The Lady with the Little Dog," in Richard Pevear and Larissa Volokhonsky, trans., *Stories* (New York: Bantam, 2000), 366.
2. Ivan Bunin, *About Chekhov: The Unfinished Symphony*, trans. Thomas Gaiton Marullo (Evanston, IL: Northwestern University Press, 2007), 21.

1 Life

1. Charles W. Meister, *Chekhov Criticism: 1880 through 1986* (Jefferson, NC: McFarland, 1988), 5.
2. Rosamund Bartlett, ed., *Anton Chekhov: A Life in Letters*, trans. Rosamund Bartlett and Anthony Phillips (London: Penguin, 2004), 175. Unless otherwise noted, references to Chekhov's letters are from this edition and are cited in the text by date.
3. In Julie de Sherbinin, *Chekhov and Russian Religious Culture: The Poetics of the Marian Paradigm* (Evanston, IL: Northwestern University Press, 1997), 4.
4. From an account of his life he sent to a fellow doctor, Grigory Rossolimo, October 11, 1899.
5. Donald Rayfield, *Anton Chekhov: A Life* (Evanston, IL: Northwestern University Press, 1997), 130.
6. Letter to Anatoly Koni, January 26, 1891. Chekhov included the same conversation in his report on Sakhalin.
7. Rayfield, *Anton Chekhov*, 394.
8. Vladimir Nemirovich-Danchenko, letter to Chekhov, April 25, 1898, in Rayfield, *Anton Chekhov*, 457.
9. Nemirovich-Danchenko, letter to Chekhov, May 12, 1898, in Rayfield, *Anton Chekhov*, 457.
10. Letter to Suvorin, September 1898, in Rayfield, *Anton Chekhov*, 461–62.
11. Maxim Gorky, letter to Chekhov, November 1898, in *Reminiscences* (New York: Pursuit Press, 1946), 87.
12. Laurence Senelick, from Anton Chekhov, *The Complete Plays* (New York: Norton, 2006), 875.

13. Anton Chekhov, letter to Olga Knipper, March 29, 1904, in Ronald Hingley, trans. and ed., *The Oxford Chekhov*, Vol. III (London: Oxford University Press, 1964), 330.

14. Janet Malcolm, *Reading Chekhov: A Critical Journey* (New York: Random House, 2002), 62.

15. Maxim Gorky, *Reminiscences of Anton Chekhov*, trans. S. S. Koteliansky and Leonard Woolf, in *Reminiscences*, 84.

2 Chekhov in context

1. Laurence Senelick, *Anton Chekhov: The Complete Plays* (New York: Norton, 2006), 1029.

2. Ronald Hingley, from *Russian Writers and Society, 1825–1904*, excerpted in Eugene Bristol, ed., *Anton Chekhov's Plays* (New York: Norton, 1977), 226.

3. "Peasants," in Constance Garnett, trans., *The Tales of Chekhov*, 13 vols. (1915–22; New York: Ecco, 2006), Vol. VI, 326.

4. Orlando Figes, *Natasha's Dance: A Cultural History of Russia* (New York: Picador, 2002), 256.

5. In Laurence Senelick, trans. and ed., *Anton Chekhov's Selected Plays* (New York: Norton, 2005), 453.

6. Letter to Pleshcheyev, February 15, 1890.

7. Simon Karlinsky and Michael Henry Heim, *Chekhov's Life and Thought: Selected Letters and Commentary* (1973; Evanston, IL: Northwestern University Press, 1997), 375.

8. Laurence Senelick, *The Chekhov Theatre: A Century of the Plays in Performance* (Cambridge: Cambridge University Press, 1997), 11.

9. November 24, 1899.

10. Maurice Valency, *The Breaking String: The Plays of Anton Chekhov* (Oxford: Oxford University Press, 1966), 249.

11. Martin Esslin, "Chekhov and the Modern Drama," in Toby W. Clyman, ed., *A Chekhov Companion* (Westport, CT: Greenwood Press, 1985), 142.

3 Early stories

1. In Avram Derman, "Structural Features in Chekhov's Poetics," in Thomas A. Eekman, ed., *Critical Essays on Anton Chekhov* (Boston: Hall, 1989), 235.

2. "Fat and Thin," Garnett, Vol. XIII, 275.

3. "Small Fry," Pevear and Volokhonsky, *Stories*, 8.

4. "A Chameleon," Garnett, Vol. XII, 207.

5. Ronald Hingley, *A New Life of Anton Chekhov* (New York: Knopf, 1976), 59.

6. "The Malefactor," Garnett, Vol. XII, 275.

7. Viktor Shklovsky, *Theory of Prose* (Moscow 1929), trans. Benjamin Sher (Normal, IL: Dalkey Archive Press, 1990).
8. Senelick, *Selected Plays*, xxviii.
9. "Boots," Garnett, Vol. XI, 186.
10. "Nerves," Garnett, Vol. XIII, 240.
11. "Overdoing It," Garnett, Vol. XI, 257.
12. "A Work of Art," Garnett, Vol. XIII, 241.
13. "In the Dark," Garnett, Vol. XI, 97.
14. "The Marshal's Widow," Garnett, Vol. XI, 154.
15. "Grisha," Garnett, Vol. XII, 47–53.
16. "The Cook's Wedding," Garnett, Vol. XII, 10.
17. "A Trifle from Life," Garnett, Vol. IV, 336.
18. Vladimir Kataev, *If Only We Could Know!*, trans. and ed. Harvey Pitcher (Chicago: Ivan R. Dee, 2002), 12.
19. "An Incident," Garnett, Vol. XII, 95–104.
20. "Kashtanka," Garnett, Vol. XII, 173–204.
21. "Vanka," Pevear and Volokhonsky, *Stories*, 45–48.
22. "Sleepy," Pevear and Volokhonsky, *Stories*, 49–54.
23. To Lydia Avilova, March 19, 1892 and April 29, 1892.
24. "Sorrow," Garnett, Vol. IX, 141–51.
25. "Misery," Garnett, Vol. IX, 55–65.
26. "Anyuta," Pevear and Volokhonsky, *Stories*, 27–31.
27. Shklovsky, *Theory of Prose*, 57.
28. "A Gentleman Friend," Garnett, Vol. VIII, 277–84.
29. "The Chorus Girl," Garnett, Vol. VIII, 1–11.
30. "The Huntsman," Pevear and Volokhonsky, *Stories*, 9–13.
31. "Agafya," Garnett, Vol. VI, 115–32.
32. "A Misfortune," Garnett, Vol. IV, 303–27.
33. "Mire," Garnett, Vol. II, 193–224.
34. Ronald Wilks, trans. and ed., *The Steppe and Other Stories* (London: Penguin, 2001), 359.
35. "The Steppe," in Richard Pevear and Larissa Volokhonsky, trans., *Anton Chekhov: The Complete Short Novels* (London: Everyman, 2004), 7. All further citations are from this edition, and page references are given in parentheses in the text.
36. William Wordsworth, "Lines Composed a Few Miles Above Tintern Abbey," line 91.

4 Early plays

1. Trans. Senelick, *Complete Plays*, 273. Unless otherwise specified, all citations from Chekhov's plays are from this edition, and page references are given in parentheses in the text.
2. Senelick, *Complete Plays*, 415.

3. Henri Bergson, "Laughter," in Wiley Sypher, ed., *Comedy* (New York: Anchor, 1956), 84.
4. Vera Gottlieb, *Chekhov and the Vaudeville* (Cambridge: Cambridge University Press, 1982), 191.
5. December 30, 1888, Senelick, *Selected Plays*, 395.
6. Donald Rayfield, *Understanding Chekhov* (London: Bristol Classical Press, 1988), 83.
7. Ibid., 84.
8. Ibid., 89.
9. *The Actor*, No. 6, 1890. Quoted in Rayfield, *Understanding Chekhov*, 90.
10. Letter to Urusov, October 16, 1899, in Avrahm Yarmolinsky, ed., *Letters of Anton Chekhov* (New York: Viking, 1973), 353.
11. December 2, 1896, in Senelick, *Selected Plays*, 419.

5 Later stories

1. Quoted in Richard Pevear, "Introduction," Pevear and Volokhonsky, *Complete Short Novels*, xiv.
2. "A Boring Story," Pevear and Volokhonsky, *Stories*, 55. The page references for all further citations from this story are given in parentheses in the text.
3. Michael Finke, *Seeing Chekhov: Life and Art* (Ithaca: Cornell University Press, 2005), 69.
4. Irina Kirk, *Anton Chekhov* (Boston: Twayne, 1981), 59.
5. Lev Shestov, "Creation from the Void," in Eekman, ed., *Critical Essays*, 18.
6. "The Fidget," Pevear and Volokhonsky, *Stories*, 139. The page references for all further citations from this story are given in parentheses in the text.
7. A. P. Chudakov, *Chekhov's Poetics* (1971), trans. Edwina Jannie Cruise and Donald Dragt (Ann Arbor: Ardis, 1983).
8. October 27, 1888, in Yarmolinsky, ed., *Letters*, 88.
9. "Gusev," Pevear and Volokhonsky, *Stories*, 121.
10. "In Exile," Pevear and Volokhonsky, *Stories*, 168.
11. "Ward No. 6," Pevear and Volokhonsky, *Stories*, 171. The page references for all further citations from this story are given in parentheses in the text.
12. Rayfield, *Understanding Chekhov*, 111.
13. "The Black Monk," Pevear and Volokhonsky, *Stories*, 224. The page references for all further citations from this story are given in parentheses in the text.
14. "Art," Garnett, Vol. XII, 271.
15. "Easter Night," Pevear and Volokhonsky, *Stories*, 41.
16. "The Student," Pevear and Volokhonsky, *Stories*, 263–66.
17. Bunin, *About Chekhov*, 21.
18. "The House with the Mezzanine," Pevear and Volokhonsky, *Stories*, 282. The page references for all further citations from this story are given in parentheses in the text.

19. Kirk, *Anton Chekhov*, 99.
20. Pevear, "Introduction," Pevear and Volokhonsky, *Complete Short Novels*, 22.
21. "The Story of an Unknown Man," Pevear and Volokhonsky, *Complete Short Novels*, 327.
22. "My Life," Pevear and Volokhonsky, *Complete Short Novels*, 436. The page references for all further citations from this story are given in parentheses in the text.
23. "The Man in a Case," Pevear and Volokhonsky, *Stories*, 300. The page references for all further citations from this story are given in parentheses in the text.
24. "Gooseberries," Pevear and Volokhonsky, *Stories*, 313. The page references for all further citations from this story are given in parentheses in the text.
25. "About Love," Garnett, Vol. V, 290. The page references for all further citations from this story are given in parentheses in the text.
26. Caryl Emerson succinctly details Chekhov's ongoing treatment of the "*Anna* plot" in *The Cambridge Introduction to Russian Literature* (Cambridge: Cambridge University Press, 2008), 161–65.
27. "The Lady with the Little Dog," Pevear and Volokhonsky, *Stories*, 365. The page references for all further citations from this story are given in parentheses in the text.
28. Vladimir Nabokov, *Lectures on Russian Literature* (New York: Harcourt Brace Jovanovich, 1981), 260.
29. Ibid., *Lectures*, 263.
30. "In the Ravine," Pevear and Volokhonsky, *Stories*, 383. The page references for all further citations from this story are given in parentheses in the text.
31. In V. S. Pritchett, *Chekhov: A Spirit Set Free* (New York: Random House, 1988), 199–200.
32. Virginia Woolf, "The Russian Background" (*Times Literary Supplement*, 14 August 1919), in Mary Lyon, ed., *Books and Portraits* (New York: HBJ), 123.
33. "The Bishop," Pevear and Volokhonsky, *Stories*, 422. The page references for all further citations from this story are given in parentheses in the text.
34. C. J. G. Turner, "Time in Chekhov's 'The Bishop,'" *Modern Language Review*, 86:1 (Jan. 1991), 131.
35. "The Fiancée," Pevear and Volokhonsky, *Stories,* 437–54.

6 Later plays

1. Robert Brustein, *The Theatre of Revolt* (1964; Chicago: Ivan R. Dee, 1991), 141.
2. Letter to Aleksey Suvorin, November 21, 1895, in Bartlett, ed., *Life in Letters*, 339.
3. Russian scholars disagree about the final vowel of Treplyov's name, since the diaeresis that would distinguish "*yo*" from "*e*" is regularly omitted from written Russian. Following Senelick's translation, I have used "Treplyov," though "Treplev" is at least as common in English versions.
4. Senelick, *The Complete Plays*, 739–40.

5. *The Seagull*, Act I, Senelick, *The Complete Plays*, 743–61.
6. S. D. Balakhuty, ed., *The Seagull Produced by Stanislavsky*, trans. David Magarshack (New York: Theatre Arts Books, 1952), 159.
7. *The Seagull*, Act II, Senelick, *The Complete Plays*, 761–74.
8. It appeared on the cover of *Fragments*, the journal to which Chekhov contributed many of his early stories, on 26 October 1896, and is reproduced on the cover of Donald Rayfield's *Understanding Chekhov*.
9. Letter to Nemirovich-Danchenko, 3 December 1899, in Senelick, *Selected Plays*, 428.
10. Balakhuty, ed., *The Seagull*, 207.
11. *The Seagull*, Act III, Senelick, *The Complete Plays*, 774–86.
12. Balakhuty, ed., *The Seagull*, 225.
13. J. L. Styan, *Chekhov in Performance: A Commentary on the Major Plays* (Cambridge: Cambridge University Press 1971), 68.
14. *The Seagull*, Act IV, Senelick, *The Complete Plays,* 786–803
15. Valency, *The Breaking String*, 157.
16. Senelick, *The Complete Plays*, 739.
17. Rayfield, *Understanding Chekhov*, 143.
18. Richard Gilman, *Chekhov's Plays: An Opening into Eternity* (New Haven: Yale University Press, 1995), 99.
19. David Magarshack, *Chekhov the Dramatist* (New York: Hill and Wang, 1960), excerpted in Bristow, ed., *Anton Chekhov's Plays*, 271.
20. Eric Bentley, "Craftsmanship in *Uncle Vanya*" (1949), in Bristow, ed., *Anton Chekhov's Plays*, 353. Emphasis added.
21. *Uncle Vanya*, Senelick, *The Complete Plays*, 865.
22. *Uncle Vanya*, Act I, Senelick, *The Complete Plays*. 819–31.
23. *Uncle Vanya*, Act II, Senelick, *The Complete Plays*, 831–46.
24. Kataev, *If Only We Could Know!*, 199.
25. *Uncle Vanya*, Act III, Senelick, *The Complete Plays*, 846–61.
26. Samuel Beckett, *Endgame*, in *The Complete Dramatic Works* (London: Faber, 1990), 101.
27. Senelick, *The Complete Plays*, 860n; the anecdote is recorded in the *Shipovnik Almanac* 23 (1914), "From Memories of A. P. Chekhov at the Art Theatre."
28. Rayfield, *Understanding Chekhov*, 173.
29. *Uncle Vanya,* Act IV, Senelick, *The Complete Plays*, 861–72.
30. Letter to Olga Knipper, September 30, 1899, in Senelick, *Selected Plays*, 426.
31. Charles B. Timmer, "The Bizarre Element in Chekhov's Art" (1960), in Bristow, ed., *Anton Chekhov's Plays*, 281.
32. Rayfield, *Understanding Chekhov*, 180.
33. Kirk, *Anton Chekhov*, 144.
34. Senelick, *The Complete Plays*, 930, 956.
35. Senelick, *The Complete Plays*, 875.
36. *Three Sisters*, Act I, Senelick, *The Complete Plays*, 883–904.
37. *Three Sisters*, Act II, Senelick, *The Complete Plays*, 904–24.

38. Valency, *The Breaking String*, 238.
39. Letter to Olga Knipper, January 20, 1901, in Senelick, *Selected Plays*, 435.
40. *Three Sisters*, Act II, Senelick, *The Complete Plays*, 924–39.
41. Styan, *Chekhov in Performance*, 200.
42. Letter to Stanislavsky, January 2, 1901, in Senelick, *Selected Plays*, 433.
43. Finke, *Seeing Chekhov*, 83–84.
44. *Three Sisters*, Act IV, Senelick, *The Complete Plays*, 939–57.
45. Senelick, *The Complete Plays*, 950n.
46. Brustein, *The Theatre of Revolt*, 157–58.
47. Gilman, *Chekhov's Plays*, 194–95.
48. Ibid., 196.
49. Chekhov to Lilina, September 15, 1903, Hingley, ed., *Oxford Chekhov*, 319.
50. The following discussion of *The Cherry Orchard* incorporates material from James N. Loehlin, *Chekhov: The Cherry Orchard* (Cambridge: Cambridge University Press, 2006).
51. *The Cherry Orchard*, Act I, Senelick, *The Complete Plays*, 980–100.
52. 5 February 1903, Hingley, ed., *Oxford Chekhov*, 318.
53. Kataev, *If Only We Could Know!*, 274.
54. Chekhov to Nemirovich-Danchenko, August 22, 1903, Hingley, ed., *Oxford Chekhov*, 319.
55. *The Cherry Orchard*, Act II, Senelick, *The Complete Plays*, 1001–16.
56. Chekhov to Knipper, September 25, 1903, Hingley, ed., *Oxford Chekhov*, 320.
57. Andrey Bely, "*The Cherry Orchard*," in Laurence Senelick, ed. and trans., *Russian Dramatic Theory from Pushkin to the Symbolists* (Austin: University of Texas Press, 1981), 92.
58. Vsevolod Meyerhold, "The Naturalistic Theatre and the Theatre of Mood," in Bristow, ed., *Anton Chekhov's Plays*, 317.
59. *The Cherry Orchard*, Act III, Senelick, *The Complete Plays*, 1016–30.
60. David Mamet, "Notes on *The Cherry Orchard*," in *The Cherry Orchard*, by Anton Chekhov, adapted by David Mamet (New York: Grove Press, 1985), vii.
61. Harvey Pitcher, *The Chekhov Play: A New Interpretation* (London: Chatto and Windus, 1973), 190.
62. *The Cherry Orchard*, Act IV, Senelick, *The Complete Plays*, 1031–43.
63. Donald Rayfield, *The Cherry Orchard: Catastrophe and Comedy* (New York: Twayne's, 1994), 88.
64. Pitcher, *The Chekhov Play*, 206.

7 Reception

1. Rayfield, *Anton Chekhov*, 101.
2. "Tolstoy's Criticism on the Darling," trans. Garnett, in *The Tales of Chekhov*, Vol. I, 28.
3. Maxim Gorky, Letter to Chekhov, January 1900, in *Reminiscences*, 99.

4. Gorky, *Reminiscences of Anton Chekhov*, 85–86.

5. D. S. Merezhkovsky, *"Chekhov kak bytopisatel"* (1907), quoted in Victor Terras, "Chekhov at Home: Russian Criticism", in Clyman, ed., *A Chekhov Companion*, 169.

6. Shestov, "Creation from the Void", 11.

7. George Calderon, "An Introduction to Tchekhof" (1912), in Senelick, *Selected Plays*, 465.

8. Ibid., 467.

9. Virginia Woolf, "The Russian Point of View," from *The Common Reader* (1925), in *Collected Essays*, Vol. I (New York: Harcourt, Brace, and World, 1967), 240.

10. Ibid., 241.

11. Ibid., 242.

12. Roberta Rubenstein, *Virginia Woolf and the Russian Point of View* (London: Palgrave Macmillan, 2009), 63.

13. Virginia Woolf, "Modern Novels", *Times Literary Supplement* (April 3, 1919), in *The Essays of Virginia Woolf*, Vol. III, ed. Andrew McNeillie (New York: Harcourt Brace Johanovich, 1988), 35.

14. Richard Ellman, *James Joyce* (Oxford: Oxford University Press, 1959), 171n.

15. Mihail Koltsov, *"Chekhov bez grima"*, *Pravda* (June 15, 1928), in Terras, "Chekhov at Home: Russian Criticism," in Clyman, ed., *A Chekhov Companion*, 171.

16. Shklovsky, *Theory of Prose*, 57.

17. Derman, "Structural Features in Chekhov's Poetics," 34–35.

18. Ibid., 43.

19. Peter M. Bitsilli, *Chekhov's Art: A Stylistic Analyis* (1942), trans. Toby W. Clyman and Edwina Jannie Cruise (Ann Arbor: Ardis, 1983), 162.

20. Jean-Louis Barrault, "Why *The Cherry Orchard*?", *The Theatre of Jean-Louis Barrault*, trans. Joseph Chiari (London: Barrie and Rockliff, 1959, reprinted 1961), 104.

21. Ibid.,105.

22. Senelick, *The Chekhov Theatre*, 271.

23. Ibid.,194.

24. Georgy Tovstonogov, "Chekhov's *Three Sisters* at the Gorky Theatre," trans. Joyce Vining, in Bristow, ed., *Anton Chekhov's Plays*, 326–39.

25. Ibid., 338.

26. Senelick, *The Chekhov Theatre*, 216.

27. John Freedman, "My Chekhov", *The Moscow Times*, January 25, 2010.

28. Robert Louis Jackson, ed., *Reading Chekhov's Text: Studies in Russian Literature and Theory* (Evanston, IL: Northwestern University Press, 1993).

29. Cathy Popkin, *The Pragmatics of Insignificance: Chekhov, Zoshchenko, Gogol* (Stanford: Stanford University Press, 1993).

30. David Allen, *Performing Chekhov* (London: Routledge, 2000); Peta Tait, *Performing Emotions: Gender, Bodies, Spaces in Chekhov's Drama and Stanislavski's Theatre* (Burlington, VT: Ashgate, 2002).

31. John Tulloch, *Shakespeare and Chekhov in Production and Reception: Theatrical Events and their Audiences* (Iowa City: University of Iowa Press, 2005).
32. Brustein, *The Theatre of Revolt.*
33. Magarshack, *Chekhov the Dramatist*; Valency, *The Breaking String*; Pitcher, *The Chekhov Play*; Richard Peace, *Chekhov: A Study of the Four Major Plays* (New Haven: Yale University Press, 1983); Gilman, *Chekhov's Plays.*

Guide to further reading

Chekhov's life and cultural context

Bartlett, Rosamund, ed., *Anton Chekhov: A Life in Letters*, trans. Rosamund Bartlett and Anthony Phillips. London: Penguin, 2004. The most recent English-language collection of Chekhov's letters, including many that had previously been censored or unavailable.

Clyman, Toby W., ed., *A Chekhov Companion*. Westport, CT: Greenwood Press, 1985. A valuable collection of essays on Chekhov's context, life and works.

Emerson, Caryl, *The Cambridge Introduction to Russian Literature*. Cambridge: Cambridge University Press, 2008. A guide to the literary world in which Chekhov wrote.

Figes, Orlando, *Natasha's Dance: A Cultural History of Russia*. New York: Picador, 2002. Provides a broad picture of Russian culture and the complex transformations of Russian's national identity.

Hingley, Ronald, trans. and ed., *The Oxford Chekhov*. Oxford: Oxford University Press, 1964. The comprehensive English-language edition of Chekhov's oeuvre.

Malcolm, Janet, *Reading Chekhov: A Critical Journey*. New York: Random House, 2002. An accessible and provocative meditation on Chekhov's life and works.

Rayfield, Donald, *Anton Chekhov: A Life*. Evanston, IL: Northwestern University Press, 1997. An important biography incorporating materials unavailable during the Soviet era.

Chekhov's short stories

Texts

Garnett, Constance, trans., *The Tales of Chekhov* (13 vols., 1915–1922). New York: Ecco, 2006. Landmark translations that introduced Chekhov's fiction to the English-speaking world.

Pevear, Richard, and Larissa Volokhonsky, trans., *Anton Chekhov: Stories*. New York: Bantam, 2000. Versions of thirty important stories by the leading translators of Russian literature into English.

    trans., *Anton Chekhov: The Complete Short Novels*. London: Everyman, 2004. The five longest prose works of Chekhov's mature career, from "The Steppe" to "My Life."

Criticism

Chudakov, A. P., *Chekhov's Poetics* (1971), trans. Edwina Jannie Cruise and Donald Dragt. Ann Arbor: Ardis, 1983. Analysis of narrative voice in Chekhov by a major Soviet critic.

Eekman, Thomas A., ed., *Critical Essays on Anton Chekhov*. Boston: G. K. Hall, 1989. A collection of essays, mostly on the prose, including works by Shestov, Derman, and Nabokov.

Finke, Michael, *Seeing Chekhov: Life and Art*. Ithaca: Cornell University Press, 2005. Penetrating psychological/biographical reading of Chekhov, focusing on the ideas of seeing and being seen.

Jackson, Robert Louis, *Reading Chekhov's Text: Studies in Russian Literature and Theory*. Evanston, IL: Northwestern University Press, 1993. Collection of essays by major Chekhov scholars, mainly focusing on individual stories.

Kataev, Vladimir, *If Only We Could Know!*, trans. and ed. Harvey Pitcher. Chicago: Ivan R. Dee, 2002. Selection of criticism by an important Russian scholar, from both before and after the breakup of the Soviet Union.

Rayfield, Donald, *Understanding Chekhov*. London: Bristol Classical Press, 1988. Revealing study encompassing the prose, drama, and life of Chekhov.

Chekhov's plays

Texts

Senelick, Laurence, trans., *Anton Chekhov: The Complete Plays*. New York: Norton, 2006. The fullest translation of Chekhov's dramatic work, including the dramatic sketches and vaudevilles.

Criticism

Brustein, Robert, *The Theatre of Revolt* (1964). Chicago: Ivan R. Dee, 1991. Powerful, readable study of Chekhov in relation to other innovators of modern drama.

Gilman, Richard, *Chekhov's Plays: An Opening into Eternity*. New Haven: Yale University Press, 1995. Insightful discussions of the major plays.

Gottlieb, Vera, *Chekhov and the Vaudeville.* Cambridge: Cambridge University Press, 1982. Definitive analysis of the short plays.

Gottlieb, Vera, and Paul Allain, eds., *The Cambridge Companion to Chekhov.* Cambridge: Cambridge University Press, 2000. Contains essays on Chekhov's drama by scholars, directors, and actors.

Magarshack, David, *Chekhov the Dramatist.* New York: Hill and Wang, 1960. Pioneering study of Chekhov as a playwright of "indirect action."

Senelick, Laurence, *The Chekhov Theatre: A Century of the Plays in Performance.* Cambridge: Cambridge University Press, 1997. Magisterial survey of Chekhov performance history.

Senelick, Laurence, trans. and ed., *Anton Chekhov's Selected Plays.* New York: Norton, 2005. Incorporates Chekhov's letters relating to the theatre as well as a good collection of critical essays.

Styan, J. L., *Chekhov in Performance: A Commentary on the Major Plays.* Cambridge: Cambridge University Press 1971. A sensitive act-by-act reading of the plays as performance texts.

Index

Cambridge Introductions to …

AUTHORS

Margaret Atwood Heidi Macpherson

Jane Austen Janet Todd

Samuel Beckett Ronan McDonald

Walter Benjamin David Ferris

Chekhov James N. Loehlin

J. M. Coetzee Dominic Head

Samuel Taylor Coleridge John Worthen

Joseph Conrad John Peters

Jacques Derrida Leslie Hill

Charles Dickens Jon Mee

Emily Dickinson Wendy Martin

George Eliot Nancy Henry

T. S. Eliot John Xiros Cooper

William Faulkner Theresa M. Towner

F. Scott Fitzgerald Kirk Curnutt

Michel Foucault Lisa Downing

Robert Frost Robert Faggen

Nathaniel Hawthorne Leland S. Person

Zora Neale Hurston Lovalerie King

James Joyce Eric Bulson

Herman Melville Kevin J. Hayes

Sylvia Plath Jo Gill

Edgar Allen Poe Benjamin F. Fisher

Ezra Pound Ira Nadel

Jean Rhys Elaine Savory

Edward Said Conor McCarthy

Shakespeare Emma Smith

Shakespeare's Comedies Penny Gay

*Shakespeare's History
    Plays* Warren Chernaik

Shakespeare's Tragedies Janette Dillon

Harriet Beecher Stowe Sarah Robbins

Mark Twain Peter Messent

Edith Wharton Pamela Knights

Walt Whitman M. Jimmie Killingsworth

Virginia Woolf Jane Goldman

William Wordsworth Emma Mason

W. B. Yeats David Holdeman

TOPICS

The American Short Story Martin Scofield

Comedy Eric Weitz

Creative Writing David Morley

Early English Theatre Janette Dillon

English Theatre, 1660–1900
    Peter Thomson

Francophone Literature Patrick Corcoran

*Literature and the
    Environment* Timothy Clark

Modern British Theatre Simon Shepherd

Modern Irish Poetry Justin Quinn

Modernism Pericles Lewis

Narrative (second edition)
    H. Porter Abbott

*The Nineteenth-Century American
    Novel* Gregg Crane

The Novel Marina MacKay

Old Norse Sagas Margaret Clunies Ross

Postcolonial Literatures C. L. Innes

Postmodern Fiction Bran Nicol